Julia Verkholantsev

# Ruthenica Bohemica

# Slavische Sprachgeschichte

herausgegeben von

Michael Moser

Band 3

LIT

Julia Verkholantsev

# RUTHENICA BOHEMICA

## Ruthenian Translations from Czech in the Grand Duchy of Lithuania and Poland

LIT

Printed with the support of the University of Pennsylvania

**Bibliographic information published by the Deutsche Nationalbibliothek**
The Deutsche Nationalbibliothek lists this publication in the Deutsche Nationalbibliografie; detailed bibliographic data are available in the Internet at http://dnb.d-nb.de.

ISBN 978-3-7000-0851-4 (Österreich)
ISBN 978-3-8258-0465-7 (Deutschland)

**A catalogue record for this book is available from the British Library**


Krotenthallergasse 10/8
A-1080 Wien
Tel. +43 (0) 1 / 409 56 61
Fax +43 (0) 1 / 409 56 97
e-Mail: wien@lit-verlag.at
http://www.lit-verlag.at

LIT VERLAG Dr. W. Hopf
Berlin 2008
Auslieferung/Verlagskontakt:
Fresnostr. 2
D-48159 Münster
Tel. +49 (0)251–62 03 20
Fax +49 (0)251–23 19 72
e-Mail: lit@lit-verlag.de
http://www.lit-verlag.de

**Auslieferung:**
Österreich/Schweiz: Medienlogistik Pichler-ÖBZ GmbH & Co KG
IZ-NÖ, Süd, Straße 1, Objekt 34, A-2355 Wiener Neudorf
Tel. +43 (0) 2236/63 535 - 290, Fax +43 (0) 2236/63 535 - 243, e-Mail: mlo@medien-logistik.at
Deutschland: LIT Verlag Fresnostr. 2, D-48159 Münster
Tel. +49 (0) 2 51/620 32 - 22, Fax +49 (0) 2 51/922 60 99, e-Mail: vertrieb@lit-verlag.de

Distributed in the UK by: Global Book Marketing, 99B Wallis Rd, London, E9 5LN
Phone: +44 (0) 20 8533 5800 – Fax: +44 (0) 1600 775 663
http://www.centralbooks.co.uk/acatalog/search.html

Distributed in North America by:

Transaction Publishers
New Brunswick (U.S.A.) and London (U.K.)

Transaction Publishers
Rutgers University
35 Berrue Circle
Piscataway, NJ 08854

Phone: +1 (732) 445 - 2280
Fax: + 1 (732) 445 - 3138
for orders (U. S. only):
toll free (888) 999 - 6778
e-mail:
orders@transactionspub.com

# Contents


***Preface and Acknowledgements*** *vii*

**Introduction.** *Lingua Ruthena in Polonia Usitata* *1*

**Chapter 1.** Czech in the Linguistic History of the Grand Duchy of Lithuania and Poland *18*

**Chapter 2.** The Ruthenian *Song of Songs* *39*

**Chapter 3.** The Ruthenian *Book of Taudal the Knight* and the Church Slavonic *Edifying Story Told by Faudal the Warrior* *52*

**Chapter 4.** The Ruthenian *Tale of Sivilla the Prophetess* *71*

**Chapter 5.** The Ruthenian *Book of Tovit* *86*

**Chapter 6.** *Ruthenica Bohemica*: Linguistic Features in Ruthenian Translations from Czech *90*

**Chapter 7.** Anatomy of Ruthenian: Linguistic Shift and Literacy Contact *128*

**Final Remarks** *148*

***Appendix* I.** The Ruthenian and Czech *Song of Songs* *154*

***Appendix* II.** The Ruthenian *Book of Taudal the Knight* and the Church Slavonic *Edifying Story Told by Faudal the Warrior* *174*

***Appendix* III.** The Latin *Visio Tundali* *180*

***Appendix* IV.** The Church Slavonic *On the Three Lawful States* *182*

***Appendix* V.** The Ruthenian *Tale of Sivilla the Prophetess* *183*

***Bibliography*** *191*

***Indices*** *206*

# PREFACE AND ACKNOWLEDGEMENTS

*Ruthenica Bohemica* is a substantial revision of a doctoral dissertation filed at the University of California, Los Angeles in 2004. Therefore, it retains many features of a scholarly thesis. While my original inclination was to write a philological study of Ruthenian translations from Czech, my position as a doctoral student in Slavic Linguistics demanded explicit linguistic content. Hence, the two parts of this study: the historical-philological examination of Ruthenian translations is presented vis-à-vis both their linguistic description and theoretical ramifications regarding the nature of their language.

In the philological study of these Ruthenian translations from Czech, I discuss the mode of their adaptation and hypothesize about historical circumstances of their emergence. In the linguistic section, I propose a new approach and a new term: literacy contact. This approach allows us to consider and study Ruthenian written language through the prism of literacy theories, an aspect that in my view has been underestimated by Ruthenian linguistic scholarship. Although some of my findings and conjectures are far from being conclusive it is my hope that they might prove useful to other scholars in the field and perhaps facilitate further study in this direction.

A note on sources and references is due. A substantial part of the dissertation was written before the year 2003, especially the linguistic chapters. While revising my manuscript I augmented footnotes with recent relevant publications but for the most part did not integrate their content into my own analysis.

If not otherwise stated all translations of quotes and titles in foreign languages are mine. In several questionable instances I consulted specialists for a second opinion (acknowledgements are in the text). However, the responsibility for accuracy is mine alone.

I should say a few words about terminology and spelling. The spelling of proper and place names is as a rule based on the contemporary division of languages: Polatsk (not Polotsk), Ostrih (not Ostrog), Kyiv (not Kiev). However, I retained the use of such terms and names as Kievan Rus' (not Kyivan Rus), Prague (not Praha), Cracow (not Kraków) due to their general use in scholarship. The spelling of proper names follows the transliteration system of the Library of Congress.

* * *

I wish to express my deep gratitude to all people and institutions who have given me support of various kinds during the writing of this monograph.

My archival research was aided by many kind and attentive librarians, curators and scholars. Thanks are due to Milada Homolková and Jaroslava Pečírková, both of the Czech Language Institute (Oddělení Vývoje Jazyka, Ústav pro Jazyk Český, Akademie Věd ČR), who offered help with locating resource materials and kindly allowed me to use their archives. I am grateful to the librarians of the Warsaw National Library (Biblioteka Narodowa) Special Collections Department, especially to Andrzej Kaszlej and Bożena Ciepłowska, for providing generous and quick access to original manuscripts. Likewise, I am grateful to many other dedicated librarians in manuscript departments at the State Historical Museum (Gosudarstvennyi Istoricheskii Muzei) in Moscow, Slavonic Library (Slovanská Knihovna), National Library of the Czech Republic (Národní Knihovna) and the National Museum Library (Knihovna Národního Muzea) in Prague.

I would like to thank Vyacheslav Vsevolodovich Ivanov for his insightful scholarly guidance and generous patronage during the writing of my doctoral dissertation and throughout my UCLA years. My heartfelt thanks go to David A. Frick of the University of California, Berkeley for his scrupulous and valuable criticism of the initial drafts of my dissertation and his invariable support and advice thereafter.

In working on this monograph, I am indebted to Edward L. Keenan and Paul Wexler who meticulously read my doctoral dissertation and provided very useful and inspiring comments. I am most grateful to them.

I would like to thank Michael Moser, the editor of the series, without whose persistent encouragement this publication would have never materialized.

I should acknowledge with great distinction Emily Weissbourd, who carefully proofread this manuscript offering constructive stylistic comments and asking many stimulating questions.

Finally, I am grateful to the University of Pennsylvania for providing me with a generous grant to support the publication of this monograph.

*To my parents, Larissa and Vladimir Verkholantsev*

## Introduction
## LINGUA RUTHENA IN POLONIA USITATA

### DEFINITION

A fifteenth-century manuscript miscellany (Q.I. 391) from the St. Petersburg Public Library contains an inscription on the margins of one of its texts, *The Passion of Christ*. It reads: "*Passio Christi versa ex Latino in Dialectum Ruthenam in Polonia usitatam*." [*The Passion of Christ*, translated from Latin into the Ruthenian dialect/language used in Poland.] This note seems to provide one of the most accurate (if long-winded) definitions of all those suggested thus far for the written language of the ethnic East Slavic[1] population of the Grand Duchy of Lithuania and Poland.[2]

Fifteenth and sixteenth-century Latin sources generally use the term *dialectus/lingua Ruthena* as an equivalent to the self-identifying Slavic terms *rus'ka (prosta) mova* and *iazyk rus'ki*. The English term *Ruthenian*, therefore, derives from the Latin historical name for this language.[3] The corpus of Ruthenian consists of texts of various genres and functions, secular and ecclesiastical, dating

[1] Here preference is given to the neutral term East Slavic (rather than Old Russian, Old Belarusian and/or Old Ukrainian) partly because I would like to stay away from any nationalistic issues (i.e. provide an ethnic attribution), and partly because, in my opinion, it is a more accurate term for the period preceding the seventeenth century. When referring to the vernacular language spoken in the discussed territory, I will use the terms "Belarusian and Ukrainian dialects."

[2] I am intentionally avoiding the term "literary language" because it is more often used in the study of contemporary normalized languages, institutionalized and enforced by general agreement, than it is in studies of pre-modern languages. Instead I am trying to characterize with an English equivalent what is in Russian terminology called "письменный язык" or, alternatively, "язык письменности," which more accurately corresponds to the nature of a non-standardized language used for writing in the pre-modern period. For more detailed summaries of this question, see, for example, Worth 1975, Corin 1993, Uspenskii 2002.

[3] However, in the terminological arena this term immediately encountered its contemporary rival, Carpatho-Ruthenian, which in scholarly discourse is usually referred to as Carpatho-Rusyn or Rusyn. Here, again, I am on shaky ground. Therefore in lieu of providing a description I will cite the self-identifying definition given by the World Academy of Rusyn Culture, the principal Rusyn organization, consisting of scholars and enthusiasts alike: "The Carpatho-Rusyns are central European people, numbering approximately 1.2 million, who live within the borders of five states: Poland, Slovakia, Ukraine, Romania, and Hungary. They have never had a state of their own. Despite disregard or suppression by most governments that ruled over them in the past, the Rusyn people have retained their identity, language and a rich culture." (http://www.rusyn.org)

from the end of the fourteenth to the seventeenth century and originating in the area that is now within the borders of Lithuania, Ukraine, Belarus and the most eastern territories of Poland.[4] Such a definition is, of course, purely philological, which is why it is still a vaguely defined linguistic concept. It is generally used more willingly by historians and literature specialists than by linguists. Ruthenian, therefore, needs to be defined linguistically as well as philologically – but this is easier said than done.

The almost two-hundred-year search for an appropriate term for Ruthenian has produced a great number of variants: it has been referred to as Lithuanian-Russian, Polish-Russian, West Russian, South-West Russian, Written Little Russian, Old West Russian dialect, (Old) Belarusian, (Old) Ukrainian, Old Belarusian-Ukrainian. Recently the Slavic historical terms *rus'ka mova* and *prosta mova*, used by sixteenth-century Ruthenians to refer to their language, have appeared in scholarly literature along with the English term Ruthenian.[5] Even a cursory examination of the variety of terms demonstrates the structural heterogeneity of this language, the ethnic diversity of its speakers and, occasionally, the political bias of an author.

## HISTORICAL AND CULTURAL SETTING

It is not the intention of this study to go into a thorough analysis of the linguistic situation in the Grand Duchy of Lithuania and the Polish-Lithuanian Commonwealth from the fourteenth to the seventeenth centuries, nor to discuss at length the linguistic relationship between Ruthenian and Polish. This has already been performed from a variety of perspectives in several other works.[6] I will therefore

[4] Defining the time span and physical borders of a language always implies a degree of approximation and convention. Although the Polish expansion into Ruthenian lands had already begun by the 1340s, the earliest beginnings of Ruthenian can symbolically be dated to 1385, the year when the first political union of Lithuania-Rus' and Poland took place in Krewo; while the formal abolition of Ruthenian transpired in 1697 when the decree of the Warsaw Sejm banned it as an official administrative language of the Commonwealth: "Pisarz po-polsku a nie po-rusku pisać powinien będzie." [A scribe must write in Polish, not in Ruthenian.]

[5] For recent studies on *prosta mova* and *rus'ka mova* see, for example, Danylenko 2006, Moser 2002, Miakishev 2000. These studies primarily deal with the language of sixteenth and seventeenth-century sources.

[6] On the general linguistic situation in the Grand Duchy of Lithuania and Polish-Lithuanian Commonwealth, see Ivanov 2005, Uspenskii 2002, various papers in *Studia Russica* 17 (1999) and 18 (2000), Morozova and Temchin 1997, Pugh 1996, Frick 1994, Labyntsev 1992, Zhuraŭski 1967 and 1982. On the Polish-Ruthenian relationship, see, for example, Łesiów 2000, Shevelov 1952 and 1980, Richhardt 1957, and Martel 1938 to name only a few.

limit myself to outlining the most important events that defined the cultural and political orientation within the discussed East Slavic lands, giving rise to the Ruthenian culture.[7]

| | |
|---|---|
| **ca. 1320–1380** | Lithuania expanded its territory to Rus' principalities. Under Grand Duke Gedyminas (1316–1341): Polatsk, Turaŭ-Pinsk, Podlachia and Volhynia. Under Algirdas (1345–1377) and Kęstutis (1345–1382): Chernihiv, Novhorod-Sivers'kyi, Briansk, Kyiv, Pereiaslav and Podolia. Thus, by 1392 the Grand Duchy extended over virtually all the Belarusian and Ukrainian lands (except Galicia) as far as the open steppe. |
| **1344–1349** | Poland under the rule of Kazimierz acquired Galicia. |
| **1385** | The treaty of Krewo (Kriavas) initiated the dynastic linkage of Lithuania and Poland (the Grand Duke Jogaila became the Polish King Władysław II Jagiełło by marrying Jadwiga, the heir to the Polish throne) and the official Christianization of Lithuania (1386). The Grand Duchy of Lithuania, however, continued to function as an independent state. |
| **1569** | The Union of Lublin started a constitutional union of the Polish Kingdom and the Grand Duchy as the Polish-Lithuanian Commonwealth (Rzeczpospolita obojga narodów). The greater part of the ethnically Ukrainian territories was detached from the Grand Duchy and annexed to Poland. It is generally considered in historiography that this act significantly affected the differentiation of Ukrainians and Belarusians. It eliminated the political frontier between Galicia and the eastern Ukraine and promoted their integration. From this time on institutions in these lands became predominantly Polish. |

Within the Grand Duchy, Ruthenian lands retained considerable cultural and even political autonomy. On the whole Orthodox Ruthenians, with their own Church organization, language and culture, constituted a considerable part of the subjects of the Grand Duchy of Lithuania.[8] In addition, prior to the end of the fourteenth century, some pagan Lithuanians, mainly nobility, were converting to Orthodoxy and assimilating into the Ruthenian way of life. For example, Enea

[7] Stone 2001, Kiaupa, Kiaupienė and Kuncevičius 2000.

[8] Out of the twelve palatinates (administrative zones) of the Grand Duchy of Lithuania and Žemaitija (the thirteenth special administrative unit) ten were populated predominantly by Ruthenians (Kiaupa, Kiaupienė and Kuncevičius 2000, 164).

Silvio Piccolomini in *De Europa* (1458) distinguishes between Orthodox Lithuanians and Lithuanian barbarians who worship idols:

*Ex Schlauis enim alij Romanam ecclesiam sequuntur, ut Dalmatae, Croatini, Carni ac Poloni. Alij Graecorum sequuntur errores, ut Bulgari, Rutheni, & multi ex Lituanis.* [...] *Alij gentili adhuc caecitate tenentur, quemadmodum multi ex Lituanis idola colentes.*[9]
[Among Slavs some follow the Roman Church, such as the Dalmatians, Croatians, Carni[10] and Poles. Others follow the errors of the Greeks, such as the Bulgarians, Ruthenians and many Lithuanians. [...] Others still remain in blindness, as for instance many of the Lithuanians, who worship idols.]

It was only some time after the official Christianization of Lithuania and the formation of the union with Poland that Lithuanian nobility began to prefer Catholicism and the Polish language that came with it. Jan Krasiński (Joannes Crasinius) in his geo-historical treatise *Polonia* (1574) introduced a social element into the ethno-linguistic characterization of the inhabitants of the Grand Duchy of Lithuania:

*Valde mihi erasse videntur illi, qui Lithuanos omnes Slauonica lingua vti scripserunt. Verum quidem est nobiliores viros Polonicum, & Roxolanicum sermonem vsurpare; sed plebs peculiare Lithuanicum idioma habet.*[11]
[Those who write that all Lithuanians use the Slavic language seem to me to be greatly in error. In fact, the nobility speaks Polish and Ruthenian but the common people have their own Lithuanian language.]

The fourteenth and fifteenth centuries are generally regarded as a "black hole" period for Ruthenia because of the scarcity of historical and literary sources. However, this time might not, on the whole, have been unfavorable for the Orthodox Church in Ruthenian lands. By the sixteenth century there were more Orthodox parishes to be found in the Grand Duchy than Catholic ones; Kłoczowski assumes there were as many as one thousand.[12] This was due in part to the general complexity of establishing a Catholic parish in the Polish-Lithuanian Commonwealth. Besides, the Orthodox Church in the Grand Duchy had a powerful advocate in Poland. The King of Poland by marriage, Władysław Jagiełło (Jogaila) was born to a Ruthenian princess, Iuliana Tverskaia, and he clearly favored Orthodox culture.[13] Frescoes Jagiełło commissioned by Ruthe-

[9] Enea Silvio [1458] 1967, 417.
[10] The Slovenes.
[11] Crasinius 1574, 98.
[12] Kłoczowski 2000, 60.
[13] Referring to several primary sources as well as to the works of Polish and Lithuanian historians, Josef Perwolf claims that Jogaila's "paganism" is a fairy tale (Perwolf 1893, 45).

nian icon-painters can still be seen in a number of Gothic Catholic churches in Poland.[14] Until his death in 1434, the Ruthenian lands that belonged to the Crown maintained a relative administrative autonomy: they had their own monetary system and used Ruthenian in administration. Moreover, Jagiełło himself issued documents relating to these lands in Ruthenian.[15] His son, Kazimierz (1427–1492) continued to favor the Orthodox Ruthenians and in 1447 bestowed on the Ruthenian gentry and clergy rights equal to those in the Polish Crown.

The Grand Duchy's administration and legal system drew heavily on Slavic customs and language.[16] Ever since the annexation of Kievan Rus' principalities to Lithuania, starting in the second half of the thirteenth century, the local variant of East Slavic with or without elements of Church Slavonic had been the language of writing in internal public affairs. Later, it became the internal administrative language of the state chancery established by the Grand Duke Vytautas. Extant archival sources show that during the reign of Alexander Jagiellończyk the international correspondence in his chancery was carried out in German with the Teutonic Order, in Latin with Poland and other West European countries, and in Tatar with the Horde,[17] while documentation of internal affairs and correspondence with Muscovy were carried out entirely by Ruthenian scribes.[18] Some of their names and places of origin are known: for example, Bohush Bohovitynovich from Podlasie, Fedko Janushkovich from Volhynia, and Kopot Vasilevich from Smolensk, to name only a few.[19]

A number of political and sociolinguistic factors aided the already well-developed Ruthenian chancery language in becoming the official language of writing in the Grand Duchy of Lithuania. The territorial expansion and political consolidation of the Lithuanian state demanded a well-organized administrative system, which, like any bureaucratic practice, was built on paper work. Developing a written Lithuanian and training scribes and clerks in it would be too grand

[14] Orthodox frescoes that date to Jagiełło's reign can be seen today in the Chapel of Saint Trinity in the Lublin Castle, in the Chapel of Saint Trinity and the Royal bedroom in the Wawel Castle in Cracow, in the Benedictine Abbey in Łyść, in the Collegiate Churches in Sandomierz and Wiślica, and in Gnieźno Cathedral. For images and a detailed study of Orthodox frescoes in the chapel at the Lublin Castle see Różycka-Bryzek 1983 and 2000.

[15] Sielicki 1997, 103.

[16] The Christianization of Lithuania in 1386 did not bring about any immediate changes in the field of writing (Kiaupa, Kiaupienė and Kuncevičius 2000, 152).

[17] Pietkiewicz 1995, 27 mentions Abrahim Tymirchyts, a member of a Tatar aristocratic family, settled in Lithuania, who was a scribe of Aleksander Jagiellończyk in the Tatar language.

[18] Pietkiewicz 1995, 16–28.

[19] For a more detailed list, see Pietkiewicz 1995; Banenis 1978, 33–35.

a task for the illiterate Lithuanian society. The Orthodox Eastern Slavs, on the other hand, possessed both the writing tradition and competent personnel. Besides, Lithuania's Slavic neighbors (Muscovy on one side and Poland on the other) made it desirable and practical to employ and develop the language of the Slavic population as a state language. Furthermore, a number of already established cultural and educational centers facilitated the continuation and further development of Slavic literacy. Even such politically and ideologically important documents as the Lithuanian chronicles were written in Ruthenian.[20]

## ORTHODOX CULTURE AND EDUCATION IN THE GRAND DUCHY OF LITHUANIA

Monasteries traditionally served in the Grand Duchy of Lithuania as repositories of Orthodox culture.[21] Among the principal ecclesiastical centers of theological thought, education, and book collection and production were Kievan Caves Monastery (founded in 1051) and Supraśl Monastery (founded in 1498 in Zabłudów). While we possess limited knowledge of monastic culture in Ruthenia in the period following the disintegration of Kievan Rus' in the thirteenth century, it is known that the number of monasteries constantly grew during the fourteenth and fifteenth centuries.[22] Antoni Mironowicz gives an extensive list of monasteries covering the whole territory of the Grand Duchy starting from the end of the fifteenth century.[23] In the territory of Polatsk alone there were fifteen monasteries. Book collections were not rare in Orthodox parish schools and churches (these could contain several dozens of books) and monasteries (the largest possessed several hundred manuscript codices).[24] The development of monasteries in the sixteenth century is documented by the construction of numerous Church objects, flourishing scriptoria and book collections, and the foundation of hospitals and schools.

The fact that monastic communities were frequently founded or supported by Ruthenian magnates shows the secular population's involvement in Orthodox cultural preservation. This patronage, in general, played a crucial role in all spheres of Orthodox life.[25] For example, the patronage of the Khodkevich family

[20] The *Genealogy of Lithuanian Princes* (ca. 1398), the *Eulogy of Vytautas* (ca. 1428), the *Chronicle of the Grand Duchy of Lithuania and Samogitia* (1565–1573).

[21] On the Orthodox Church in the Polish-Lithuanian Commonwealth see Bednov 2002, Mironowicz 2001 and 2003a.

[22] Hrushevs'kyi 1955, 261–266.

[23] Mironowicz 2001, 40–42.

[24] Topolska 1984, 202–204.

[25] Topolska 2004.

was of great significance for the survival and restoration of Orthodox cultural tradition in Lithuania. The estates of this old and influential family of Ruthenian magnates were located in Podlachia, the region on the westernmost edge of Orthodoxy in Lithuania. At the end of the fifteenth century Alexander Khodkevich founded what became one of the most prominent intellectual centers of Orthodoxy in the Polish-Lithuanian Commonwealth, the famous Supraśl Monastery. In 1567 Hryhoryi Khodkevich founded an Orthodox school in Zabłudów. Here, in Zabłudów, the largest printing house in Lithuania was established where Ivan Fedorov and Petr Mstislavets were active in the 1560s. The Orthodox center in Zabłudów continued to thrive after the enactment of the Lublin Union in 1569 and maintained connections with other centers of Orthodox culture in Kyiv, the Balkans, and Mount Athos.[26]

Prince Konstantyn of Ostrih, palatine of Kyiv and founder of numerous Orthodox schools, churches and monasteries, also occupied a prominent position in the dissemination of Orthodox culture and education. One of his ambitious plans was to transfer the seat of the patriarch of Constantinople to Ostrih, where he founded an Orthodox Academy and printing house in 1580, and where a year later the famous *Ostrih Bible* was published.[27]

The important role of maintaining religious unity and spreading culture and literacy belonged to the Orthodox brotherhoods.[28] Initially they were organized to counteract the Catholic orientation of the guilds and the obligatory participation of guild members in the Catholic Church. The first brotherhoods were founded in 1439 in L'viv and around 1450 in Vilnius within the furriers' guild.[29] By and large, craftsmen founded them in order to maintain religious solidarity. Subsequently, the growth of cities encouraged the growth of the brotherhoods. From the second half of the sixteenth century on their role expanded, and they began to include other social classes.

Unfortunately, we do not possess much information about the system of education in Ruthenia in the period preceding the mid-sixteenth century. There were no governmental schools; elementary education was carried out in the monastery, parish, and private schools. Children of the gentry most probably received private instruction. For the most part, the number of monastic schools be-

[26] For more details and a bibliography, please refer to Labyntsev and Shchavinskaia 1996.
[27] Isaevich 1990.
[28] For more information on the brotherhoods in Ruthenia, see Mironowicz 2003b, Isaevich 1966, Morzy 1959, Medynskii 1954.
[29] Mironowicz 2003b, 188–192.

gan to grow from the end of the fifteenth century.[30] Nevertheless, numerous signatures on documents belonging to various social strata suggest that literacy at that time was not a very uncommon phenomenon. At the end of the sixteenth century a new type of educational institutions – the brotherhood schools – began to emerge.[31]

The quality of instruction and the scope of the curriculum at Vilnius Jesuit Academy, founded in 1570, attracted many Ruthenians (whether of Catholic, Protestant or Orthodox confessional orientation) among its students.[32] The Academy continued the mission of Cracow University of "conversion and enlightenment of Lithuania"[33] and became a center of humanist sciences, new philosophy and theology, modeled on Western universities.

Starting from the 1580s the Ruthenian language was officially included among the disciplines studied at the Academy.[34] The extract from *Index lectionum* states: "Every morning and afternoon reading and writing in Ruthenian, then translating selected texts from the Gospel or the Catechism and learning them by heart."[35] No doubt this was a working lab where a written Ruthenian crystallized. An examination of study materials and "notebooks" would shed some light on the pedagogical technique and theoretical principles of the development of Ruthenian as an "academic" language.

## LINGUISTIC SITUATION

With Lithuania's official adoption of Christianity and the political federation with Poland in the late fourteenth century, the Orthodox Slavs, previously a dominant and influential group in the Lithuanian state, started losing their privileged position in the state's social and political life to the ruling Catholic group. This process was further assisted by the fact that many of the Ruthenian nobility were willingly converting to Catholicism. As the public prestige of Catholicism increased, so did the prestige of Polish culture and language. By the sixteenth century Polish literary language had reached its "Golden Age" and was in vogue among Ruthenian intellectuals and literati. The end of the sixteenth century is

[30] Mironowicz 2001, 46–52.

[31] Mironowicz 2001, 50–51 provides detailed reference concerning this issue.

[32] Piechnik mentions students with Ruthenian last names (Piechnik 1984, 114–115; 1983, 89) among whom was Simeon Polotskii (93–95). Meletii Smotryts'kyi attended the Academy for some time (on this controversial issue, see Frick 1995, 31–37).

[33] Piechnik 1984, 184–185.

[34] Piechnik 1984, 83; Fałowski 2001, 198.

[35] Piechnik 1984, 83.

usually marked as the time when Polish became an influential language in all spheres of public life in the Polish-Lithuanian Commonwealth.

It should be noted that Polonization in the Grand Duchy during the fifteenth and sixteenth centuries occurred largely within the culture of magnates and szlachta, state officials, clerks, churchmen, and well-to-do burghers – i.e. the "educated" classes. Polish was one of the major languages of the Royal Court and, therefore, the language of social prestige. Ruthenian, as a language of writing, was a language of learned people and, as such, culturally and socially marked. It is intriguing that the dissemination of Polish language and culture among East Slavic speakers in Lithuania-Rus' does not seem to be connected with a significant migration of the Polish population (not so in Galicia, of course). On the contrary, the Ruthenians (as well as the ethnic Lithuanians)[36] were most ardently opposed to Polish political dominance. For instance, Article 12 in Chapter 3 of the Lithuanian Statute of 1588 banned the distribution of lands and state offices among foreigners.[37] Ruthenian urban areas outside Galicia also did not contain a predominating Polish populace.[38] Nevertheless, it is remarkable that the Polonization of the educated classes spread very quickly in the Ruthenian lands of the Grand Duchy, facilitating its allegiance to Catholicism.

When studying pre–1569 Ruthenian writing one should bear in mind that the circumstances surrounding educated Ruthenians' cultural and linguistic contact with Polish language inherently differed, for instance, from the contact between the speakers of Belarusian, Ukrainian, and Polish borderland dialects. In the latter case, to a certain extent, the regular physical contact between speakers of these dialects took place unaccompanied by stylistic constraints or intentional socially induced language accommodation (though these two different contact situations may have produced some similar linguistic results).

It is of equal importance that, having Ruthenian written sources as an object of study, we recognize that we deal with a language of writing, the production of which is linguistically essentially different from that of speech.[39] Therefore, the rules that operate in the various cases of dialect contact and are inferred

---

[36] Ochmański 1986, 303.

[37] This ban was primarily directed against the Polish nobility, who were trying to occupy state and ecclesiastical offices and the lands that came with them (Iukho 1978, 68).

[38] Hrushevs'kyi 1955, 249.

[39] Among the voluminous literature on differences between spoken and written language see, for example, Ong [1982] 1988; Tannen 1982; Downing, Lima and Noonan 1992; Olson 1994; Jahandarie 1999.

in the research on extant dialects may not be unconditionally applicable to the language contact realized in writing. The medieval culture of the written word involved a number of extra-linguistic aspects, a fact which puts a narrow linguistically-oriented analysis in a rather weak position. We must further bear in mind that a large portion of Ruthenian texts are translations and relexifications,[40] with all that these circumstances entail (dependence on the language of the source, textual corruption, linguistic interference, strict observance of the grammatical structure of the original, etc.). Therefore, the theoretical principles connected with the mixed and transitional dialects on the borders between Poland, Belarus, and Ukraine will not be involved in our method. This question has been studied both in synchronic and diachronic perspectives elsewhere and continues to draw the attention of dialectologists.[41] Likewise, questions concerning the formation of literary Belarusian and Ukrainian and the development of individual dialects lie outside of this study's scope.[42]

## Introducing a New Concept: Literacy Contact

In order to understand the mechanisms of a written language one must penetrate the mentality of a literate mind. One may view Ruthenian literacy as a composite. At its core lies the multifaceted relationship between vernacular and literary languages. As a result, each constituent of this composite is not homogenous but is itself composed of multiple interacting components. One may further think of two mechanisms within the apparatus of Ruthenian literacy: one mechanism is the interaction between vernacular dialects (Belarusian and Ukrainian) and "Church Slavonic"[43] writing practice, which I will henceforth call Cyrillic literacy; another is their relationship with Polish literacy. Since this interaction seems to represent a classic contact situation, I suggest in Chapter Seven of this monograph that we view written Ruthenian as a result of literacy contact. The term "literacy contact" that I propose is reminiscent of the term "language contact" but refers to a different function (manifestation) of language, that of writ-

[40] On the concept of relexification see Wexler 1991, 2002 and 2006.

[41] See, for example, Woolhiser 1995 (includes extensive bibliography on the subject); various articles in Warchoł 1986, 1989 and 1993; Czyżewski 1986 and 1998, Smułkowa 1988, Shevelov 1952.

[42] More on these subjects can be found in Łesiów 2000, Rusanovskii 1998, Pritsak 1984, Strumins'kyj 1984, McMillin 1980, Pliushch 1971, Shevelov 1953.

[43] I use the generic term "Church Slavonic" here to denote both the language of ecclesiastical texts written in traditional Church Slavonic and the non-ecclesiastical language of administrative and historiographic texts that started developing in the Kievan period.

ing. In this light, it stands between the term "language contact," that emphasizes the linguistic systemic relationship between participating languages, and the semiotic term "text contact" that emphasizes the relationship between complete texts. On the macro level the term "literacy contact" indicates the contact of literacy conventions in one language with literacy principles in another language. Conversely, on the micro level "literacy contact" reflects a situation of contact between two writing systems in the mind of a literate individual.[44]

In order to understand how this complicated mechanism of relationships works it is crucial to take into account the "human" and "social" aspects of Ruthenian. In other words, one should begin with an examination of the linguistic practices and language attitudes of Ruthenian writers. This would reveal in what manner these attitudes depended upon their literacy skills and linguistic competence and also what influence their political and religious views had on their linguistic preferences.

Apropos of the dichotomy between the vernacular and Church Slavonic we should perhaps revise the assertion that is often voiced about Ruthenian clergymen's alleged ignorance of Church Slavonic in the sixteenth century. We do not possess any first-hand accounts from the fifteenth century. The most widely cited criticism of such ignorance dates from the second half of the sixteenth century. This is Piotr Skarga's condemnation of the Church Slavonic culture in his treatise *O jedności Kościoła Bożego pod jednym Pasterzem* (*On the Unity of the Church under One Pastor*, 1577):

> Z słowieńskiego języka nigdy żaden uczonym być nie może. A już go teraz przecie prawie nikt doskonale nie rozumie. Bo tey na świecie naciey nie masz, któraby im tak, jako w księgach jest, mówiła a swych też reguł, gramatyk i kalepinów do wykładu niema, ani już mieć może. Ztąd popi waszy, gdy co w słowiańskim chcą rozumieć, do polskiego się udać muszą po tłumactwo.[45]
> [No one can ever be a learned man through the Slavonic language. And almost nobody understands it perfectly now. For there is no nation in the world that would speak it the way it is in the books; and this language has not, and can no longer have, its rules, grammars and Calepinos. Hence your priests have to turn to Polish for translations if they want to understand anything in Slavonic.][46]

Whether Skarga's condemnation reflected reality or not one should keep in mind that his treatise promoted an ideological agenda. In fact, the citation in

[44] An individual may also be literate in only one language and project his knowledge of literacy in this language onto his writing in another.

[45] Cited from Martel 1938, 69.

[46] Cited from Strumins'kyj 1984, 10.

question is taken from the broader context of Skarga's argument in favor of using either Greek or Latin as an ecclesiastical language, rather than Slavonic. Besides, his criticism may not even be relevant to the linguistic situation of fifteenth-century Ruthenia.

That the Ruthenian laity and occasionally even clergy at the end of the sixteenth century had difficulty understanding Church Slavonic texts is evident not only from remarks of the opponents of Orthodoxy, such as Piotr Skarga, but also from the criticism of Ruthenian intellectuals themselves.[47] However, evidence from fifteenth and sixteenth-century manuscripts shows that Ruthenian men of letters had by no means lost competence in Church Slavonic.[48] Numerous biblical, liturgical, and edificatory manuscript books in Church Slavonic of Ruthenian provenance dating from that period are to be found in the largest repositories of the Ruthenian written legacy, such as, for example, the National Library in Warsaw, the National Library in Vilnius, and the State Historical Museum in Moscow.[49] Evidence of scribes' proficiency in Church Slavonic lies in the many notes and comments in these manuscripts.[50] At the same time, already at the end of the fifteenth and even more so in the sixteenth century (since manuscripts are more numerous from this period) we find many inscriptions and texts in the Ruthenian vernacular.[51] This proof of the coexistence of Church Slavonic and Ruthenian literacy suggests that the use of Ruthenian in many instances might have been a conscious choice and not a consequence of Church Slavonic illiteracy.[52] I will return to this supposition later in this study.

The increase in the use of the Ruthenian vernacular in writing comes with the rise of polemical literature at the time of religious disputes between the Orthodox and Uniates at the end of the sixteenth century. Unfortunately, texts from this period do not allow us to form a definite judgment about the beginnings of Ruthenian since they are already written in an elaborate language. Even so, the

---

[47] Strumins'kyj 1984, 10; Frick 1994 termed this phenomenon "Ruthenian self-hatred."

[48] Of course, this depends on our notion of "competence" and what extent of linguistic knowledge we can accept as sufficient or relevant. For example, the humanistic Latin also became very corrupted and differed significantly from its parent, Classical Latin.

[49] See, for example, Dobrianskii 1882, Shchapov 1976a, Turilov 1986, Naumow and Kaszlej 2004.

[50] Although these compositions may not necessarily be of the highest style, I leave the question of quality of style outside of this discussion.

[51] Karskii [1897] 1964, Perets 1903.

[52] At the same time, one should not forget that Ruthenian was still somewhat functionally limited to non-liturgical texts, although individual translations of biblical and even liturgical texts started appearing already in the fifteenth century (see Chapter Two). However, these translations were not programmatic and doctrinal.

large variety of Ruthenian texts composed in that period illustrates the diverse spectrum of linguistic preferences and views of Ruthenian authors. In his article on religious polemical literature in the Ruthenian lands, Ihor Ševčenko distinguished between three factions of Orthodox polemicists: the traditionalists (Ivan Vyshens'kyi and Vasyl' of Surazh), the progressive wing (Marcin Broniewski) and those in between (the anonymous author of the *Perestroha*).[53] Incidentally, the distribution of these factions reflects the spectrum of linguistic attitudes connected with the Polish-Ruthenian cultural and ideological confrontation:

> The differences between these three factions are to be sought not in their (uniformly negative) attitudes toward Catholic dogma, but in the literary norm employed in their works and in their views on modern ways of education and learning. The traditionalists wrote in a less Polonized form of Church Slavonic, or in a Church Slavonic mixed with Ukrainian vernacular, and used Byzantine or para-Byzantine – in both cases, outmoded – polemical texts in Slavonic translation. They distrusted Latin and extolled the virtues of Church Slavonic. People in between, like the author of *Perestoroha*, wrote in a heavily Polonized vernacular and extolled the values of education, including worldly learning. Finally, the "progressives" wrote in brilliant Polish, betrayed Latin modes of thought in their prose, quoted Latin phrases, and dealt with questions of authenticity on the basis of whether the original of the incriminated text was written in Greek or in Latin.[54]

Also of interest are the linguistic preferences of Syl'vestr Kosov, an Orthodox archimandrite, metropolitan of Kyiv, native of the Vitebsk region, and an opponent of the union with Muscovy. Of his four published works, three are written in Polish.[55]

Fiodar Eŭlashoŭski (1546–1619) is another interesting historical figure whose literary work illustrates the linguistic behavior of the Ruthenian nobility. Born to an Orthodox family of a minor landed gentry of the Brest region, Eŭlashoŭski was attracted to the ideas of the Reformation and became a Calvinist. Eŭlashoŭski's name is generally associated with his memoirs, usually entitled the *Historical Notes*. This account of personal experience amidst the political life of the Polish-Lithuanian Commonwealth marks the beginning of the genre of diaries and memoirs in Ruthenia.[56] Eŭlashoŭski's notes are valuable because they contain first-hand information about private life in the Grand Duchy and, specifically, about the education of a Ruthenian courtier. Thus, we know that

---

[53] Ševčenko 1996.

[54] Ševčenko 1996, 151.

[55] Moszyńska 1998, 138–139.

[56] Sviazhynski 1990. Eŭlashoŭski's *Historical Notes* were finished in 1604.

Eŭlashoŭski learned Ruthenian and Polish, and also that he was conversant in Hebrew letters:

**а в пѧто$^{м}$ рокꙋ почато мє бави$^{ть}$ наꙋкою рꙋскою, кгды$^{ж}$ в ты$^{х}$ часєх в тє̑ нашє̑ стронє нє было єщє и$^{н}$ши$^{х}$ наꙋкъ и длѧ того$^{ж}$ пришло ми зоста$^{ть}$ з рꙋскою и по$^{л}$скою наꙋкою и по жидо$^{в}$ски написа$^{ть}$ ꙋмєло$^{м}$**[57]

[And in my fifth year I was entertained with Ruthenian letters, since at that time there were no other letters in our land and therefore I was to learn the Ruthenian and Polish letters and I also could write in Hebrew.]

Eŭlashoŭski occupied various important administrative positions that, among other responsibilities, demanded proficiency in the administrative language. Moreover, he was close to the Polish Court and in constant contact with Polish officials and nobles.[58] We find the mark of his professional activity in the language of his *Historical Notes*. In characterizing his text, one can hardly describe it as East Slavic. Were it not written in Cyrillic characters it could have been taken for Polish; the graphic representation, orthography, and, occasionally, the morphology are East Slavic whereas the rest of the linguistic levels are largely Polish. This becomes evident when we compare it to a contemporary Polish translation made by E. Ciemniewski. His translation technique, which does not seem to be very intricate, resembles Eŭlashoŭski's Ruthenian text, only written in Polish letters. For example, the above quoted fragment is translated in the following way:

W piątym roku poczęto mnie zajmować nauką języka ruskiego; a że w owym czasie w naszych stronach innych nauk wcale jeszcze nie było, musiałem poprzestać na znajomości tegoż oraz polskiego języka.Umiałem także pisać po żydowsku...[59]

The study of the language of Meletii Smotryts'kyi, another famous Ruthenian man of letters, has also provided valuable information about the linguistic behavior of a Ruthenian intellectual.[60] Analyzing the writing technique of Smotryts'kyi and his other contemporaries, David Frick comes to the conclusion that at the beginning of the seventeenth century the boundary between Polish and Ruthenian "was porous in both directions."[61]

A striking example of the porous Polish-Ruthenian boundary is represented in the text of the Lithuanian Statute "translated" into "Polish," or, rather,

---

[57] Sviazhynski 1990, 90.
[58] Sviazhynski 1990, 25.
[59] Pollak 1966, 353.
[60] Frick 1995, Pugh 1985 and 1996.
[61] Frick 1995, 185.

transcribed into Latin characters from the Cyrillic. This is a copy of a Mamonich 1595 edition of the Statute of 1588 described by Miakishev 2001. Compare for example the title pages of the Ruthenian 1588 edition and the Polish 1595 edition[62] (N.B. the retention of the pleophonic form in "Polish"):

| | |
|---|---|
| STATUT WIELIKOHO KNIAZTWA | **СТѦТȢ ВЕЛІКОГО КНꙖТВѦ** |
| LITOVSKOHO, OD NAIASNEŸ | **ЛІТОСКОГ ѿ** наꙗснеⷮшего г҇дра |
| SZOHO HOSPODARA KOROLA | королѧ его м҇лсти |
| IEHO MILOSTI, ZŸGIMONTA TRE | жикгимонта третего на |
| TIEHO NA KORONACŸI W KRAKO | коронацыи въ кракове выданы |
| WIE WŸDANŸ ... ROKU 1595 | рокȣ ,а҃ ф҃ пи҃ . |

[The Statute of the Grand Duke of Lithuania, His Most Serene and Excellent Majesty, King Zygmunt III, issued on the occasion of his coronation and published in Cracow in the year 1588 (1595 in Polish).][63]

Miakishev comes to the conclusion that the transcription was carried out "by ear" (*на слух*). The scribe was most likely equally proficient in Ruthenian and Polish. The Polish interference is evident in his occasional use of nasals; in the use of the Polish preposition and prefix *od* instead of the Ruthenian *ot*; generally, in the adherence to the rules of Polish orthography, particularly the Cracow tradition; and in the use of Polish variants of cognate words.[64] This text is a valuable source of information about the sixteenth-century Ruthenian sound system, since the transliteration seems to reproduce the actual pronunciation.

The above mentioned texts represent different manifestations of the Ruthenian written language's relationship with Polish. These differences depend on the author's cultural background, education, occupation, language attitude, and linguistic proficiency. They show that we may have to submit to the fact that written (literary) Ruthenian is a collection of idiolects and individual translations, characterized by their source languages. Whatever the case may be, the social history of Ruthenian has yet to be written.

Most evidence about the East Slavic-Polish linguistic relationship in Ruthenian literacy that has been studied so far dates to the mid-sixteenth century at the earliest. What, then, happened during the two hundred year gap between the fading of Kievan Rus' cultural tradition and the acknowledged Polish cul-

---

[62] The transcription is mine and is based on the title pages reproduced in Miakishev 2001, 182–183.

[63] The Polish King Zygmunt III Waza was crowned on December 27, 1587 at the Wawel Cathedral in Cracow.

[64] Miakishev 2001, 187–191.

tural dominance in the Grand Duchy of Lithuania at the second half of the sixteenth century? Unfortunately, we possess very limited knowledge of the vernacular of that period, and what we know is primarily based on the chancery language of administrative and legal documents.[65]

This sought-after evidence may be found in the Ruthenian manuscript miscellanies containing religious and literary texts, which present a valuable source for the study of both the Ruthenian language and the literary history of future Ukrainian and Belarusian lands. These miscellanies consist of compilations of texts generally copied and collected for private use, either edificatory or devotional. Some of them contain translations into Ruthenian, usually made by anonymous authors as early as the fifteenth century, providing evidence of a much earlier transmission of Czech and Polish texts into Ruthenia than is customarily supposed.

## RUTHENIAN TRANSLATIONS

Until the fifteenth century the main focus of Rus' bookmen had been on the textual corpus of Byzantine Christianity, Greek being the primary source language of new translations. After the Grand Duchy entered into a dynastical and later a constitutional union with the Polish Kingdom, forming the Polish-Lithuanian Commonwealth, it became more involved in the cultural and political life of Central Europe than before. As an open venue for both cultural and commercial imports, the multi-ethnic Lithuanian state, almost simultaneously, experienced Greek Orthodoxy, Roman Catholicism, Reformation, Counter-Reformation, Humanism, and Protestantism.[66] Historians have noted that much Ruthenian political and cultural history has been shaped by a spirit of tolerance and the lack of absolutist tendencies in dogmatic and ecclesiological differences between the Eastern and Western Churches.[67] This open-mindedness vis-à-vis the confes-

[65] A question that we should probably pose here is how close the administrative language was to the fifteenth and sixteenth-century Ruthenian vernacular? If we consider the distinction between the bureaucratic style and the literary or spoken register in modern languages as a point of reference we should allow a great difference.

[66] In his study on the "lost" continent of Dniprovia (lost to historical imagination), Edward Keenan emphasizes the role of the political prosperity and especially economic efflorescence of the whole region, that created conditions for this cultural diversity. Keenan believes that the fragmentary evidence of attested great works (he cites the *Peresopnytsia Gospel*, Crimean school of Armenian miniature paintings, European romance translations and biblical translations from Hebrew) is a sign of a great civilization, of which only a small fraction can be seen today (Keenan 2007).

[67] For example, see Gudziak 2001, 49.

sional divide between Catholic and Orthodox in the dogmatic sphere in Ruthenia was mirrored by a similar situation in the textual repertoire of Ruthenian bookmen. Translations of Christian texts dating from that period reflect this cultural and religious broadmindedness.

In the fifteenth century, Ruthenian men of letters started viewing Western Christian texts as a source for the replenishment of ecclesiastical literature in a Slavic tongue, whether in the sacred Church Slavonic or in the profane Ruthenian vernacular. Unfortunately, not many of the texts that were then translated from Latin and other Slavic vernaculars (such as Polish and Czech) have been thoroughly studied. The omission of these texts from comprehensive linguistic and literary examinations has several reasons. One of the impediments to linguistic analysis stems from the fact that these Ruthenian texts are translations, whose linguistic examination requires foregoing philological research and establishing source texts, which in many instances are problematic.

Another important impediment to the study of translations has been a persistent notion of a national literature, imposed by nationalist ideologies of the Romantic era. This notion still often operates in many approaches to literary culture, leading scholars largely to ignore and underestimate the role of translated texts in framing a national literary history. Ruthenian translations, however, are to a great degree a product of the idiosyncratic and diverse cultural climate that reigned in the Grand Duchy of Lithuania and Polish-Lithuanian Commonwealth, and they deserve to be treated as rightful representatives of the Ruthenian literary corpus.

In the chapters that follow, readers will find a study of four fifteenth-century Ruthenian translations from Czech focusing on the historical context of their transmission. A historical and philological examination of each translation has been supplied with a linguistic analysis and a discussion of translation technique. This multifaceted approach allows us to make assumptions about possible circumstances of translation, and about the linguistic mechanisms that led to the creation of these Ruthenian texts. A brief account of the status and circulation of the Czech language in fifteenth and sixteenth-century Polish and Lithuanian lands precedes the study of the Ruthenian translations.

# Chapter One
# CZECH IN THE LINGUISTIC HISTORY OF THE GRAND DUCHY OF LITHUANIA AND POLAND

Czech developed very early as a vernacular literary language.[1] It had already taken shape as a language of writing at the beginning of the fourteenth century, and continued to mature during the reign of the Czech King and the Holy Roman Emperor Charles IV (1346–1378), whose cultural-political program promoted the development of Czech as the national language of scholarship and administration.[2] Over the course of the fourteenth century, literary Czech made its way into most areas of cultural, religious and political life. Emerging first as a language of religious and didactic prose, it also entered such secular genres as poetry, legends, epic stories, and chronicles that described and glorified national history. In time, its vocabulary became sufficiently elaborate to be used in theological and scholarly prose.[3] In fact, legal and administrative documents were being written in Czech as early as the second half of the fourteenth century. Gradually, it transcended ethnic borders and became a language of administration in Polish Upper Silesia (which was added to Czech lands in 1355) and in adjacent areas.[4] By the end of the fourteenth century a rich literature in Czech had been created, which became a model for neighboring Slavic literary languages.

## THE AUTHORITY OF CZECH IN POLAND

The end of the fourteenth century marks the beginning of Czech's influence on the emerging Polish vernacular literary tradition.[5] The first Polish texts had primarily religious content, translated from Latin with the help of corresponding Czech translations. Even original works imitated Czech models: for example,

[1] Auty 1980, Cuřín 1985, 17–56.

[2] Michálek 1975.

[3] Latin-Czech lexicons compiled by Claretus de Solencia (Bartoloměj z Chlumce) were most probably intended for authors to assist them in their Czech composition. See Michálek 1989 for more details.

[4] Havránek 1939.

[5] Scholarly literature about Czech influence on Polish is abundant. The following selected studies summarize the most important issues and provide further literature on the subject: Orłoś 1993, Mayenowa 1984, Schenker 1978, Jakobson 1953, Florovskii [1946] 1988, Havránek 1939, Jansen 1939.

many scholars argue that the oldest attested Polish religious song, *Bogurodzica, dziewica*, bears signs of Czech linguistic influence.[6] Czech words and phrases also enhanced the language of secular genres. Similarly, Latin texts of Polish provenance were also shaped by Bohemian examples.[7] Along this route of influence Silesia played a considerable connecting role. Silesian lands, under constant cultural influence from Bohemia, were of great importance in Polish medieval learning and culture.

In the second half of the fourteenth and the beginning of the fifteenth centuries, the cultural superiority and prestige of Prague in Central Europe attracted the intellectual elite from many countries. Many Polish academics studied at Prague University, founded in 1348 by Charles: the majority of professors who took posts at Cracow University, founded sixteen years later, had received their degrees in Prague.[8] The spread of Hussite ideas and writings in the beginning of the fifteenth century, although not as intensive (especially after 1420) as nineteenth-century and Marxist historiography suggests, nevertheless also bore a share of the responsibility for the Czech linguistic influence on Polish.[9]

In the sixteenth century, we find testimonies that Czech began influencing not only written literary Polish but also the learned spoken language. The use of Czech words and expressions in Polish became a sign of good taste. The works of Polish humanists concerned with the language question note that Czech was used, both intentionally and unintentionally, to shape the Polish literary language. One of the most frequently cited examples is an opinion of Łukasz Górnicki in *Dworzanin Polski* (*The Polish Courtier*, 1566):

*... a czasem drugi, chocia nie będzie w Czechach, jedno iż granicę śląską przejedzie, to już inaczej nie będzie chciał mówić, jedno po czesku, a czeszczyzna, wie to Bóg, jaka będzie. A jeśli mu rzeczesz, żeby swym językiem mówił, to powieda, iż zapomniał abo że mu sie przyrodzony język prawdziwie gruby widzi, czego dowodząc, wyrwie jakie staropolskie z Bogarodzice słowo a z czeskiem jakiem gładkiem słówkiem na sztych je wysadzi, aby swego języka grubość, a obcego piękność pokazał; na koniec i z tym na plac wyjdzie, że niemal każdy w polskim języku wymowca czeskich słów miasto polskich używa, jakoby to było naschwał*

---

6 František Mareš offered a comparative study of the Old Polish *Bogurodzica* and the Old Czech *Hospodine, pomiluj ny*, showing numerous similarities between these two old religious songs (Mareš 2000, 450–454).

7 Jansen 1939, 48–49.

8 See, for example, Barycz 1948. The Prague University was established for four “nations”: Czech, Saxon, Bavarian and Polish.

9 For a recent analysis of the extent of the Hussite movement in the fifteenth-century Poland, see Kras 1998.

*dobrze.*[10]
[... and sometimes another one, although not yet in Bohemia, as soon as he crosses the Silesian border, he will not wish to speak otherwise but in Czech, and what a Czech language that will be, God knows. And if you tell him to speak his own language he will say that he has forgotten it or that his native language sounds truly coarse to him and to prove that he will take an Old Polish word from *Bogurodzica* and compare it with some polished Czech word in order to show the crudeness of his own language and beauty of the foreign. Finally, he will go so far as to say that almost every speaker in Polish uses Czech words instead of Polish, as if that was wonderfully good.]

Although Górnicki censures the use of Czech words when Polish equivalents exist, he advises employing them to enrich Polish as needed:

*A tak przystępując do rzeczy, kiedy dworzaninowi polskich słów nie zstanie, dobrze uczyni, iż pożyczy z czeskiego języka, rychlej niż z drugich, a to dla tego, że już ten sam u nas jest wzięty i policzony za najcudniejszy...*[11]
[And so in speaking, when a courtier lacks Polish words, he will do well if he borrows them from Czech rather than from other languages, because this language is accepted among us and considered to be the most beautiful...]

The employment of Czech models in literary Polish was one of the main issues in the polemic between translators and writers Jan Sandecki-Małecki and Jan Seklucjan in the 1540s.[12] Jan Sandecki-Małecki was convinced that literary Polish should be modeled after Czech, especially in biblical translations, as evidenced by this passage from his *Defensio verae translationis* (*The Defence of Accurate Translation*, 1547):

… I well know that the Polish language (within the limits of possibility and necessity) should be corrected and enriched with the help of Czech. You certainly know that whoever wishes to translate the Holy Writings into the Polish language accurately and properly cannot manage without the aid of a Czech text. While making such translations we should turn to this language as to an encyclopedia and compose with its help individual Polish expressions and phrases… for our language is for the most part corrupted to such an extent that no one can accurately and properly speak it if he does not know the Czech well.[13]

Sandecki-Małecki then gives several examples of Latin words that could not be translated into Polish without the knowledge of Czech. This piece of evidence,

[10] Górnicki 1954, 75–76. Górnicki's treatise is a relatively free adaptation of Baldassare Castiglione's *Il Cortegiano* (*The Courtier*, 1516). This passage paraphrases Castiglione's remark on the pretentious use of Old Tuscan words in Italian. On the Górnicki's text and its relationship with the Italian original, see Introduction by Roman Pollak in Górnicki 1954, iii–cxxxiii.

[11] Górnicki 1954, 82.

[12] Mayenowa 1984, 343.

[13] Cited and translated from Janów 1947, xxxix–xl.

as described by a sixteenth-century Polish philologist, is extremely valuable because it shows that there had been an established (and even predictable) linguistic pattern in the application of Czech models to Polish ("... whoever wishes to translate the Holy Writings into the Polish language accurately and properly (*vere ac proprie*), cannot manage without the aid of a Czech text").

Sandecki's son, Hieronim, inherited his father's ideas. In the introduction to his translation of Luther's *Postylla domowa* (*The House Postil*, 1574), which he modeled on Czech, he wrote:

*Czechowie są pirwszy niżeli Polacy w przekładaniu Bibliej i innych ksiąg Luterowych na swój czeski język, a dlategoż my Polacy musieliśmy wiele słów od Czechów brać i dzisiejszego czasu, a zwłaszcza w teologiej wiele ich brać i onych używać musimy.*[14]
[The Czechs are more advanced than the Poles in translating the Bible and other books of Luther into their language, and therefore we Poles had to take many words from the Czechs even today, especially in theology we must take and use a lot of their words.]

## The Mark of Czech in Ruthenian

While language contact between Czech and Polish is relatively well documented and has received scholarly attention, the influence of Czech on Ruthenian is traditionally regarded as merely indirect, exerted almost exclusively through Polish. Accordingly, all "Bohemisms" are thought to have been transmitted through the mediation of Polish and are therefore considered Polonisms.[15] Although the direct influence of Czech on Ruthenian should not be overestimated, one should at the same time be cautious about rejecting its existence. The cultural authority of the Czech language and the dominance of Czech literary production spread more or less throughout the whole Polish-Lithuanian Commonwealth. Given this fact, it would be inaccurate to suppose that they affected only ethnic Poles, while leaving the Ruthenian population untouched.

### Direct Contacts between the Czechs and the Ruthenians

Direct contact between the Czechs and Ruthenians, although not as intensive as that between the Czechs and Poles, is nevertheless worth noting during the history of the Grand Duchy of Lithuania. It was present in various socio-political and

[14] Cited from Orłoś 1993, 26.
[15] See, for example, Schenker 1983.

cultural spheres of public life – in diplomacy, trade, education, arts and scholarship, and even in military craft.[16]

Established in 1348, the Prague University quickly became an educational hub in Central Europe, attracting students from neighboring countries, including the Grand Duchy. Young people from Lithuania made up a significant percentage of the regular students at Prague University, as is evident from the fact that in 1397 the Polish Queen Jadwiga established a special College in Prague for "Lithuanian" students.[17] The term "Lithuanian" at that time included all residents of the Grand Duchy, both ethnic Lithuanians and Ruthenians. Conversely, it is documented that Czech clergy and lay people resided in Lithuania and Ruthenian lands; we know of Canon Jan Čech (Johannes Bohemus) in Vilnius in 1398 and of a certain Mikuláš Čech, who built a chapel in L'viv in 1406 in honor of Sts. Václav, Vít and Prokop. Jeroným Silván (Pražský), a Catholic missionary and scholar, was active at the court of the Polish King Władysław Jagiełło and in Lithuania at the end of the fourteenth century.[18]

With the rise of the Hussite movement, the Czech clergy became attracted to the Orthodox ecclesiastical tradition, in which they saw the foundation of the original, uncorrupted Christian Church. Their interest resulted in a visit to the Ruthenian dioceses in 1412–1413 by Jerome of Prague (Jeroným Pražský), a friend and associate of Jan Hus (who is not to be confused with Jeroným Silván Pražský, a passionate adversary of Hussitism).[19] This trip turned out to be decisive in Jeroným's condemnation and execution at the Council of Constance in 1416, where he was accused of heresy and sympathy for the Orthodox Church.

The Ukrainian historian Mikhailo Hrushevs'kyi attached exceptional importance to the influence of Hussite ideas on the Ruthenian linguistic and literary culture. He asserted that although direct evidence of such influence has not been preserved, the vernacularization of both language and literature in fifteenth-century Ruhenia was nurtured by the Hussite linguistic and religious outlook.[20] At the same time, Antonii Florovskii spoke of the Hussite influence in Ruthenia with some reserve.[21]

---

[16] The most detailed account of contacts between the Czechs and the Eastern Slavs is given in Florovskii 1947.

[17] Hrushevs'kyi 1995, 61–62, Pervolf 1874, 181–182.

[18] Florovskii 1935, 341–343.

[19] Florovskii 1935, 341–363, Jakubec 1911, 135 and 137; Perwolf 1893, 56–59.

[20] Hrushevs'kyi 1995, 73–83.

[21] Florovskii [1946] 1988, 160–163.

In his two-volume monograph *Chekhi i vostochnye slaviane* (*The Czechs and the Eastern Slavs*), Florovskii offered extensive data documenting multilateral economic relations between Bohemia and the Ruthenian communities in the Grand Duchy of Lithuania and Polish-Lithuanian Commonwealth.[22] He also discussed at length the circumstances of the migration of Czechs to Ruthenia, as well as the role Czech noblemen, craftsmen and the military played in Ruthenian economy and culture as early as the thirteenth century.[23] In this context circulation of and familiarity with Czech texts in the Ruthenian milieu would certainly have been expected and natural.

## Czech Influence on Administrative Ruthenian

Scholars have repeatedly suggested and then discarded the possibility of the direct influence of Czech on the Ruthenian administrative language. Linguistically speaking, the main difficulty in resolving this question lies in the fact that Czech also exerted influence on Polish. Therefore, many of the Czech features and even phraseological expressions in Ruthenian are often explained by Polish interference. While Iakovliv, Hrushevs'kyi, Ohienko, and Havránek spoke in favor of a direct Czech influence,[24] studies carried out by Christian Stang of the Ruthenian chancery language of Polatsk and Vílnius and by Władysław Kuraszkiewicz of Galician and Volhynian documents (*gramoty*) do not mention Czech linguistic influence.[25]

According to Josef Macůrek, the author of a number of articles on the language and composition of Galician-Volhynian diplomatic documents, fourteenth and fifteenth-century *gramoty* show dependence on Czech archetypes.[26] Macůrek studied the structure of these documents and arrived at the conclusion that *gramoty* originating in the territory of Galicia, Volhynia and Moldavia differed from the Vilnius, Novgorod, Pskov and Northeast Russian documents of that time and were based on West European examples (Czech and Polish-Latin). He argued that they not only resembled the structure of Czech documents, but also contained similar verbal expressions. He attributed the presence of the West Slavic component primarily to Czech influence. Macůrek's reason for discarding

---

[22] Florovskii 1947, 99–267.

[23] Florovskii 1947, 268–333.

[24] Iakovliv 1929, Ohienko 1930, Havránek 1939, 56-57, Hrushevs'kyi 1995.

[25] Kuraszkiewicz 1934, Stang 1935 and 1939.

[26] Macůrek 1960a, 1960b, 1968. See also Humets'ka 1967 for a review and criticism of Macůrek's studies.

Polish interference came from his observation that in the fourteenth and fifteenth centuries the language of administration in Poland was Latin, whereas literary Polish was still in the making.

Following up Macůrek's studies, Josef Anderš reintroduced the subject of direct Czech influence on the language of Ukrainian documents. He provided, however, very little new data.[27] Overall, I would follow Florovskii in concluding that we do not possess enough facts to either accept or refute with certainty the statement that Czech influenced the language of Ruthenian administration directly, without Polish mediation. Nevertheless, we ought not to exclude its possibility, at least until further research confirms or disproves it.

Although Florovskii rejects the validity of any decisive conclusions about the linguistic influence of Czech on administrative Ruthenian, he nevertheless answers the question of whether Czech law had an impact on Ruthenian legislation in the affirmative.[28] While the impact of Czech on Ruthenian administrative writings can be disputed, at least one record of Ruthenian legislation exhibits obvious Czech involvement. This text is the Ruthenian translation of the Wiślica Statute of Kazimierz the Great (1347), one of the most important Polish legal documents.[29] It was commissioned by a nobleman, Vanko Kirdeevich of Kvasilov, a castellan of Chełm, who ordered a translation of this statute to be made from the original Latin. The Ruthenian foreword to the text of the statute says:

... ѻ то быль сталъ абы тыто книги прав польских҄ из латыны были в часк8 ричь и в тых҄то стронах҄ на дальнеи земли р8скїи выложены ... и тыи книги праведныи статочне стоꙗлъ абы ем8 моглы изъ чески изъ латыны выложены быть небо латыны и чески невмѣше але литер8 р8ск8 добре чтꙗше.[30]

[... he was concerned that these books of Polish law be translated from Latin into the Czech language in these lands, on the distant Ruthenian soil... and persistently sought that these books of law be translated from Czech and Latin since he did not know Latin and Czech but could read Ruthenian script well.]

One way or another, the translation implicated the Czech language. This is apparent from the inclusion in the foreword of the following passage, which describes the similarity of Czech to Ruthenian:

---

[27] Anderš 1976 and 1998.

[28] Florovskii 1947, 51–59.

[29] On this text, see Perwolf 1886, Florovskii 1947, 52–54. Unfortunately, I was unable to study this text personally because the St. Petersburg archive, in which it is kept, is closed for renovation.

[30] Citation from Florovskii 1947, 52.

далеко сѹть от себе тыито земли, чехи а рѹси за лѣсы, иже сѹть чехове люди на западе слонца на горахъ, а люди довцепны, мало от рѹскаго ıазыка отторгнены, а рѹсь есть люди близки ричи свы ıазыка ческа подъ ѹсходемъ слонцемъ.[31]
[These lands of the Czechs and Rus' are far away from each other, beyond the forests. The Czechs are people in the west in the mountains, and a clever people, not much separated from the Rus' people, and the Rus' are the people in the east, in their idiom close to the Czech language.]

Josef Jireček assumed that a Czech version of the Wiślica Statute existed at some point, which was then used as a source text for the Ruthenian translation.[32] This, though, does not seem likely. It is more probable that a Czech scribe, who, unlike his Ruthenian colleagues, was versed in Latin, carried out or collaborated on the Ruthenian translation. Remarkably, the West Slavic lexical component, although it could have crept into the text due to Czech interference, reflects Polish pronunciation rather than Czech: the Ruthenian довцепны is more similar to the Polish *dowcipny*, 'clever, quick, intelligent,' than to the Czech *dovtipny*; the Ruthenian отторгнены imitates the Polish *odtargnąć*, 'tear off, separate, take apart' rather than the Czech *ottrhnúti*; the Ruthenian на западе слонца obviously reproduces the Polish *słońce*, 'sun,' instead of the Czech *slnce* (*slunce*); the Ruthenian station стронах derives from the Polish *strona*, 'side, land,' rather than from the Czech *strana*; whereas the Ruthenian статочне could come from either the Polish *stateczny*, 'brave, manly, dignified, significant, persistent, constant, sufficient,' or the Czech *statečný*.

There are at least two possible explanations for this outcome. First, the Polish phonological dress of these words could be due to a later transformation of Czech borrowings into more familiar Polish forms during recopying. Second, if the Czech translator worked on the translation with a Ruthenian colleague, then Polish forms could be "Ruthenian" equivalents of Czech introduced by the Ruthenian scribe. A translation practice, involving several translators, was not uncommon at that time (cf. the translations of Maxim Grek, who collaborated with several translators and scribes).

Further, another fact suggests that Czech was used in administrative practice in the Grand Duchy of Lithuania. In the 1831 issue of the *Časopis Českého Museum*, František Palacký published two letters from the Grand Duke of Lithuania Švitrigaila, written in Czech in 1431. Švitrigaila was then plotting against his brother, the King of Poland Władysław Jagiełło, and turned for help to the

[31] Florovskii 1947, 52.
[32] Jireček 1875, 168. Perwolf 1886 provides convincing evidence against this assumption.

Czech Hussites.[33] While it is improbable that Švitrigaila himself was proficient enough in Czech to dictate a letter, he apparently employed scribes at his chancery who were capable of writing and translating into Czech.

## Czech Biblical Books among Ruthenians

That Czech biblical books circulated among Ruthenians is evident from the fact that they are found in private and monastic libraries. For example, several Czech (as well as Ruthenian) books in the private library of Olbracht Gasztołd are regarded as the property of his father, Marcin, a palatine of Kyiv.[34] Similarly, the Czech biblical and other religious books have been recorded in the Supraśl monastic library, in the library of the Grand Duke of Lithuania and in the library of the L'viv brotherhood.[35]

Among the various works of Czech manuscript production, the Bible received the most attention in both the Polish and Ruthenian literary milieus. Of all the Slavs, the Czechs were the first to translate the entire Bible into vernacular. These translations were well known in Poland; in fact, the first Polish Bible emerged under Czech influence.[36] It appears that the Czech biblical translations also circulated among the Ruthenians. According to the testimony of Balthasar Hostovinus (Balthasar Hostounský, 1534–1600), a Czech Jesuit who took active part in the organization of the Jesuit College in Vilnius, both Poles and Ruthenians were familiar with the Czech Bible:

*La Bohemica benché nella pronuncia sia di quanto differente et men se intende, et in duo ò tre mesi si potrà far tanto, che si potrà predicare. Anzi appresso molti Poloni et Rutheni che non sapevano, se non leggere, la Bibia Boëmica.*[37]
[Although the Czech language is somewhat different in pronunciation and is less widely un-

[33] Palacký 1831, 280–282. Since Palacký's publication is extremely rare and hard to obtain I am citing here an excerpt from one of these letters:
*Osweczeny knyeze, Synowcze nas zmilely!*
*Yakož gsi k nam poslal sluhu sweho werneho Meczka, zakazuojcze sye nam, y jako slybugicze nam pomahaty protiw naſſim neprzetelom, sewſſemy kohozby mohl przemoczy; a take kterak na to drziff wſſecky wiſſe pany y Capitany, aby nam pomoczny byly na naſſe neprzetele: z toho dyekuyeme twemu Oswyeczeny, ponewaz tak naſſe dobre gednaſs y radyſs, a my take toho protyw tobie nechczeme zapomenuty, ale wſſeczkym dobrym odczynyty, y take zasie pomahaty, kdež tobie potrzebie bude.*[...]

[34] Topolska 1984, 205.

[35] Florovskii [1946] 1988, 163–164.

[36] Urbańczyk 1946, Florovskii [1946] 1988.

[37] This extract is from Hostovinus' letter to the general T. J. Lainez from Lemberg (L'viv), October 17, 1564 (Archivum Romanum Societatis Iesu /ARSI/, Rome).

derstood, nevertheless it is possible to make it so that in two or three months we will be able to preach. It is apparent with many Poles and Ruthenians, who could not read anything except the Czech Bible.][38]

Another trace of the circulation of the Czech Bible among Ruthenians is contained in a manuscript miscellany at the Vilnius Public Library (#47).[39] It comprises a collection of books of the prophets with exegesis, some part of which might have been translated with the help of the Czech Bible. The first leaf is inscribed: **прєдсловиє исаїна пророчєства с҃ счєскои библїи написано** (Introduction to the *Prophecy of Isaiah* written from the Czech Bible).[40] Finally, the translation of the *Bibliia Rus'ka* carried out by Frantsishak Skaryna definitely reflects an interest among Ruthenians in Czech biblical texts.[41] One of the sources which Skaryna consulted extensively for his Ruthenian *Bibliia* was a Venetian edition of the Czech Bible (1506).

Yet even before Skaryna undertook his grand work, Czech texts had started penetrating the Ruthenian Orthodox milieu and had left their mark on Ruthenian translations. Several translations from Czech of individual biblical books, popular and edificatory stories, legends and prophecies are preserved in fifteenth and sixteenth-century Ruthenian manuscripts.[42] The appearance of at least some of these translations could be explained by the presence in East Central Europe of the Croatian Benedictine Glagolite monks (*Glagoljaši*) and their possible proselytizing activity among the Orthodox Ruthenians.

## CROATIAN GLAGOLJAŠI AND RUTHENIAN TRANSLATIONS FROM CZECH

### The Croatian Glagolite Monks

The common Slavic language played an important role in cultural, economic and political contacts among the Slavs. Although individual Slavic vernaculars were

---

[38] I am grateful to Marco Clementi, Pietro Dini and Felix Heinzer for their comments regarding the translation of this record.

[39] This is an old catalogue number, according to Dobrianskii 1882, 58.

[40] Dobrianskii 1882, 58–60. Unfortunately, I have not had the opportunity to examine this manuscript. I suspect that the phrase **с҃ счєскои** may be a corruption of **грєчєскои**.

[41] Among the voluminous literature on Skaryna's work are, for example, studies by Vladimirov [1888] 1989, Sidorov 1979, Bulyka, Zhuraŭski and Sviazhynski 1990, Labyntsev 1990.

[42] The question of Ruthenian translations from Czech (some of which are mentioned in this study) and familiarity of Ruthenians with Czech literary sources is also discussed in Florovskii 1939, 1947 and [1946] 1988; Perwolf 1874, 250–256; Hrushevs'kyi 1960, 103–107, 117–119; Karskii 1921, 29–30.

already fairly diversified by the fourteenth century, to a certain degree all Slavs understood Church Slavonic. While Eastern and Southern Orthodox Slavs used Church Slavonic written in Cyrillic as an ecclesiastical language, Western Catholic Slavs generally used Latin in the church. A small community of Catholic Slavs in southern Croatia and Dalmatia, however, retained the use of Church Slavonic and the original Glagolitic writing.

Since the middle of the thirteenth century only a few dioceses in Dalmatia were allowed to hold Roman Catholic liturgy using a Slavic language and letters. More precisely, they used a Croatian variant of Church Slavonic written in the Glagolitic script, the first Slavic alphabet devised by Saint Cyril in the ninth century during the "Moravian" mission (hence their name "the Glagoljaši," the Glagolite monks). Glagoljaši's liturgical books (breviaries and missals) contained the original Cyrillo-Methodian translations, albeit complemented and modified by translations from Latin to conform to the Roman Mass. Pope Innocent IV first granted the right to use Church Slavonic in liturgy to the bishop of Senj in 1248, as a tribute to Saint Jerome, a celebrated Church Father, biblical translator and monastic leader. Croatian clergymen claimed that Saint Jerome was a native of Dalmatia and, therefore, a Slav.[43] They further maintained that Saint Jerome had not only translated the Bible into Latin, but also translated the Holy Mass into Church Slavonic and invented the Slavic (i.e. Glagolitic) letters. After the pope gave official permission to use Slavonic in liturgy and before the end of the thirteenth century, three orders in the regions of Senj, Zadar, and the Kvarner islands – the Benedictines, the Third Order Franciscans, and the Order of St. Paul – became centers of Slavonic liturgy. Saint Jerome's posthumous career as a Slav and as the inventor of Slavic letters had begun, and he became the official patron saint of the Croats.[44]

## The Prague Emmaus Monastery

The alleged Slavic origin of Saint Jerome turned out to be of considerable use in another part of the Slavic world as well. The myth traveled from the Dalmatian coast to Prague along with eighty Benedictine Glagolite monks. The idea of a Slavonic liturgy according to the Roman Rite also appealed to the Czech King, later the Holy Roman Emperor Charles IV, who attached great significance to the Slavic tongue in the ecclesiastical sphere. Charles embraced the belief that

[43] Saint Jerome was born in the mid fourth century in the town of Stridon situated on the border between Dalmatia and Pannonia.

[44] Smržík 1959, 46–60; Ostojić 1960, Fine 2000.

Saint Jerome was the author of the Slavic liturgy and the inventor of the Slavic Glagolitic letters. In his letter to Pope Clement VI Charles used this as an argument to gain the pope's consent to establish a Slavonic monastery in Prague. In 1347, having received the pope's permission to introduce the Slavonic liturgy in Prague, he invited a group of the Benedictine Glagoljaši from the island of Pašman and the diocese of Senj to establish the Prague Emmaus Monastery *Na Slovanech.*[45]

Charles had been familiar with the Benedictine Glagoljaši since 1337, when, as the Margrave of Moravia, he visited the Dalmatian coast and the diocese of Senj, where he witnessed firsthand their impoverishment caused by wars and other misfortunes. After Charles became King, he wished to support and spread the Slavonic liturgy, which was then allowed only in Dalmatian dioceses. He may have brought the Glagoljaši to Prague merely for this purpose. It is also possible, though, that his plan to establish Roman Slavonic liturgy in Prague was a part of a more far-reaching and specific objective.

Historians hypothesize and argue about the possible reasons for the foundation of the Slavonic monastery in Prague. Among the frequently proposed motives is Charles' intention to conduct the apostolate among heretics (Balkan Bogomils) and/or "schismatics" (the Eastern and Southern Orthodox Slavs). It has been suggested that Charles, a zealous Catholic and an advocate of a united church, contemplated missionary work in non-Catholic Slavic countries. He may have intended to use the Roman Slavonic liturgy and the common Slavic language as a means of introducing Roman Christianity among Eastern and Southern Slavs.[46]

I am, however, inclined to agree with scholars who view the foundation of the Emmaus Monastery *Na Slovanech* in the broader cultural context of

[45] Ostojić 1960. This monastery was also known as the Monastery *Na Slovanech.* The name shows that the Glagolite monks were perceived in Prague as the "Slavs," the custodians of Slavic traditions.

[46] This interpretation is primarily based on Charles' own explanation in his letter to the Pope. For example, considerations of a mission to "schismatics" have been suggested by Paulová 1950, Hamm 1971, 96, Huňáček 1975, 177–179. That Charles held the cause of church union dear to his heart can also be seen in his letter of 1355 to the Serbian Czar Stefan Dušan, who was then negotiating with the Pope about a possible union between the Serbian and Roman churches. In his letter, Charles supported Dušan's aspirations and emphasized the Slavs' advantage in being able to celebrate Divine Liturgy in their vernacular. In this letter, he also pointed out that the prominent and dignified Slavic language would help Serbian clergy to convert to Catholicism. Unfortunately for Charles, Czar Dušan died very soon and the negotiations about the union were abandoned. Then again, Trajdos 1988 is skeptical about the relevance and even technical possibility of such a mission for a monastery based in Bohemia.

Charles' dynastical-political program for the Bohemian Kingdom under the rule of the House of Luxembourg.[47] To support his dynastic aspirations in Bohemia, Charles required not only an intellectually and culturally thriving capital, into which Prague was gradually transforming during his reign. He also needed an ideological justification for the historical importance of the Bohemian state. To assist this goal, he urged and inspired historians to elevate the role and place of Bohemia in world and biblical history. A number of historical treatises, commissioned by Charles, substantiated the ancient and noble origin of the Slavs and Czechs. They traced back the descent of Bohemian rulers to Great Moravia, and the origin of the Bohemians to the Tower of Babel.

One such work is the *Cronica Boemorum* (*The Czech Chronicle*) by the Franciscan friar Giovanni dei Marignolli (Jan Marignola), which he composed as Charles' court historian after returning from his famous journey to China in 1353. Written in the Joachimite prophetic tradition, the chronicle traced the lineage of Charles back to Nimrod, a legendary biblical hero and the founder of the Babylonian Empire. It also included Roman Emperors Diocletian and Maximian among the ancestors of the Slavs, referred to the Slavs as "the people of the sun" and generally demonstrated their ancient and distinguished origins.[48]

Another historical work that emphasized and glorified Bohemia's Slavic heritage, the *Czech Chronicle*, was compiled by Přibík Pulkava from Radenín in 1374. It was first written in Latin and then appeared in Přibík's own loose translation into Czech. To portray the Slavs as foremost among Christian people, Přibík's chronicle gives a detailed account of Saint Cyril's request to the Pope to use Slavonic language in liturgy. At the beginning, the Pope did not take Cyril's application seriously. However, when, according to the chronicle, Cyril entered into an argument with bishops and cardinals about the Slavonic liturgy a voice from heaven was heard commanding them to celebrate God in all languages, the whole scene reminiscent of the Pentecostal gift of tongues:[49]

*Kterúžto prosbu papiež v smieh jest obrátil. A když pak o to s kardinaly a s mnohými biskupy mnohé řeči a rozmysly byly, ihned v rychlosti hlas povzněl s nebes a řka: Všelikterý duch chval Hospodina a všickni jazykové jemu sě vyznávajte. Tehdy papež ten div veliký uslyšav, na věky ustanovil jest, aby slovanským jazykem mše svaté, jiné také službv božie slúženy byly...* [50]

[47] Paulová 1950, Michálek 1975.

[48] Chadraba 1975, Cinke 1975.

[49] On the Pentecostal justification of the Slavonic liturgy, the Cyrillo-Methodian mission and the beginning of national self-determination among the Slavs see Jakobson 1985, Ševčenko 1991, Obolensky 1994.

[50] Emler 1893, 221.

[The Pope turned this request into a joke. But later when there were long disputes and discussions with cardinals and bishops about that there suddenly was heard a voice from heaven saying: "Every spirit praise the Lord and all languages profess Him." Then, after having heard this great miracle, the Pope established forever that the Holy Mass, as well as other divine services, be celebrated in the Slavic tongue.]

This episode was later also repeated by Enea Silvio Piccolomini in his *Historia Bohemica* (written in 1457, first edition in 1475).[51]

Charles made every effort to cultivate and glorify Slavic cultural accomplishments in order to advance his dynastic policy in Bohemia. About four centuries after the Slavic Apostles' famous dispute, Charles also asked for papal permission to institute the Roman Slavonic liturgy in Prague. However, this time it was not the Pentecostal idea that he employed in his request. As the Glagolite bishop of Senj had done formerly, Charles used Saint Jerome's alleged authorship of the Slavonic Bible and liturgy as an argument. In the act Charles issued at the monastery's foundation, he reiterated that the Slavonic liturgy was respected in honor and memory of Saint Jerome, who translated the Holy Scripture from Hebrew into Latin and Slavonic.[52] Charles declared the Croatian Slavonic of Saint Jerome to be the original language of the Slavs and a proto-language of the Czech vernacular:

*... ob reuerenciam et memoriam gloriosi confessoris beati Jeronimi, Stridonensis doctoris egregii et translatoris interpretisque eximii sacre scripture de ebrayca in latinam et slauonicam lingwas, de qua siquidem slavonica nostri regni Boemieydioma sumpsit exordium primordialiter et processit.*[53]

[... on account of respect for and in the memory of the glorious Confessor, Blessed Jerome, Stridon's illustrious doctor and distinguished translator and interpreter of the Holy Scripture from Hebrew into Latin and Slavonic, since indeed from it the Slavic language of our Bohemian Kingdom takes origin and proceeds (originated and developed).]

The connection between the Slavic language of the Bohemian Kingdom and the original Slavonic of Saint Jerome, pointed out by Charles in his letter to Pope Clement, was fundamental to Charles' cultural reforms. The Saint Jerome legend provided a sacral authentication of the Czechs and Slavs as privileged people. This very idea is elaborated in a work of the Břevnov Benedictine Jan of Holešov, the *Exposicio cantici sancti Adalberti*, a treatise on the religious hymn *Hospodine, pomiluj ny* (*Lord, have mercy on us*).[54] In his treatise, Jan of Holešov

[51] Enea Silvio [1458] 1998, 42.

[52] More precisely, Croatian Church Slavonic.

[53] The act of November 21, 1347 in Nürnberg (Helmling and Horcicka 1904, 9–10).

[54] The manuscript of the treatise is dated to 1397 (The National Library, III D 17).

provided a quasi-scholarly linguistic proof of the relationship between Croatian and Czech languages. He claimed that the hymn contains many Croatian words and used this to argue that the Czech language and people are Croatian in origin:

> ... *nos Bohemi et genere et lingua originaliter processimus a Charvatis, ut nostrae chronicae dicunt seu testantur, et ideo nostrum boemicale ydioma de genere suo est charvaticum ydioma...*[55]
> [...we, Bohemians, both by origin and language stem from the Croatians as our chronicles relate and testify, and therefore our Bohemian language by its origin is the Croatian language...]

The gift that the Benedictine Glagoljaši received from Charles upon the foundation of the Prague Emmaus Monastery was indeed royal – a part of the Gospel written in the Cyrillic of East Slavic provenance, dating from the mid twelfth century. This manuscript was believed to be an autograph of Saint Procopius (Prokop), the founder and abbot of the Sázava Monastery in eleventh-century Bohemia, which cultivated the Byzantine Slavic liturgy and maintained contacts with Rus'. Saint Procopius was also celebrated as one of the patrons of the Czech lands. The incomplete Cyrillic Gospel was later lavishly bound together with a lectionary, written in Glagolitic in the Emmaus Monastery and finished in 1395. This codex is known in modern scholarship as the Reims Gospel.[56]

The compilation of two parts, Cyrillic and Glagolitic, into one codex is not accidental, and the illumination of the newly written Glagolitic part does not leave doubts about its programmatic character. One of the illuminated initials features an image of Saint Jerome curing a lion; another initial shows Saint Procopius.[57] In this way, the codex symbolized the unity of Cyrillic writing, believed to have been created by Saint Cyril and cultivated in Bohemia by Saint Procopius, and the Glagolitic letters, believed to have been invented by Saint Jerome. The instructor of the Reims Gospel illuminator left another illumination

[55] Cited from Hercigonja 1975, 63. František Mareš provided a detailed study of this Old Czech hymn (Mareš 2000, 403–476).

[56] The story of this Emmaus codex is remarkable as is its provenance and mission. When the Emmaus Monastery fell to the Hussites in 1419 they also inherited this manuscript. Following the condemnation of Hussitism at the Council of Florence (1439–1442), the moderate Utraquists turned for help to the patriarch of Constantinople and presented him with the precious Emmaus Gospel as a gift (1452). After the fall of Constantinople the manuscript turned up in private hands and finally ended up in France, in the Reims Cathedral, where it became a *Texte du sacre,* the Gospel on which French kings took their oath during coronation. The codex was thought to be Greek until the visit of Peter the Great to Reims in 1717 when one of his retinue identified the Cyrillic part of the codex.

[57] Petr and Šabouk 1975, plates 42 and 43.

of Saint Jerome instructing the Emmaus monks in a Latin Emmaus Bible of ca. 1360.[58]

Patron saints chosen for the Emmaus Monastery also emphasized general Slavic and Czech heritage. The monastery was dedicated to the patron of the Croatian Glagoljaši Saint Jerome, the Slavic Apostles Saints Cyril and Methodius, Saint Procopius of Sázava, and the first Prague bishop and the patron of the Czech lands, Saint Vojtěch.

Whatever the emperor's intentions may have been, Charles well understood the potential of the Slavonic liturgy and cultural tradition in both ecclesiastical and political affairs. His expectations were justified. The Emmaus Monastery had a considerable impact on the development of the Czech vernacular in religious writings. A number of Czech texts written in Glagolitic were created and translated in the monastery, among them the Czech Bible.[59]

**Oleśnica and Kleparz Slavonic Monasteries**

Charles IV was not the only Slavic ruler with an interest in Slavonic liturgy, and the Glagoljaši did not confine their scribal and literary endeavors to Prague. Long before their return to the Dalmatian coast, a number of Glagolite monks left their Prague base and traveled east. In 1380, they were invited to the Silesian Oleśnica (Olešnice) by the Piast Prince Konrad II, although Stanisław Rybandt suggests that the main ideologue of the Oleśnica Corpus Christi Monastery's foundation was Jan of Prague, the abbot of the Wrocław Augustinians.[60] Ten years later, in 1390, the Prague Glagolite monks were solicited by the Polish Queen Jadwiga and King Władysław Jagiełło to settle in Kleparz, a suburb of Cracow, in the Monastery of the Holy Cross.[61] The Polish chronicler, Jan Długosz, explicitly mentions Jadwiga as the main patroness and the initiator of the monastery's foundation.[62]

The creation of both monasteries that used Slavonic liturgy according to the Roman Rite served the political and cultural agendas of their patrons. Prince Konrad II hoped to stimulate Slavic cultural and religious life in Silesia to coun-

[58] Petr and Šabouk 1975, plate 40.

[59] For information on the Czech texts created by the Glagoljaši at the Emmaus Monastery, see Pacnerová 1975, 2000, 2001, 2002; Havránek 1975, Mareš 1972 and 1975, Michálek 1975. The best sources on Czech biblical translations are Kyas 1997 and Pečírková 1998.

[60] Rybandt 1970, 666–670.

[61] Długosz 1864, 227–229 (foundation documents), Krukowski 1886.

[62] Trajdos 1988, 73–74.

tervail the influence of German colonizers and Teutonic knights, as well as to strengthen economic and cultural ties with Bohemia and Lithuanian Rus'.[63] Following his marriage to the Polish Queen Jadwiga in 1386, the former Lithuanian Grand Duke Władysław Jagiełło accepted Catholicism and took on the task of Christianizing (or rather Catholicizing) Lithuania, with its large Ruthenian Orthodox population. Jadwiga and Jagiełło could have regarded the Prague Benedictines as valuable partners in that cause.

Jadwiga's partiality for the Glagolite monks has not been sufficiently explained. Possibly she was familiar with the Slavonic ecclesiastical tradition and the Croatian Glagoljaši through her mother, Elizabeth of Bosnia, and so could have understood their importance in advertising the Roman Rite among the Orthodox Ruthenians. Likewise, she was well informed about Prague's cultural and religious life, and could have known about the activity of the Emmaus monks there.[64]

While we may only make assumptions about Jadwiga's intentions, it is well documented that Władysław Jagiełło, like Charles IV, was an advocate of a union between the Catholic and Orthodox Churches. That Jagiełło was not at all ill-disposed towards the Orthodox faith is evident from the fact that in 1384 he almost accepted a proposition from Muscovy of a dynastical union with the daughter of Grand Prince Dmitrii Ivanovich (Donskoi), Sofia. In exchange, Jagiełło was expected to Christianize Lithuania in the Orthodox Rite. The counter offer of the Polish Queen Jadwiga's hand and Roman Catholicism in the following year changed his plans. This union not only made Jagiełło a King of Poland, it also strongly protected his native Lithuania from the claims of the Teutonic Order.

As a King of Poland in the 1390s, Jagiełło had already entered into rather fruitless negotiations with the Constantinopolitan patriarch about a church union.[65] Despite the fact that these negotiations fell short of Jagiełło's expectations, he did not abandon his aspirations. He further appealed to the Council of Constance that took place in 1414–1418. One of his letters from 1417 relates his efforts to bring the Ruthenian Orthodox Church ("*illa veterna Grecorum rebellio*," as Jagiełło puts it) round to a union with Rome.[66] In another letter, Jagiełło notifies the Council of a mission that he entrusted to Metropolitan Gregory Tsam-

[63] Rybandt 1970.

[64] Trajdos 1988, 75–76.

[65] Mironowicz 2003a, 150–151.

[66] ["that old rebellion of the Greeks."] Sokołowski and Lewicki 1876, v. 2, Letter # 77, 92–93.

blak ("*metropolitus tocius Russie ac plage orientalis*"),[67] whom he sent to Constance to negotiate for a union.[68] Could it be that the Orthodox frescoes, which Jagiełło commissioned for several Catholic churches and Royal Castle chapels, were also a part of his unitary efforts?

The conversion of Orthodox believers to Catholicism was not a part of Jagiełło's official policy. Nevertheless, his intention to expose the Ruthenian Orthodox community to the Roman Rite may have motivated him to follow the examples of Charles and Konrad in inviting Prague Glagolite monks to Cracow in 1390.[69] Indeed, he could have been thinking about his Ruthenian attendants, who had followed him to the Polish Court from Lithuania several years before, and now needed intelligible instruction in their new Catholic faith.[70] Jadwiga and Jagiełło, too, understood the power of a comprehensible Slavic idiom in the religious sphere – in the fifteenth century, the liturgical language of Croatian Glagolites still had a similar sound to that of the Orthodox Ruthenians. By founding the Slavonic Benedictine monastery in Kleparz they may have hoped that the monks' use of Slavonic would help the newly converted Ruthenians gain familiarity with the Roman liturgy. They also may have expected that it would entice Orthodox Ruthenians to convert to Catholicism or, at least, to regard the Catholic Rite more favorably.[71]

Another detail suggests that the Kleparz Slavonic Monastery was founded with a mission in mind. In contrast with the Emmaus Monastery *Na Slovanech*, which was dedicated to the Slavic Saints, the Slavonic Benedictine monastery and chapel in Kleparz were named first after the Passion of Christ and then after

---

[67] ["Metropolitan of All Russia and Eastern parts."] In reality, the council of Ruthenian bishops appointed Gregory metropolitan of Kyiv and Vilnius.

[68] Sokołowski and Lewicki 1876, v. 2, Letter # 81, 98–100. However, although Gregory did indeed go to Constance he was not inclined to discuss church union with Rome.

[69] Trajdos rejects Řeháček's representation of Jagiełło as a principal patron of the Glagolite monks and his diminishing of Jadwiga's role in this foundation (Trajdos 1988, 74; Řeháček 1975, 216).

[70] In fact, in his decree regarding the foundation of the monastery Jagiełło explicitly counted on subsequent community support of the monastery, and provided his own funding only for the construction and a very modest annual income (Wyrozumski 1982, 121–122.). Providing only initial donations was a usual policy of the Polish King in the foundation of new monasteries (Trajdos 1988, 86). Jadwiga and Jagiełło obviously hoped that Slavonic liturgy would be in demand among Cracow Ruthenian residents.

[71] Trajdos is skeptical about Řeháček's opinion regarding a dynamic Ruthenian community in Cracow (Řeháček 1975, 217; Trajdos 1988, 84). While Řeháček describes Cracow as a center of trade with Ruthenian cities and a locale of Ruthenian "element," Trajdos maintains that the number of Ruthenian residents in Cracow was minimal and that both Cracow and Kleparz were dominated by Poles and Germans.

the Holy Cross, implying the task of the apostolate.[72] Although the monks themselves could not conduct outreach to the Ruthenians of the Grand Duchy, the monastery could possibly serve as a repository and scriptorium for Slavonic texts and as a workshop for potential missionaries to the Orthodox Ruthenians.

If a mission was not planned for the Kleparz Monastery then the Emmaus Glagolite monks must have had some other important reason for arriving in Cracow. Otherwise, why would they leave their comfortable Prague home, where they were surrounded by king's favor and attention, to settle in a Cracow suburb with rather questionable living conditions, where no one cared for them? All the new Kleparz site had to offer was a small chapel and a wooden construction for the monks' residence, with no convenient amenities for living or worshipping. The financial situations of the Prague and Kleparz monasteries were also incomparable both in terms of their incomes and their social status. In addition to a secure yearly income and regular royal donations, the Prague Emmaus Monastery owned several farms, villages, and city businesses, whereas the Kleparz monks obtained a small initial subvention and could only rely on a very small yearly income (about twenty times less than that received in Prague).[73] Given all of this, theirs could not have been an accidental expedition and there had to be some rationale for the settlement of the Emmaus Glagolite monks in Kleparz.

## The Legacy of the Slavonic Monasteries in Prague, Oleśnica and Kleparz

Unfortunately, none of the Benedictine Slavonic Glagolite monasteries remained in East Central Europe for a long time.[74] The Slavonic Glagolitic liturgy in the Prague Emmaus Monastery disappeared during the Hussite wars, when the monastery sided with the Hussite Utraquists.

The fate of the Kleparz Monastery of the Holy Cross was also short-lived. Initially, the monastery was planned on a grand scale: it was supposed to occupy an extensive mansion and house thirty monks. However, the construction of the

[72] Trajdos 1988, 83. The Holy Cross was also a personal cult of Jagiełło as a baptizer of Lithuania. At the same time, Trajdos sees no reason and need for a mission by the Glagolites because, he argues, their modest numbers and resources could not come even close to the volume of missionary work already being carried out at that time by the orders of Dominicans and Franciscans in the Grand Duchy of Lithuania (Trajdos 1988, 82).

[73] Wyrozumski 1982, 120–122; Trajdos 1988, 86.

[74] On the history of the foundation of the Emmaus, Oleśnica (Olešnice) and Kleparz Monasteries and the Glagolite monks see the following works: Krukowski 1886, Paulová 1950, Moszyński 1971, Stejskal 1974, Petr and Šabouk 1975 (collection of articles), Wyrozumski 1982, Trajdos 1988.

monastery was never finished, and after Jadwiga's death in 1399 the Glagolite monks lost royal patronage. According to Długosz, the Slavonic liturgy was still read during his life time in the monastery but disappeared in the years 1470–1480.[75] The ambivalence of the state and ecclesiastical authorities as well as the lack of wealthy benefactors resulted in its decline throughout the fifteenth century. The original chapel existed until 1528, when it was destroyed in a fire along with the Glagolitic library.[76]

The Oleśnica Slavonic Monastery also suffered decline, finally ceasing to exist in 1505 when it became a part of the parish church of St. George, which then belonged to the Augustinians.[77] Unfortunately, as yet no literary or written works have been found connected with the Benedictine Glagolite monks from Oleśnica.

If historians question the missionary vocation of the Kleparz Slavonic Monastery it is because most believe that the Glagoljaši did not leave any traces of their activity in Poland. In my view, all existing historical hypotheses regarding the Kleparz Glagolites are inconclusive because they are insufficiently supported by evidence from written sources – literary artifacts of the Glagolites' assumed activity. Although the Kleparz Slavonic Monastery disappeared from the cultural and political arena and the mission – if indeed there was such a mission – was never fully realized, traces of the Glagolite monks' contact with the Orthodox Ruthenians do exist. They can be found in several Ruthenian translations from Czech and Croatian Church Slavonic, as well as in Latin prayers and liturgical texts transcribed in Cyrillic.[78]

By the time the Prague Emmaus Glagolites came to Silesia and Poland, they had begun writing and translating into Czech and must have brought Czech manuscripts with them to Oleśnica and Kleparz. The examination of several fifteenth-century Ruthenian translations from Czech suggests that their emergence could be associated with the Glagolite monks in Kleparz, who provided Czech manuscripts as sources. These Ruthenian translations, therefore, may serve as textual evidence of the proselytizing activity of the Catholic Glagoljaši among Orthodox Ruthenians as envisioned by Jadwiga and Jagiełło.

In the next four chapters I will describe the language, identify the sources and reconstruct the textual history of four Ruthenian translations from Czech:

---

[75] Długosz 1864, 226; Krukowski 1886, 21–22.
[76] Trajdos 1988, 89.
[77] Rybandt 1970, 677; Wyrozumski 1982, 122.
[78] Mareš 1976 (the Ruthenian translation of the *Marian Mass* from Croatian).

the *Song of Songs*, from a late fifteenth-century Ruthenian miscellany,[79] and three texts from the Swidziński Miscellany of Lithuanian chronicles: the *Book of Taudal the Knight* (к҃нига ѿ таоꙋдаλе рыцари), the *Tale of Sivilla the Prophetess* (сказаниє҃ ѿ сивиλλе п҃р҃очици), and the *Book of Tovit* (книга товиѳъ).[80]

[79] Gosudarstvennyi Istoricheskii Muzei (The State Historical Museum), Sinodal'noe sobranie (Moscow Synod Collection) # 558, (Gorskii and Nevostruev 1862, 763–765).

[80] Biblioteka Ordynacji Krasińskich (Krasiński Collection) # 82, (Pułaski 1915, 76–78).

# Chapter Two
# THE RUTHENIAN *SONG OF SONGS*

A copy of one of the earliest Ruthenian translations from Czech, of the *Song of Songs*, has been preserved in a fifteenth and sixteenth-century Ruthenian manuscript miscellany (Moscow Synod Collection, # 558) on ff. 39–45.[1] The text is arranged in the form of a dialogue between the 'Soul' or the 'Bride' the Church and the 'Bridegroom' Jesus Christ, according to the medieval allegorical exegetic tradition. The biblical book is preceded by a short explanation of its spiritual meaning and is followed by an extensive contemplative and instructional treatise (ff. 45–55v) that recommends different ways to inspire and invigorate one's love of God, suggesting prayers for this purpose.

## CZECH SOURCE

A textological comparison of the Ruthenian *Song of Songs* with the Czech Bible shows that the source text has been taken from one of the Czech Bibles of the third redaction.[2] This redaction, executed most likely sometime during the second and third decades of the fifteenth century, is generally associated with the Hussite movement. The *Padeřovská Bible* (1432–1435) is generally regarded as the best specimen of the Czech Bible's third redaction. It is therefore quite unsurprising that, among the dozen or so extant manuscripts of the third redaction which I have examined, it stands closest to the Ruthenian translation.[3] However,

---

[1] This manuscript is a part of the State Historical Museum's Moscow Synod Collection (Moskovskaia Sinodal'naia biblioteka, Gosudarstvennyi Istoricheskii Muzei); it is described by Gorskii and Nevostruev 1862, 763–765. The date given by Gorskii and Nevostruev (sixteenth or seventeenth century) is incorrect. The manuscript should be dated to the fifteenth-sixteenth centuries, while the quires with the *Song of Songs* date to the last quarter of the fifteenth century (Turilov 1986).

[2] There are four redactions of the Czech Bible. The term *redaction* denotes a version of translation of the Biblical text that is revised, improved, altered, or translated anew. The classification into redactions of the Czech Bible does not imply merely the correction of previous mistakes but also accounts for different sources of revision, i.e. different versions of the Latin Vulgate. A comprehensive discussion of the Czech Bible translations and bibliography may be found in Kyas 1997 and Pečírková 1998.

[3] An assumption that a Czech Bible close to the *Padeřovská Bible* could have served as a source text for the Ruthenian *Song of Songs* had already been made by Alekseev 1983, 285.

a few variants in other manuscripts of the same redaction show that there had been another Czech version even closer to the Ruthenian *Song of Songs* than that of the *Padeřovská Bible*. For example, several Czech Bibles of the third redaction (*Klementinská, Fojtův Starý Zákon, Lobkovická, Nymburská, Talmberská*) retain the word *prudkoſti*, which is "translated" in the Ruthenian *Song of Songs* (**пр8дкостїю**) but is not present in the *Padeřovská Bible*:

| | |
|---|---|
| **(4:15)** | **Колодѧ^з затве̏рженыи про гл8бин8 во^д живы^х . которыи жь текоуть быстринѧми пр8дкостїю ѿ ливана** |
| **Padeřovská:** | *Studnicie zahradnie pro hlubnie wod żiwych . kterež teku z libana* |
| **Other Bibles:** | *Studnicie zahradnie pro hlubnie wod żiwych . kterež teku prudkoſti z libana* |

A transcription of the Czech *Song of Songs* from the *Padeřovská Bible* with relevant variants from other Czech Bibles is given in Appendix I along with an edition of the Ruthenian *Song of Songs*.[4]

## Translator's Technique

In general, the Ruthenian *Song of Songs* is a literal translation that closely follows the Czech source and for the most part keeps the same word order. It is characterized by the following techniques:

### Pseudo-Translations

The translator left many Czech words and expressions untranslated, instead rendering them literally as transcriptions and pseudo-translations. For example: **ѐдинаго кождого** (3:8),[5] cf. Czech *gednoho każdeho*, **вып8канїа** (4:13), cf. Czech *wypukanie*, **ѡ҆глѧдала** (6:11), cf. Czech *ohledala,* **рѣпи̏чка оу҆гла^ж енаѧ** (7:2), cf. Czech *řepice vhlażena*, **по̏рканы** (8:9), cf. Czech *prkany*.

### Lexical Doublets

From time to time, the translator supplied pseudo-translations with their Ruthenian equivalents, producing lexical doublets. For example:

---

Alekseev based his assumption on excerpts from the *Padeřovská Bible* published by Vladimír Kyas. I was not familiar with Alekseev's article while carrying out this research project. My ignorance, therefore, obliged me to conduct a thorough examination and comparison of all available Czech Bibles, which I was able to access with the help of many considerate curators at several archives and especially employees of the Czech Language Institute at Prague.

[4] Both texts are revised editions from my earlier publication in Verkholantsev 2003.

[5] Numbers next to Ruthenian citations indicate the chapter and verse as designated in Appendix I. Czech examples are taken from the *Padeřovská Bible*.

| | **Czech** | **Ruthenian** |
|---|---|---|
| **(2:8)** | *přeſkakuge pahorky*<br>skips upon the hills | а̀ перескакиваючи погорки. и̂ холмъı<br>and skipping upon the hills and hills |
| **(2:11)** | *přewal od'ſel y odſtupil*<br>the rain is over and gone | превалъ лютости ѿшоⷧ҇ и̂ ѿстꙋпиⷧ҇<br>the rain of rage is over and gone |
| **(3:9)** | *Wečeřadlo včinil ſobie kral*<br>*ſalomun z dřieuie libanſkeho*<br>The dining room King Solomon made for himself of the wood of Lebanon. | прⷭ҇тлъ вечерѧдло ѹ҆чинилъ собѣ<br>цр҃ь соломонъ з древа ливанова<br>The throne, dining room King Solomon made for himself of the wood of Lebanon. |
| **(8:8)** | *w den kdyžto namluwana ma byti*<br><br>on the day when she shall be spoken for | въ дн҃ь коли ж то маѐть быти намоⷡвлена а̀любо смовлена<br>on the day when she shall be spoken for or spoken for |

## Lexical Variation

In some cases the translator hesitated over a choice of either a pseudo-translation or a Ruthenian word, which resulted in several Ruthenian variants for a Czech counterpart: заграда, ѡ҆городокъ and ѡ҆городъ for Czech *zahrada*, 'garden;' пріѥтелка and милаѧ for Czech *přietelnice*, 'beloved;' глѧдала and и̂скала for Czech *hledala*, 'sought;' зернатаⷽ(ѧ) ꙗблка and раиска(ѧ) ꙗблка for Czech *zrnata yablka,* 'pomegranates.' The last example perhaps deserves a separate discussion. The borrowing зерната(ѧ) ꙗблка appears only once, whereas the Ruthenian equivalent раиска(ѧ) ꙗблка is used in the other five occurrences (4:3, 6:7, 6:11, 7:12, 8:2). The choice of a borrowing in this case might have had stylistic grounds. Let us look at the context:

| | | |
|---|---|---|
| **(4:13)** | **Czech** | *Wypukanie twa rag zrnatych yablek* |
| | **Ruthenian** | вып8каніа твоа раи зернѧтыⷯ ꙗ̀блѡⷦ҇<br>Thy plants are an orchard of pomegranates |

Were the translator to use the Ruthenian equivalent in this context, the neighboring word раи would create a tautological expression раи раискиⷯ ꙗ̀блѡⷦ҇. It is noteworthy that the translator demonstrated such stylistic sensitivity by avoiding repetition and using the Czech word instead.

When the same word occurred several times within a sentence or passage, the translator used a pseudo-translation at the beginning but then tried to find a more exact Ruthenian equivalent. For example:

| (3:1–2) Czech | Ruthenian |
|---|---|
| *Na ložci mem po nocech hledala ſe(m)* | на ложи моѐмъ ѷночи глѧдала ѐсмь |
| *gehož miluge du˙ſie ma .* | ѐгоⷤ милꙋеть дш҃а моѧ . |
| *hledala ſem geho a nenalezla ſem .* | искала ѐсми ѐго а не нашла . |
| *Wſtanu a obegdu mieſto po rynciech* | ѷстанꙋ ѝ ѡ̀боидꙋ мѣсто по рынцѣⷯ |
| *a po vliciech* | ѝ по ѹлицаⷯ |
| *hledati budu gehož miluge du˙ſie ma .* | ѝскать боудꙋ еⷮ ѐгоⷤ милꙋеть дш҃а моѧ̀ |
| *Hledala ſem geho a nenalezla ſem .* | ѝскала ѐсми ѐго ѝ не нашла ѐсми . |

By night on my bed I sought him whom my soul loveth: I sought him, but I found him not. I will rise now, and go about the city in the streets, and in the broad ways I will seek him whom my soul loveth: I sought him, but I found him not.

## Mistranslations

In several cases the translator did not understand the Czech text:

| (2:3) | Czech | Ruthenian |
|---|---|---|
| | *tak mily moy mezi ſyny* | такъ милыи мои межи станы |
| | So is my beloved among the sons | So is my beloved among the estates |

While **станы** in place of **сыны** may also be a later scribal error made during copying, the Czech variant reading *ſtieny* ('shadows') in the *Lobkovická Bible* shows that the Czech Bibles lacked uniformity and clarity in this reading and could have caused this mistake, i.e. *stieny* ('shadows') could have been easily confused with *stany* ('tents, marquees').

| (4:8) | *z hlawy amana z wrchu ſanir* | почен҄ъши ѿ головы ѝ маючи |
|---|---|---|
| | *a hermon* | наверхꙋ саниⷬ ѝ гермонъ |
| | from the top of Aman, from the | starting from the top and having |
| | top of Sanir and Hermon. | at the top Sanir and Hermon |

The translator did not understand the proper name *amana,* which led to a misinterpretation of the whole sentence.

| (8:13) | *Kteraž bydliś w zahradach* | котораѧ живешь ѹ̀ виноградѣⷯ милого . |
|---|---|---|
| | *přietele poſluchagij hlaſu tweho .* | послꙋхаю голоса твоеⷮ |
| | You who dwell in the gardens, | You who dwell in the gardens of the beloved, |
| | the companions listen to your voice. | I listen to your voice. |

The above mentioned translation techniques, as well as errors and mistranslations, suggest that the translator did not understand the Czech in a few instances and, therefore, probably was a Ruthenian.

## Date of Translation

The quires of the Ruthenian miscellany where the *Song of Songs* is found date to the last quarter of the fifteenth century.[6] The Ruthenian *Song of Songs* seems to be a copy of an original translation that should be dated to an earlier period. Several scribes applied their hands to it. The biblical book is for the most part written by one hand with a single insertion (by a very uneven and unrefined hand) on f. 39v. The commentary has more insertions made by various hands (for example, four lines on f. 45v and about ten lines on f. 53). In addition, several folia in the commentary fluctuate in the number of lines (from thirty one to twenty nine). The scribes' writing sometimes looks hasty, with occasional slips, especially in the commentary. Finally, some scribal errors seem to have been caused by the similarity or illegibility of letters. These corruptions could have originated as a result of copying that was made from another manuscript, not by dictation. For example words свѣста and поѹⷫ are clearly corruptions of невѣста and поѹⷮ in свѣста хⷭва дш҃а поѹⷫ ѡ̇ своеⷨ милоⷨ женисѣ хⷭѣ (f. 43v).

In all probability, the protograph of the Ruthenian *Song of Songs* was translated in the second quarter or the middle of the fifteenth century when use of the third redaction of the Czech Bible was widespread. The translation of the Ruthenian *Song of Songs* is unlikely to date from the end of the fifteenth century or later because at that time a translator would have preferred to use one of the printed Czech Bibles as a source. The printed Czech Bibles, however, already reflected the text of another, fourth redaction. The first printed Czech Bible – the *Pražská Bible* – appeared in 1488, and was followed by the Kuttenberg Bible (the *Kutnohorská Bible*) in 1489 and the Venetian Bible (the *Benátská Bible*) in 1506. For instance, a translation of the *Song of Songs* in Frantsishak Skaryna's printed *Bibliia Rus'ka* (1518) was based on the Venetian edition of the Czech Bible.

The treatise-commentary, which frames the Ruthenian *Song of Songs* and clarifies its allegorical meaning, probably originated at the same time as the

---

[6] Turilov 1986. The text of the *Song of Songs* is on ff. 39–45, followed by an instructional treatise on ff. 45–55. The quires that contain the text are ff. 39–46 and 47–54. The watermarks (a Gothic Y, with cloverleaf tail and a cross above) are on ff. 39 and 44, f. 41 and 46, f. 48 and 53. This watermark was very common for the period of the 1460s–1480s (Piccard 1961, ## 30283, 30334, 30305, 30418 and Likhachev 1899, ## 2519–2521 to give only a few examples with different dates). The watermarks on the folia, following the text of the *Song of Songs* (bull's head with a single line shaft above, ending in a five or six-petal flower and with a triangle below) are also very wide-spread and date to the 1460s–1480s.

translation. Its language differs from that of the *Song of Songs* in that it does not reveal any apparent Czech influence. Most likely, it was added as an original composition or as a translation of a so far unidentified treatise.[7]

So, the Czech source of the Ruthenian translation of the *Song of Songs* suggests that it was made before the end of the fifteenth century. But let us also examine the manuscript context in which the Ruthenian *Song of Songs* is attested, as it may provide us with further clues for establishing the date and provenance of the Ruthenian translation.

## Manuscript Context

The miscellany from Moscow Synod Collection #558 is an assortment of various texts written by a number of scribes. Only folia 9–165 are of Ruthenian provenance. Other Ruthenian texts in that part include a copy of the Bulla of Pope Eugene IV at the Florentine Council, the Ruthenian *Life of Alexis, the Man of God* (**житїє и жи$^{з}$нь чл҃ка бж҃їа ѿлеѯїа**), and the Ruthenian translation from Polish of the *Legend of Three Persian Kings* (**ѡ житїи и ѡ хо$^{ж}$нїи тре$^{х}$ короле$^{в}$ перси$^{л}$скы$^{х}$**). It also contains several other texts of especial interest to us since they could have been translated at the Kleparz Monastery of Holy Cross from sources that belonged to the Glagolite monks.

The text that follows the Ruthenian *Song of Songs* and is copied by the same hand is a Ruthenian translation of the Catholic Mass in honor of the Virgin Mary (ff. 55v–59). František W. Mareš studied the *Marian Mass* and showed that it had been translated from one of the Croatian missals. He suggested that the translation took place at the Monastery of the Holy Cross in Kleparz, a home of Croatian and Prague Glagolite monks.[8] The translator, in his opinion, was a Ruthenian (or a Belarusian, as Mareš called him),[9] a layman brother who lived in the monastery and was familiar with both Roman Catholic and Slavic Orthodox liturgy, Glagolitic and Cyrillic scripts, Church Slavonic, and Polish. That the translator, or a copier, was an Orthodox and not a Catholic can be seen from his comments on the mass, in which he started by using Catholic terminology but then switched to the Orthodox terms. For example, he started using **аменъ** but

---

[7] The identification of a source of this commentary would most likely clarify the origin of the Ruthenian *Song of Songs*. I am leaving this task for a future separate study.

[8] Mareš 1976, 295–362.

[9] Mareš characterized the language of the translation employing the modern division of languages into Belarusian, Russian, Ukrainian, and Polish. However, all linguistic features that he describes could be seen as simply Ruthenian.

later in the text switched to **аминь**. At the beginning, his first comment says "**капланъ речеть**" but in the rest of the text we find "**попъ речеть**." The Ruthenian *Marian Mass* follows the Croatian Church Slavonic text very closely in its choice of syntax and lexicon, suggesting that the need for a "translation" was not so much linguistic as graphic (from the exotic Glagolitic into understandable Cyrillic) and confessional (from Catholic terms into recognizable Orthodox concepts).

The Monastery of the Holy Cross (in which the translation of the *Marian Mass*, according to Mareš, took place) was founded by the King of Poland Władysław Jagiełło and Queen Jadwiga in 1390. Intended for the Benedictine Glagolite monks, it was modeled on the Emmaus Monastery in Prague.[10] One of the royal couple's primary objectives in inviting the Prague Glagoljaši could have been to promote the Roman Slavonic liturgy among the Orthodox Ruthenians, whose liturgical language was very close to that of the Glagoljaši.

Further, Mareš proposed that the Ruthenian translation of the *Marian Mass* with explanations of the liturgical service was prepared for Jagiełło's fourth wife, Zofia Holszańska (ruled 1422–1461). An Orthodox princess, Zofia converted to Catholicism in order to wed the King of Poland Wladysław Jagiełło and needed instruction in her new faith. According to Mareš, the *Marian Mass* was translated for this purpose around the year 1422, when Zofia arrived at the Cracow Royal Court.

The Ruthenian *Marian Mass* and the *Song of Songs* are preserved in the same manuscript and are copied by the same hand. Could it be then that their provenance is related, and that the Ruthenian *Song of Songs* was also translated at the Kleparz Monastery?

Several decades after the Ruthenian *Marian Mass* was most likely translated, namely in the second quarter of the fifteenth century, Queen Zofia Holszańska commissioned a translation of the whole Bible into Polish. The translation, also from Czech, was made by several translators and scribes, among them the queen's chaplain Andrzej of Jaszowice. However, the result of this enterprise, the Szaroszpatak Codex of 1455 (usually referred to as the *Biblia królowej Zofii, The Bible of Queen Zofia*), reveals a different Czech source.[11] The authors of the *Biblia królowej Zofii* critical edition, Stanisław Urbańczyk and Vladimír Kyas, compared it to Czech versions and arrived at the conclusion that the

---

[10] For a detailed discussion of the historical circumstances related to the foundation of the Holy Cross Monastery see Chapter One.

[11] Unfortunately, only a part of the Old Testament has been preserved and the *Song of Songs* is not in it.

source for the Szaroszpatak Codex was an unknown Czech Bible with text fluctuations between the first and second redaction.[12] It seems that the third redaction did not circulate among Polish bookmen.[13] Instead, it is most likely that the third redaction of the Czech Bible should have been known to the Glagoljaši in Kleparz who maintained close connections with the Emmaus Monastery. The Emmaus Benedictine monastic community was the only Catholic commune in Bohemia that sympathized with the linguistic ideas of the Hussite movement and consequently might have had in their possession a manuscript of the third, Hussite redaction of the Czech Bible.[14] This fact may also serve as a likely explanation as to why the *Biblia królowej Zofii*, although dated from a later period, was not based on the third redaction but on an earlier version. The Hussite movement was generally unpopular among Polish Catholics and the team of translators of the first Polish Biblical Codex could have deliberately chosen an earlier, non-Hussite redaction of the Czech Bible.

## THE RUTHENIAN *MARIAN MASS* AND THE *SONG OF SONGS*

It is not accidental that the *Song of Songs* and the *Marian Mass* are found next to each other in the same manuscript, since they are linked thematically. The cult of the Virgin Mary as a symbol of the heavenly bride is frequently associated with the *Song of Songs*.[15] Since Origen's influential commentary on the images of virginity in the *Song of Songs*, this biblical book has been interpreted in Christian exegesis as describing the mystic union between the church and Christ or the soul and the Word (Logos, Verbum Dei) under the appellations of the Bride and Bridegroom. The "church" and "soul" have been therefore allegorically connected with the virginity of Mary. Furthermore, the *Song of Songs* contributed several important symbols to the Marian cult.

The Marian symbols taken from the *Song of Songs* include "the sealed fountain" and "the enclosed garden" (which symbolize the seal of Mary's virginity that was left unbroken by the birth of Christ), the tower of David (which signifies Mary's inviolate chastity and strength), and the lily (which symbolizes

---

[12] Kyas 1955; Urbańczyk and Kyas 1965, V. For the parallel edition of Czech sources the editors chose the *Cardův Starý Zákon* (first redaction) and the *Táborská Mlynářčina Bible,* (second redaction) supplementing them with occasional variants from Bibles of the third redaction.

[13] Polish Bibles of the sixteenth century were already translated from the fourth redaction of the Czech Bible (first edition of the *Severýn Bible*, 1529).

[14] Sakař 1975, 187–188.

[15] Astell 1990, Matter 1990.

Mary's purity).[16] These symbols, for instance, have inspired Marian iconographic representation. Brian Daley has observed that a new iconographic convention emerged at the beginning of the fifteenth century. The Virgin began to appear in a garden surrounded by walls, and crammed with various symbolic objects, animals and plants. He has proposed to look for an explanation of this iconographic style in the Marian exegesis of the *Song of Songs* (verse 4:12): "A garden enclosed is my sister, my spouse; a spring shut up, a fountain sealed."[17]

That a copier or a later reader of the Ruthenian *Song of Songs* connected it with the Marian cult is apparent from an encircled comment on the manuscript's margin on f. 43 which reads:

пр҇ч҇тєи дв҃ци марии разоумнѣи"
[interpret as the Most Holy Virgin Mary].

This comment is located next to the following verse (6:10):

ѡ҆дна є҇с голꙋбо҇чка моꙗ доконалаꙗ моꙗ є҆дина є҇с. мт҃ри свои выбрана родитєльници своє҆и.
[My dove, my perfect one, is only one, the darling of her mother.]

Mareš analyzed the orthography of the *Marian Mass* and concluded that the translation was made optically, not from dictation; that is, that the translator himself interpreted the Glagolitic script of the original. As evidence he pointed to a couple of mistakes in the Ruthenian translation, which resulted from misunderstandings of the script, as well as consistent use of the same abbreviations as in the Croatian Glagolitic text. Mareš's main example is consistent use of the abbreviation –ѡ҇г in Ruthenian Genitive singular adjectival endings, to render the corresponding Croatian ending *–oga* and its abbreviation in Glagolitic, instead of the expected –а҇г (i.e. єдинѡ҇г instead of єдина҇г ). This abbreviation, he claims, is not common in the Orthodox Church Slavonic orthography but is typical for Croatian Glagolitic.[18] According to Mareš, the distribution of abbreviations with –а҇г and –ѡ҇г corresponds to the distribution of the same abbreviations in the Glagolitic Hrvoje Missal, which stands very close to the source text.

The Ruthenian *Song of Songs* also contains the abbreviation with an "omega" in the word и҆нѡ҇г on f. 43. This fact either undermines Mareš's argument about the obscurity of this abbreviation among Ruthenian scribes or sug-

[16] Cope 1959, 166.
[17] Daley 1986.
[18] Mareš 1976, 316–317.

gests that both texts could have been translated by the same translator, influenced by Croatian Glagolitic orthography.

If indeed the translator of the *Marian Mass* possessed all those skills that Mareš mentioned – the knowledge of Croatian Church Slavonic and of Glagolitic and Cyrillic scripts, as well as familiarity with Orthodox and Catholic liturgy – this would imply that the Prague Emmaus Glagoljaši indeed succeeded in reaching out to some local Ruthenians and training them in the Glagolitic script and Roman liturgical practice. It is not surprising then that in the same manuscript, following the *Marian Mass* on ff. 59-60, there are several Latin prayers and liturgical texts transcribed in Cyrillic.

The first three texts, *Pater noster*, *Ave Maria* and the short version of the *Credo* (the *Apostles' Creed*, *Symbolum Apostolorum*) are also supplied with Church Slavonic translations.[19] Both prayers and the *Credo* are among the most important texts of Western Christianity, which every faithful layman had to know and recite by heart during liturgy or in private.[20] Particularly, the short version of the *Credo* was very common in Catholic practice but absolutely unknown in Orthodox liturgy. It was even often condemned as alien to the Orthodox faith. For example, in a seventeenth-century Ruthenian manuscript from the Moscow Synod Collection # 294 there are several articles that express disapproval of this text (f. 326):[21]

ѡ҆ ап҃ⷭлскомъ глемомъ сѵмволѣ . новоѡбрѣтаетсѧ нѣкїи сѵмволъ чꙋждь сꙋщъ стыѧ мт҃ре нашеѧ православныѧ восточныѧ цр҃кве толкованныи не ѿ ꙋченїи ниже словеⷭ и҆ разꙋмѣнїи стых҃ъ дхⷪоносныхъ ѿцевъ .

[On the so called Apostolic Symbol. There is a certain symbol, alien to our holy mother Eastern Orthodox Church, which is not interpreted by the teaching, words and comprehension of the holy spirit-bearing fathers.]

Transcriptions of Latin liturgy and prayers, and particularly the short version of the *Credo*, demonstrate that their Ruthenian author was not only interested in the Roman Slavonic liturgy per se but was trying to gain familiarity with the Roman Rite in general.

---

[19] I am currently preparing a study of these texts.

[20] For example, in the Ruthenian *Marian Mass* the translator indicated only the incipit of the *Otche nash*, which is recited during the mass, probably relying on the universal knowledge of this prayer.

[21] Gorskii and Nevostruev 1862, 437–445.

## ORTHODOX OR CATHOLIC?

In light of the above, a question suggests itself about the confessional dress of the Ruthenian translation of the Czech *Song of Songs.* In other words, is this translation Catholic or Orthodox?

The translator of the Ruthenian *Song of Songs* appeared untroubled by the fact that the Czech source was a Roman Bible (the Czech Bible was originally translated from the Paris version of the Vulgate), albeit with a Hussite twist.[22] This is noteworthy because later Ruthenian miscellanies are abundant in anti-Catholic tracts denouncing Latin biblical translations and defending the Septuagint. For example, in the already mentioned seventeenth-century Ruthenian miscellany (Moscow Synod Collection, # 294) on f. 347 there is a *Preface to the Bible,* which says:

**предсловїє на библїю йли паче лжесловїє на седмдесѧть сты҃ѧ преводникы ѐже писа ѐрѡнѵмъ латiнскїи ꙋчитель .**
[The foreword to the Bible, or, more accurately, a "false-word" on the Seventy Holy translators, which Jerome, the Teacher of the Latins, wrote.]

The language of the Ruthenian *Song of Songs* reveals no Catholic tinge and suggests that the text was probably adopted by an Orthodox scribe. The spelling of proper names is consistently Orthodox: [v] substitutes [b], [f] substitutes [t], [s] substitutes [z], and [k] is used in place of [ts]:

**ливана** vs. *libana* (4:8), **ливанова** vs. *libanſka* (7:4);
**зевоне** vs. *ezebon* (7:4);
**ѧминодавовы** vs. *aminadabowy* (6:12);
**веѳиль** vs. *betel* (2:17);
**дщери йѐрꙋсолимьскїа** vs. *dcery geruzalemſke* (5:16); **йѐр҇лмъ** vs. *geruzalem* (6:3);
**кипр̑ски** vs. *ciprſky* (1:13).

However, the dialogical structure of the Ruthenian *Song of Songs* is somewhat unusual; it is absent in all other Slavic Orthodox translations of the *Song of Songs.*[23] The biblical book is staged as a dialogue between the 'Soul' or the

[22] This, of course, would happen again several decades later, when the Archbishop of Novgorod Gennadii would commission a team of learned men to compile and translate the complete Bible. Then their main resource would also be a Latin Bible – the Vulgate (Cooper 2003, 127–134).

[23] For comparison, none of the following translations of the *Song of Songs* published in Alekseev 2002 has a dialogical structure: a "Methodian" reading translation (четий перевод), a combined text from Croatian Glagolitic breviaries and missals, an exegetical translation (толковый перевод) ascribed to Philo of Carpasia, an Old Russian translation from Hebrew, a

'Bride' (the Church or Mary) and the 'Bridegroom' (Jesus Christ), reproducing the composition in the Czech Bible. The rubrics in the Ruthenian translation are more extensive than in the Czech Bible. Although in several places they expand upon the Czech version, they consistently follow the structure of the dialogue. The breakdown of the passages or the speeches (and therefore the interpretation) is, with a few exceptions, the same as in the Czech Bible of the third redaction.

To summarize, the Ruthenian *Song of Songs* seems to have been translated by an Orthodox translator who was not particularly fastidious about its Roman Catholic source. His primary concern was clarity, precision of language and proper spiritual interpretation. Evidently, the use of the Cyrillic orthography and Orthodox names was sufficient to recommend the translation to an Orthodox readership.

## CONCLUSION

The Ruthenian *Song of Songs* was translated from one of the Czech Bibles of the third redaction most likely by an Orthodox Ruthenian, sometime in the second quarter or the middle of the fifteenth century. It is, therefore, an apograph removed from the original by several decades. Yet it retains its Bohemized idiom, which apparently did not disturb the copyist(s): there is no trace of an attempt to Slavonicize the text.

Why was a translation from Czech into Ruthenian needed? Could it have been that a biblical text written in a West Slavic vernacular, be it Polish or Czech, was more understandable to a literate Ruthenian than a text written in Church Slavonic? An affirmative answer to this question would suggest that the existing Church Slavonic versions of the *Song of Songs* were either unavailable or not comprehensible enough to serve as a usable inspirational source for an instructional treatise. It is also possible that the translator was attracted by the dialogical structure of the Czech source, which suggested and assisted appropriate interpretation.

The relation of the Ruthenian *Song of Songs* to other texts in the manuscript, specifically to the *Marian Mass* and Cyrillic Latin prayers, suggests that its emergence may be connected with the activity in Poland of the Benedictine Glagolite monks from the Prague Emmaus Monastery.

---

Ruthenian translation from Hebrew, Constantine Kostenecki's translation, Skaryna's translation and the *Ostrih Bible* translation.

I am in no hurry to follow František Mareš and consider both Ruthenian translations, as well as transcriptions of Latin, to be texts prepared for Zofia Holszańska. After all, the Ruthenian princess Sonka was most likely illiterate before she arrived at the Royal Court. However, it is possible to remark with confidence that what characterized the translator(s) and the copier(s) of these texts was a spirit of confessional open-mindedness: an active interest in the Catholic Rite was accompanied by apparent adherence to the Orthodox faith.

## Chapter Three
## THE RUTHENIAN *BOOK OF TAUDAL THE KNIGHT* AND THE CHURCH SLAVONIC *EDIFYING STORY TOLD BY FAUDAL THE WARRIOR*

The *Book of Taudal the Knight* (**кн҇ига ѿ таоу҆дале рыцари**) from an early sixteenth-century miscellany is another Ruthenian translation from Czech that may be associated with the activity of the Prague Emmaus Glagoljaši among Orthodox Ruthenians. It is the only attested Ruthenian version of the *Visio Tundali* or *Visio Tnugdali*, a vision of the other world, one of the highly popular texts of the late Middle Ages. Among others, this text influenced Dante's *Divine Comedy* and Bosch's forceful depiction of Purgatory's horrors. It recounts the story of the Irish knight Tundal, who after leading a sinful life was suddenly struck dead during a feast. His soul, guided by a guardian Angel, journeyed to the other world, where it saw the World of Darkness (Hell) and the World of Light (Paradise). There it witnessed and suffered many kinds of terrible torments and was subsequently shown the way to salvation. Because a part of his body retained some warmth, Tundal was not buried and remained for three days in a state that today we would describe as a coma. When his soul returned to his body, he came back to life and recounted what he had seen while he was asleep, glorifying the power and mercy of God. After that he gave away all his possessions to the poor and lived the rest of his life in piety.

### MANUSCRIPT CONTEXT

The Ruthenian *Book of Taudal the Knight* came down to us in an early sixteenth-century Swidziński Miscellany of Lithuanian Chronicles #82 (ff. 92–106).[1] Apart from Lithuanian chronicles, this miscellany contained other historical, apocalyptic, and eschatological texts, including several translations from Czech. As if to deprive scholarship of one of the finest Ruthenian specimens of eschatological compilation, Providence condemned the Swidziński Miscellany to destruction in a World War II fire, along with the greater part of the Krasiński Collection to which it then belonged. Fortunately, in 1881, Alexander Brückner published several fragments from the Ruthenian *Book of Taudal the Knight*, which allow us to form an opinion about this text.[2]

---

[1] This manuscript used to be a part of the Krasiński Collection (Pułaski 1915, 76–78).
[2] Brückner 1881, 199–212.

While the manuscript itself is lost for examination, a brief paleographic description left by Evfimii Karskii and Franciszek Pułaski as well as several published texts and fragments give an idea of its contents and language.[3] Karskii, a Belarusian philologist and authority on Belarusian medieval writing and linguistic culture, dated the manuscript to the first half of the sixteenth century and suggested that most of the texts, including the *Book of Taudal the Knight*, were copied from an earlier protograph, which he placed shortly before the year 1492.[4] According to Karskii, the manuscript was written in a single handwriting (large *poluustav*), characteristic of the first half of the sixteenth century. The various types of pagination suggest that the individual texts must have been rebound and reorganized several times. It is likely that the original collection was different and could have included other texts as well. The manuscript bore signs of frequent use and diligent study; its leaves were worn from reading and contained numerous notes and comments in the margins. The contents of this collection provide a valuable context for the study of the text in question and deserve to be listed here. In addition to the Lithuanian chronicles the manuscript contained various legends, edifying stories and prophecies:

The beginning and the end of the manuscript are lost.
ff. 1–11v. (in original pagination f. 54) continuation of *Alexandria*, the last part:
**ѾѾ пришествїи̇ а̇лекса҃ндровѣ ко ц҃рци свое҃м рокъсанѣ. И̂ ѡ см҃рти е̇го**;
ff. 12–20v. (in original pagination f. 64) **лѣтописецъ великого кня̆зьства литовъского и̇ жомойцьского**. *The Chronicle of the Grand Duchy of Lithuania and Samogitia (Žemaitija)*;
ff. 21–39v. **кр̆оиники ѿ великихъ кн҃зе҃х литовъскыхъ**. *The Chronicles of Grand Princes of Lithuania*;
ff. 39v–76. **хоженїє данила игꙋмена въ ст҃ый гра҃д Ісе̇р҃слмъ**. The *Pilgrimage of Daniel the Abbot to the Holy City of Jerusalem*, complete text (long redaction);
ff. 77–91v. **книга товиѳъ** (Pułaski provides the spelling as **Товиѳъ**). The Ruthenian *Book of Tovit*, translated from Czech;
ff. 92–106v. **кн҃ига ѿ таоўдале рыцари**. The Ruthenian *Book of Taudal the Knight*; the text is unfinished, translated from Czech;
ff. 107–119v. **ре҃ч ѿ тре҃х ставехъ**. *On the Three States*. This is an account of St. Augustine's discourse on the three conditions of virginity, marriage, and widowhood;
ff. 119v–124v. **сказаниѐ ѿ сивил҃ле пр҃о рчици**. The Ruthenian *Tale of Sivilla the Prophetess*, translated from Czech;

---

[3] Karskii 1894, 6–19; Pułaski 1915, 76–78; Brückner 1881 (*The Book of Taudal the Knight*, **кн҃ига ѿ таоўдале рыцари**), Karskii 1898 (*The Tale of Sivilla the Prophetess*, **сказаниѐ ѿ сивил҃ле пр҃о рчици**), Karskii 1894 (*The Book of Tovit*, **книга товиѳъ**).
[4] Karskii 1894.

ff. 125–177v. пророчениа҆ с҃тыхъ пр̑ркъ ѿ х҃ѣ і҆с҃ѣ. пр̑рчество моѵ̈сеѡво законодавца, пр̑рчество солѡ̆моне. *Prophecies of Jesus Christ*, *The Prophecy of Moses the Law-maker* and *Solomon's Prophecy*;
ff. 178–180v. слово ѡ̀ послѣднем времени ѡ̀ михаиловѣ црс҃твѣ. *On the Last Times, On the Kingdom of Michael*. This could be a translation of the *Apocalypse of Pseudo-Methodius of Patara*; the text is unfinished.

According to Karskii's paleographic description, the miscellany did not bear any indication of the author's identity, but the content, as Karskii described it, speaks lucidly about his interests and educational background. Although sometimes articles in a miscellany can be very diverse in subject matter, justifying the term, the texts in the Swidziński Miscellany are related in that they reflect the interest of the compiler in both the factual history of Lithuania-Rus' and the Christian interpretation of divine history in general. Most texts belong to historical, apocalyptic and eschatological literature; and several of them differ from the traditional Orthodox repertoire and come from Western sources.

## Sources and Historical Context. The Latin and Czech *Visio Tundali*

The Latin *Visio Tundali* originated in a congregation of Irish Benedictines in Ratisbon (or Regensburg, Bavaria) in the second half of the twelfth century. Its composer, a monk named Marcus, claimed that he heard it from Tundal himself. Since then the vision circulated in several versions: Marcus' original and a number of short, abridged adaptations which were included in various encyclopedias, collections of legends and annals. By the end of the fifteenth century the *Visio Tundali* enjoyed wide circulation and had been translated into the major European vernaculars,[5] and among Slavic languages into Croatian, Czech, Ruthenian and Church Slavonic. Although numerous studies are devoted to describing the textual history and circulation of the *Visio Tundali* and its translations, they generally omit Slavic material from the discussion, and so remain insufficiently known among Slavic medievalists.

Karskii dated the Ruthenian *Book of Taudal the Knight* to the end of the fifteenth century, connecting its translation with eschatological expectations right before the year 1492 (i.e. the year 7000 from the Creation of the World according to the Orthodox ecclesiastical calendar). In addition, several historical facts and names mentioned in another text in the Swidziński Miscellany, the

[5] These include German, English, Dutch, Swedish, Icelandic, Provencal, French, Italian, Spanish, Catalan, and Portuguese.

Ruthenian *Tale of Sivilla the Prophetess* (сказаниѐ ѿ сивиллє прⷪ҇рчици), further influenced Karskii's dating. Karskii argued that many texts collected in the Swidziński Miscellany, and especially those translated from other languages, would have been of particular importance to a translator in the period of the approaching end of the seventh millennium. Although some of Karskii's assumptions regarding the events in the Ruthenian *Tale of Sivilla the Prophetess* were erroneous (see discussion in Chapter Four) his reasoning seems plausible. Indeed, this date stirred the minds of Orthodox ecclesiastical officials and ordinary clergy and laymen alike. They all tried to find a proper theological interpretation of its meaning (whether it meant the accession of the Antichrist or the Second Coming of Christ and the Last Judgment).[6] For those fearing and preparing for the Last Judgment, the *Vision of Tundal* gave a vivid first-hand account of the torments awaiting sinners of all kinds.

The three fragments of the Ruthenian *Book of Taudal the Knight* published by Alexander Brückner give a fair idea of its language and textological features.[7] Brückner, who at that time was able to see the whole original text in the manuscript, concluded that the Ruthenian *Book of Taudal* is a translation of Vincent de Beauvais' *Visio Tundali*, one of the most widespread short versions of the vision. Originally, this short version was adapted by Helinand de Froidmont for his *Chronicon*[8] and was later borrowed by Vincent de Beauvais for his *Speculum Historiale* (under the year 1149).[9] The published fragments of the Ruthenian *Book of Taudal* indeed show a faithful translation of the corresponding chapters of Beauvais' work.[10] Brückner was also the first to point out and substantiate a Czech source of the Ruthenian *Book of Taudal*. Citing numerous examples from the published fragments and the rest of the text (which, alas, remained unpublished) he showed that the language of the Ruthenian translation

[6] Mil'kov 1999 provides a comprehensive account of how the historical consciousness of Medieval Rus' was nourished by eschatological and apocryphal literature; see especially the chapter *Istoriia v zerkale apokrifa* (*History through the Mirror of Apocrypha*), pages 253–329. On the history of various interpretations of eschatological expectations, see Beliakov and Beliakova 1992. Some scholars believe that differences in calculation and interpretation of the end of the world were the main issue in the dispute of heretical Judaizers with Orthodox ecclesiastical officials; see Lur'e 1995, Taube 2004b.

[7] Brückner 1881, 199–212.

[8] Helinand de Froidmont 1855 (written between 1211 and 1223).

[9] Vincent de Beauvais [1624] 1964, book 27, chapters 88–104. Hypothetically, it is possible that the Ruthenian *Book of Taudal the Knight* was translated from a German version of Vincent de Beauvais' text; but my research has not yet revealed a match among the described German versions (Palmer 1982).

[10] See Appendices II and III.

abounded with Bohemisms on all linguistic levels (lexical, syntactical and morphological).[11]

## Translator's Technique

Since the Czech source text of the Ruthenian *Book of Taudal the Knight* has not yet been located, it is impossible to conduct a textological comparison and examine the translator's technique properly as has been done for the Ruthenian *Song of Songs* in the previous chapter. However, we can make certain assumptions about the translation method of the *Book of Taudal* and find similar parallels with the translation method of the Ruthenian *Song of Songs*.

### Pseudo-Translations

The translator sometimes literally rendered Czech words in Ruthenian as transcriptions or pseudo-translations:

словоутного родоу (T 9),[12] cf. Czech *slovutný*, 'noble,' and Church Slavonic бл҃гороу^д^ноу радителю (CS 10);[13] [в] ритеръствѣ (T 15), cf. Czech *rytieřstvo*, 'knighthood,' and Church Slavonic ѿ вои^н^ (CS 16); [ѡ] реча^х^ (T 20), cf. Czech *řeč*, 'thing'; пышныхъ (T 62), cf. Czech *pyšný*, 'proud,' and Church Slavonic грьды^х^ (CS 55); досы^т^ (T 80), cf. Czech *dosyt*, 'enough'.

### Lexical Doublets

Similar to the Ruthenian *Song of Songs*, there are lexical doublets in the Ruthenian *Book of Taudal* for a single word in the Latin source text – a Czech word and a Ruthenian equivalent:[14]

(T 39) 'very': силно – велми (cf. Czech *velmi*, Polish *wielmi*):

| **Ruthenian** | **Latin** |
|---|---|
| ветръ велми силно великыи | *ventus horribilis* |
| wind very very strong | wind terrible |

(T 43-44) 'again': и ѡпѧть – засѧ (cf. Czech *zasě*, Polish *zasię*):

| | |
|---|---|
| оувращахѫ ихъ въ ѡгонь<br>иѡпѧть засѧ въ моукы | *mittebant eas in ignem, & e conuerſo.* |
| they pulled them into fire again<br>again into tortures | sent them into fire and back. |

[11] Brückner 1881, 199–212.

[12] A number next to the letter "T" indicates a line number in the edition of the Ruthenian *Book of Taudal* in Appendix II.

[13] A number next to the letters "CS" indicates a line number in the edition of the Church Slavonic *Edifying Story* in Appendix II.

[14] Latin examples are taken from Vincent de Beauvais [1624] 1964, 1127.

As Alexander Brückner has demonstrated in his study of the Ruthenian *Book of Taudal the Knight*, this text is linguistically reliant on its Czech source. In order to test this linguistic argument, I indulged in a bit of scholarly hooliganism by imagining how this text would have looked in an Old Czech translation. To reconstruct the Czech text I used both the Latin and Ruthenian versions. While we must keep in mind that the following passage is a linguistic reconstruction, other historical linguists have identified it as a conceivably authentic fifteenth-century Czech text:[15]

**Old Czech Hypothetical Translation**

*Z toho města byl jest muž, jemuž jmě bylo Tundal, rodu slovutného, ale děl velmi nedobrých, po tělu vítěžný a velmi smělý, a o spasení svéj duše málo nebo nic sě nestaráše. To jemu biesě přěliš protivně, aby kto mu chtěl málo o spasení duše poviedati. Do cierkve takež nechodieše a žebráky nenávidieše před sebú, ale jhráčóm, pištcóm a hudcóm vydal jest co měl.*

**The Ruthenian** ҝнига ѿ таоу҆дале рыцари

С того мѣста былъ есть моуⷤ родомъ, емоуⷤ имѧ было таоудалъ, родоу словоутного але дѣлъ велми недобрыхъ, по тѣлоу витѧⷤный а велми смѣлый, а ѡ спасенїи своеа дш҃а мало ибо ничого не смотрѧше. то емоу прелишь бѧше противно, а штобъ хто ѐмоу хотѣлъ мало ѡ҆ спасенїи дш҃и повѣдати . до цр҃кви такеⷤ не ходѧше а нищихъ ненавидѧше преⷣ собою, але играцемъ и пистцоⷨ а гоуⷣцомъ выдалъ есть что мѣлъ .

In either the Czech or Latin version, the *Visio Tundali* was clearly known in Bohemian lands. For example, we find an entry, "*Tungdalus visionem vidit,*" in twelfth-century Prague Annals (*Annales Pragenses*) under the year 1149.[16] Likewise, an East Middle German translation of the long Marcus version is found in a fifteenth-century manuscript of Bohemian provenance.[17] Still, the Ruthenian translation under examination is the only evidence that there once existed a Czech translation of the *Visio Tundali* (though, who knows, perhaps it will be discovered some day in one of the hitherto unknown Czech manuscripts).

## THE CROATIAN *NARRATION OF THE GOOD KNIGHT DUNDUL*

Unfortunately, it is only possible to hypothesize about records in anonymous and approximately dated medieval manuscript miscellanies. Unlike scientists of the

---

[15] I am especially grateful to Dr. Milada Homolková of the Czech Language Institute at Prague for allowing me to use their archives for verification of the Czech lexical material, and for making valuable comments on this speculative reconstruction.

[16] Wagner 1882, xiv.

[17] Palmer 1982, 263–267.

natural world, philologists must work with circumlocutory evidence, often providing interpretations that are vulnerable to contradiction. Given the potential risks, I find it necessary to examine the Ruthenian *Book of Taudal the Knight* and the historical circumstances of its translation and transmission against other medieval Slavic translations of the *Visio Tundali*, which exist (or once existed) in Croatian, Czech, and Church Slavonic. Closer scrutiny suggests that these translations could have been associated with a common source.

If indeed the Czech version existed, the Czechs were not the only Catholic Slavs who were familiar with the *Visio Tundali* in a Slavic language in the fifteenth century. At least two versions and three copies of the *Visio Tundali*, translated from Italian and Latin, are attested in fifteenth and sixteenth-century Croatian manuscripts. Of most interest to us is the Croatian translation from Latin, entitled *The Narration of the Good Knight Dundul* (*Čtenie dobroga viteza Dundula*), from the fifteenth-century Glagolitic Petris Miscellany (*Petrisov zbornik*).[18] Its Latin source is most likely a copy of Vincent de Beauvais' short adaptation of the *Visio Tundali*, the same version that was used as a source for the Ruthenian *Book of Taudal the Knight*. Although these translations use the same source, the Croatian translator's technique is noticeably different from that of the Ruthenian. Both translators followed the Latin text fairly closely, but the Croatian translator also added brief personal remarks and details not present even in Marcus' complete text.

Despite the apparent difference in translation techniques, there is reason to suppose that the Croatian and Ruthenian texts are nevertheless related. The Petris Miscellany in which the Croatian *Čtenie dobroga viteza Dundula* is preserved contains several texts of Czech origin.[19] It is usually connected with the Benedictine Glagolite monks, who returned from Prague's Emmaus Monastery after residing there from the middle of the fourteenth century.[20] While some texts in this collection have Czech textual prototypes,[21] others – the *Čtenie dobroga viteza Dundula* among them – are believed to show apparent Czech linguistic interference.[22]

[18] This manuscript is described in Milčetić 1911, 271–272 and Štefanić 1960, 355–397. Currently, it is a part of the Special Collections Department at the National and University Library at Zagreb and is being prepared for publication (Jurić 1993, 124–127, #957).

[19] Among them are fragments from the Old Czech *Pasionál*, a reworked variant of the Latin *Legenda Aurea.*

[20] Hercigonja 1975, 66–68, 370.

[21] *Čtenie kako e usěčena glava Ivanu Krstitělju* (f. 183–184), *Čti na Pasku evanĵeli* (f. 250v–254v), *Ot žit'ě svetih trih krali* (f. 288v–291v), see Hercigonja 1975, 66.

[22] Hercigonja 1975, 67–68.

Given that the Glagolite monks were familiar with the *Vision of Tundal* in Croatian, they also could have had in their possession a Czech translation of this vision. This brings us to hypothesize that Kleparz was the site of the Ruthenian translation of the *Visio Tundali* from Czech. Another important consideration, apart from the textological similarity and fitting historical circumstances, speaks in favor of this hypothesis. Research on the circulation of the *Visio Tundali* in various countries points to the importance of Benedictines in transmitting the vision.[23] Since the Croatian Glagoljaši belonged to the rule of St. Benedict, it is not surprising that they possessed a Slavic translation of the vision. Conversely, it is quite plausible that they could have played a part in the transmission of the *Visio Tundali* to the Slavic East. Finally, the fact that the *Vision of Tundal* is absent from the Polish textual inventory until the late seventeenth century suggests that it reached the Ruthenian milieu without Polish mediation, and by an independent agent foreign to a Polish environment.[24]

## THE CHURCH SLAVONIC *EDIFYING STORY TOLD BY FAUDAL THE WARRIOR*

The *Vision of Tundal* clearly circulated among Ruthenians and entered the Slavic Orthodox textual repertoire in a Church Slavonic translation entitled *The Edifying Story Told by Faudal the Warrior* (**повеᶜᵀ полезна сиѧ̇ сказаⷩ҇ ѐ фаоуда-лоⷨ воꙵноⷨ**).[25] It is found on ff. 259–288 in a Ruthenian miscellany from the Zamojski Collection, dated to 1495–1505.[26] The Church Slavonic version is textologically close enough to the Ruthenian *Book of Taudal the Knight* to suggest that we may be dealing with the same textual redaction. The heavily Bohemized language of the Ruthenian version clearly suggests a Czech source, virtually excluding the possibility of any other, let alone a Church Slavonic source. Still, both the Ruthenian and Czech versions could have provided a basis for the Church Slavonic *Edifying Story*. The translator of the *Edifying Story* was quite careful in his choice of the Church Slavonic language and hardly allowed any

---

[23] Palmer 1982, 17 (fn. 29).

[24] In Polish the *Vision of Tundal* appeared in verse adaptation only at the end of the seventeenth century in Klemens Bolesławiusz's work *Przeraźliwe echo trąby ostatecznej* (Poznań 1670).

[25] An edition of the corresponding fragments of the Church Slavonic *Edifying Story Told by Faudal the Warrior* is given in Appendix II.

[26] The National Library (Warsaw), Biblioteka Ordynacji Zamojskich (BOZ) #92. This manuscript is briefly described in Shchapov 1976a and 1976b.

other linguistic features in his translation, leaving us with very few clues about the source language.[27]

In his review article on Ruthenian translations from Latin and West Slavic languages, A. A. Turilov describes the Ruthenian *Book of Taudal the Knight* and the Church Slavonic *Edifying Story Told by Faudal the Warrior* as two independent translations, suggesting a Latin or a Polish source for the Church Slavonic translation.[28] If we exclude a Czech or Ruthenian source, a Latin source would seem more plausible than a Polish.[29] However, a number of textological considerations suggest that the translator of the Church Slavonic *Edifying Story Told by Faudal the Warrior* could have used the Ruthenian version as a source. Let us therefore examine this possibility more thoroughly.

A Church Slavonic translation made from a Ruthenian vernacular source is remarkable and almost without precedent in the fifteenth century. Let us therefore peruse carefully the features – mostly textological – that illustrate the immediate link between the Ruthenian and Church Slavonic texts, and suggest the possible direction of the translation from Ruthenian (or Czech) to Church Slavonic. A chart outlining the relationship between the translations under question can be found at the end of the chapter.

**Tundal's Name**

The modification of Tundal's name – rendered as 'Taudal' in the Ruthenian and 'Faudal' in the Church Slavonic texts – suggests a common source. The corruption of 'Tundal' into 'Taudal' could most likely have occurred during a translation made from a Czech text written in Latin Gothic script (in which it is easy to confuse the combination of letters 'un' and 'au') into Ruthenian, whereas the substitution of an 'F' for a 'T' in the rendering of 'Faudal' seems to have been a deliberate adaptation of the name 'Taudal' to Orthodox pronunciation in the subsequent translation into Church Slavonic. (Compare, for example, the Latin name *Thomas* and its Church Slavonic equivalent *Foma*, Latin *Theophanes* and Church Slavonic *Feofan*, etc.) Otherwise, it is very difficult to explain the corruption of Tundal's name into 'Taudal' and 'Faudal' in two independent transla-

[27] Several orthographic features suggest that the translator and/or a copier were of Ruthenian, or at least East Slavic, origin: more or less consistent use of the third person Present Tense ending in –ть, the use of ч instead of щ (e.g. что), оу instead of ж (e.g. въскоую instead of въскжѭ).

[28] Turilov 1998, 60.

[29] A Polish source is highly unlikely. Besides, as I have already mentioned there had been no prosaic versions of this text in Polish manuscript tradition at this time and the Church Slavonic translation betrays absolutely no trace of Polish influence.

tions. None of the described Latin versions uses a modified name 'Taudal' and a modification of this name in two independent versions is very unlikely.[30]

## The Frame of the Story

Tundal was an Irish nobleman and presumably a real figure. He was born in the town of Armagh in the Irish see of Cashel. Monk Marcus, the author of the Latin vision, informs us that the vision occurred in the year 1149: the second year of the expedition of Conrad, king of the Romans, to Jerusalem, the fourth year of the pontificate of Pope Eugene III, and the same year that he returned to Rome from the regions of Gaul. Also that year, Malachy, archbishop of Armagh, bishop of Down, died at the Clairvaux Monastery on his way to Rome.[31] The Ruthenian version, although evidently following the *Speculum Historiale*, corrupts and condenses this historical information:

**Vincent de Beauvais, *Speculum Historiale***

*Anno domini 1149.*
*qui fuit annus ſecundus expeditionis Hieroſolymorum, Conradi Regis Romanorum, & annus quartus Eugenii Papæ, in quo anno ipſe Papa de partibus Galliarum Romam reuerſus eſt, in quo etiam anno ſanctus Malachias in Clareualle defunctus eſt, viſa eſt hæc viſio. Duę ſunt Metropoles in Hibernia, Ardiacha (Ardmacha) ſeptentrionalium Hibernenſium, Auſtralium Caſelenſis, de qua ortus fuit vir quidam, Tundalus nomine.*

This vision was seen in the year 1149 A.D., which was the second year of the expedition of Conrad, king of the Romans, to Jerusalem and the fourth year [of the pontificate] of Pope Eugene, and the same year that the Pope returned to Rome from the regions of Gaul, in which year St. Malachy passed away at the Clairvaux

**The Ruthenian *Book of Taudal the Knight***[32]

лѣта ѿ нарожені́а с҃на б҃жиа́го тисѧчаго
триⷣцатого девѧтого было дрѫгое лѣто ц҃рѧ
таврата цесарѧ римъского валеⷱного ишто есть
валькоу про ерⷭлимъ мѣлъ, а четвертаго лѣта,
ꙗкоже есть еѵгенїюсъ папежемъ былъ воленъ, в
томъ лѣте тако еѵгениюсъ папеⷤ възратилсѧ
есть былъ до рима з влаⷯ ишто словоу галлїа а
тогоⷤ лѣта стыи малахиа́ въ манастыри, иже
то слове глозоналъ, изшелъ с того свѣта.
С того мѣста былъ есть моуⷤ родомъ, емоуⷤ
имѧ было таоудалъ.

In the year one thousand and thirty nine from the Nativity of the Son of God, it was the second year of the Czar Tavrat (sic!), the great Roman Caesar, who went to a war for Jerusalem, and the fourth year that Eugene was elected pope, also in this year Pope Eugene returned to Rome from Italy, which is called Gallia, and the same year St. Malachy left

[30] Even if there existed a so far unknown Latin version of the *Visio Tundali* that employs the modified name 'Taudal', in order to lend this name to both Ruthenian and Church Slavonic translations independently it would have to be a source for a Czech translation too. This seems most unlikely.

[31] Marcus 1989, 110.

[32] This passage is taken from Karskii 1898, 16, where it is transcribed with more paleographic details.

Monastery. There was a city in Hibernia, Armagh, in northern Ireland, the southern see of Cashel, from this place there was a man by the name of Tundalus.

this world in the monastery which is called Glozonal. From this place there was a man whose name was Taudal.

The Ruthenian version contains several textual corruptions. In addition to modifying the date of the vision from 1149 to 1039, the Ruthenian version distorts the name of *Clareualle* (the Latin name for the Clairvaux Monastery) into **глозоналъ** (*Glozonal,* perhaps misreading the Czech *Clareval*?), mangles Conrad as Tavrat, and completely omits the geographical information about Tundal's place of birth. Nevertheless, it does not fail to translate faithfully the phrase "*de qua ortus fuit vir quidam, Tundalus nomine*":

**С того мѣста былъ есть моуж родомъ, емоуж имѧ было таоудалъ.**
[From that place there came a man, named Taudal.]

Although it is probable that the passage about Tundal's birth place was already missing in the Czech version, the corruption most likely occurred in Ruthenian, since a Czech Catholic translator would attach more importance to such a detail as the location of an ecclesiastical see. By contrast, this omission would not be unexpected from a Ruthenian Orthodox translator, who knew little about distant Western lands and Catholic Church eparchies, and who would therefore have little interest in the geographic particulars of the vision.

By the same token, the translator into Church Slavonic would have been even less interested in precise geographical and historical details. The Church Slavonic *Edifying Story Told by Faudal* omits the whole introductory passage containing historical facts and names, substituting for it a succinct synopsis of the story and its edifying meaning. The vision itself opens with the sentence:

**Поведавы нам сиа̀ и̓меноуѐмы фаоудал. рожение̇ и̓ воспитанїе̇ ет. въ градии римстим.**
[A man who told us this, named Faudal, by birth and education was from the city of Rome.]

It is not difficult to guess a possible motivation for shifting Tundal's place of birth to Rome. The omission of Tundal's Irish birthplace in the Ruthenian translation – whether original or copied from Czech – created an ambiguous context from which it could be inferred that Tundal was born in Rome since that city was the last one mentioned in the narrative right before the phrase "From that place there came a man, named Taudal." This corruption shows that by the time the vision wound up in the hands of the translator of the Church Slavonic *Edifying Story*, its text was reduced to the version represented in the Ruthenian *Book of Taudal*, which omitted the Irish place of birth and suggested Rome instead.

## Textological Idiosyncrasies

The following examples demonstrate that the Church Slavonic translation (CS) replicates the idiosyncrasies of the Ruthenian translation (R), elements that exist neither in the original Latin text (L) nor in the Croatian (C) version.

**(i).** … among whom [friends] he had ('a favorite' in R and CS) one who along with military service owed him three horses.

**L** *inter eos habebat unum, qui co(m)militonis debito, trium equorum debitor erat*

**C** meju kimi prijatelji njegovimi biše mu jedan dlžan tri konje

**R** и любимого ймѣлъ ѐсть товариша єдиного в ритеръствѣ, тотъ ємоу былъ должеⷩ҇ три кони .

**CS** но ѡ҆баче ѐдинъ ѿ воиⷮ҇ любл҄ѧше · ѝскрено ѐмоу же ѝ долъженъ бѣ три конѧ

Both the Ruthenian and Church Slavonic versions (in contrast to the Latin and Croatian texts) add information about a debtor stating that he was a favorite of Tundal. It is possible that this addition had already been present in the Czech translation from Latin.

**(ii).** ... there was an iron cover ten (in R and CS) ~ six (in L and C) cubits thick.

**L** *operculum ferreum habens spissitudinis sex cubitorum*

**C** I biše na tom dolu pokrivalo želězno. i tlstota želězna běše šest sat lakat

**R** а на том долоу покрывало желѣзноє толъстотою на десѧть локотъ

**CS** ѝ на неⷨ҇ покрывало желѣзно. толъ.сто лакти десѧть

The Ruthenian and Church Slavonic translations deviate from the Latin source, transforming the number from "six" (*sex*) to "ten" (десѧть) for no apparent reason. The Croatian translation also modifies the Latin source but preserves the principal numeral, multiplying it by one hundred (šest sat, 'six hundred').

**(iii).** ... a very long plank stretched across a deep valley from one mountain to the other like a bridge; it measured a mile in length and one finger (in R and CS) ~ foot (in L and C) in width.

**L** *ibi erat tabula longissima de uno monte in alium montem porrecta, in modum pontis super vallem extensa, quae mille passus habebat in longitudine, in latitudine pedem unum.*

**C** I tu biše prik toga dola ot brěga do brěga jedna brv vuska za jednu nogu širine, a jednu milju běše dlga hoditi.

**R** тоу пакъ бѧше єдна лавичька велми длъга съ єдиноє горы но дроугоую ꙗко мостокъ черезъ долъ преглоубокїй оу даль на милю а единъ вширинȣ перъстень мосток ити

**CS** ѝ тоу бѧше лава долготою. велика ѿ горы к то дроузей горе ꙗко мостъ. чересъ ровъ преглоубокий. долготою ꙗко пѧтьма поприщй. и широка ѿ прьстей ѐдиномъ

The Ruthenian and the Church Slavonic translations modify the unit of measurement used in the Latin text from "one foot" (*pedem unum*) to "one finger" (єдинъ перъстень, ѿ прьстей єдиномъ), whereas the Croatian version follows the Latin source (jednu nogu).[33] It is a matter of speculation where in the chain of translations – Czech or Ruthenian – this corruption occurred.

In general, the Ruthenian version follows Latin more accurately than the Church Slavonic. There are textual features present in the Latin and Ruthenian translations but not in the Church Slavonic. Based on the preserved Ruthenian fragment, there are no cases when a certain textual feature would be present in Latin and Church Slavonic but not in Ruthenian.

## MANUSCRIPT CONTEXT. *ON THE THREE LAWFUL STATES*

The manuscript context also offers insight into the relationship between the Ruthenian and the Church Slavonic translations of the *Visio Tundali*. The BOZ #92 Miscellany, like the Swidziński Miscellany, is a collection of various hagiographical and eschatological compositions:[34]

f. 1. An ending of *The Life of Basil the New*;
ff. 2–122. Andrew of Caesarea's *Exegesis on the Apocalypse of John*;
ff. 123–231. *The Life of Basil the New* and his student Gregory's *Revelation about the Second Coming of Christ*;
ff. 231–259. *The Revelations of Pseudo-Methodius of Patara*;
ff. 259–288. повєст полєзна сиѧ сказан є фаоудалом воином. *The Edifying Story Told by Faudal the Warrior*;
ff. 288–289. ѿ трех ѡзаконєниꙗх, *On the Three Lawful States*. This is a short homily on the three conditions of virginity, marriage, and widowhood, and on the sin of fornication. This text is omitted from Shchapov's description of the manuscript in Shchapov 1976a.
ff. 290. Blank
ff. 291–411. моука гса нашего ӏсса хса и из мртвых востаниє. The Ruthenian translation of the *Passion of Christ*;[35]
ff. 411–452. слово стго андрѣѧ о цариградѣ. Epiphanius' *Life of St. Andrew*;
ff. 452–458. Extracts from the *Books of the Four Patriarchs* (on John Chrysostom and Cyril of Alexandria, the Philosopher).

---

[33] The Church Slavonic перъстень, 'ring', may be either a result of Brückner's incorrect transcription or a corruption from перъстъ or перъстеи which could have occurred either in Czech or Ruthenian.

[34] Its contents are briefly described in Shchapov 1976a, 40–43 and 1976b, 267.

[35] The same version is in the miscellany Q.I. 391 (St. Petersburg Public Library) and in the Moscow Synod Collection Miscellany #558, which contains the Ruthenian translations of the *Marian Mass* from Croatian Church Slavonic and the *Song of Songs* from Czech.

Unlike that of the Swidziński Miscellany, the history of the BOZ #92 manuscript is somewhat better known. Shchapov includes it among the manuscripts in the Polatsk St. Sophia Cathedral library. These were taken to Poland by Jan Zamojski in 1579, when Polatsk fell to the army of Stefan Bathory.[36] Unfortunately, it is unclear whether the manuscript had been copied in Polatsk or had been brought there by one of the cathedral scribes or library keepers.

Now let us turn to the text on ff. 288–289, ѿ тре$^{х}$ ѣзаконенига$^{х}$ (*On the Three Lawful States*), which has escaped Shchapov's notice. This is a short homily on the three states of virginity, marriage, and widowhood, and of avoiding the sin of fornication.[37] It can, indeed, be easily overlooked because its opening initial does not differ from any other chapter initials in the preceding text. The homily *On the Three Lawful States* is written in the same hand, and at the first glance seems a continuation of the *Edifying Story Told by Faudal the Warrior*. The only mark that gives away its independent status is the word ѧминь (*Amen*) at the end of the *Edifying Story Told by Faudal*.

If we turn to the contents of the Swidziński Miscellany from the Krasiński Collection, in which the Ruthenian *Book of Taudal the Knight* is found, we will see that it is also followed by the same text:

**BOZ #92 Miscellany**

ff. 259–288. пове$^{ст}$ полезна сиа̀ сказа$^{н}$ ѐ фаоудало$^{м}$ войно$^{м}$. The Church Slavonic *Edifying Story Told by Faudal the Warrior*;
ff. 288–289. ѿ тре$^{х}$ ѣзаконенига$^{х}$, *On the Three Lawful States*. This is a short homily on the three conditions of virginity, marriage, and widowhood, and the sin of fornication.

**Swidziński Miscellany**

ff. 92–106v. книга ѿ таоу́дале рыцари. The Ruthenian *Book of Taudal the Knight*, the text is unfinished, translated from Czech;
ff. 107–119v. ре$^{ч}$ ѿ тре$^{х}$ ставехъ, *On the Three States*. This is an account of Augustine's discourse on the three conditions of virginity, marriage, and widowhood.

For the homily *On the Three States* (ре$^{ч}$ ѿ тре$^{х}$ ставехъ) in the Swidziński Miscellany, Karskii has given several *incipit* examples, which leave no doubt regarding the content and authorship of this text:[38]

(f. 159) починаѐтсѧ ре$^{ч}$ ѿ тре$^{х}$ ставехъ. сты$^{и}$ ѧоугоустинъ. въ свои$^{х}$ слове$^{х}$ на стрѣтенїе га нашего его їу ха глеть. иже который хр$^{с}$тианъ маеть быти ... ;
(f. 159v) починаетсѧ первы$^{и}$ ставъ сѹщимъ въ браце моужe$^{м}$ и жена$^{м}$ хр$^{с}$тиганомъ;
(f. 161v) вторый ставъ ѐсть вдовъскїи;
(f. 165) тѹто сѧ починае$^{т}$ ѿ ставѹ девиче$^{м}$.

[36] Shchapov 1976b, 267.
[37] The full transcript of this text can be found in Appendix IV.
[38] Karskii 1894, 16.

[(f. 159) Here begins [a homily] on the three states. Saint Augustine, in his sermon on the feast of the Presentation of Jesus at the Temple, says: if a Christian has to be…
(f. 159v) Here begins a passage on the first state of married Christian men and women;
(f. 161v) The second state is widowhood;
(f. 165) Here begins a passage on the state of virginity.]

Church Slavonic translations of Saint Augustine's writings are definitely not abundant. According to Francis Thomson, so far the only known Church Slavonic translation of any of Augustine's writings is an insignificant excerpt (as yet untraced) in a florilegium in *Izbornik of 1073*.[39] This fact makes the discussed account of Saint Augustine's teachings among Ruthenians very notable.

That these two texts, each fairly unusual for the Orthodox repertoire, should by mere coincidence appear in the same sequence in two seemingly unrelated manuscripts must seem suspect, even to a skeptic. Rather, it is more likely that both texts, the Ruthenian *Book of Taudal the Knight* and the homily *On the Three States* (рє͡ч ѿ трєх ставєхъ) migrated together and reappeared in the BOZ #92 manuscript as the Church Slavonic *Edifying Story Told by Faudal*, and *On the Three Lawful States* (ѿ прєх въ͏законєниѧх) respectively. The text of *On the Three Lawful States* (ѿ прєх въ͏законєниѧх) is much shorter than that of *On the Three States* (рє͡ч ѿ трєх ставєхъ), which suggests that the former was summarized from the latter. Furthermore, during its reduction and adaptation this short homily also lost its author, Saint Augustine. The homily *On the Three Lawful States* is not only graphically perceived as a single whole with the Church Slavonic *Edifying Story Told by Faudal* but seems to function as a commentary on it, bringing forward apocalyptic messages related to the sin of fornication. To conclude, the fact that Saint Augustine's *On the Three States* is found alongside the Ruthenian and – in a condensed form – alongside the Church Slavonic versions of the *Vision of Tundal* strongly suggests that the Church Slavonic *Edifying Story Told by Faudal* was translated or adapted from the fifteenth-century Ruthenian *Book of Taudal the Knight*.

If only to play devil's advocate, I ought to admit the possibility that both the Church Slavonic and Ruthenian translations could have arisen independently from a common Czech or even Latin source. As regards the Czech source, one could argue that, theoretically, all of the above mentioned textological and linguistic features could have already occurred in Czech, including the manuscript context resemblance. Further, I would venture to offer an alternative scenario, in which the Czech *Vision of Tundal* never existed, and the Ruthenian translation

[39] Thomson 1999, I, 119.

could have been made by a Czech translator directly from a Latin source (and, as would be more likely, with the help of a Ruthenian scribe). That would explain both the presence of Czech linguistic elements in the Ruthenian text and the absence of a Czech source. However, I will not pursue this line of argument further, both because it is in itself implausible and because I cannot offer any supporting evidence except by referring to other precedents.[40] Were a Czech *Vision of Tundal* ever to be discovered it would shed considerable light onto this question.

Another scenario would stage the Ruthenian *Book of Taudal* as translated from a Czech source, and the Church Slavonic *Edifying Story* as translated from a Latin source. Although such a scenario is not completely impossible, it is highly problematic because it would have to satisfy the following conditions: first, both texts would have to reflect the same version of Vincent de Beauvais' *Visio Tundali*; secondly, both Czech and Latin source texts would have to contain the same textological corruptions and modifications, described above under "Tundal's Name," "The Frame of the Story," and "Textological Idiosyncrasies;" finally, both Czech and Latin source manuscripts would have to contain Saint Agustine's discourse on the three states of virginity, marriage and widowhood that follows the Ruthenian and Church Slavonic versions of the *Vision of Tundal*. In order to satisfy these conditions a Czech text would have to be copied from the same Latin manuscript that was used as a source for the Church Slavonic *Edifying Story Told by Faudal*, and this would still not account for the modification of Tundal's name (to the Church Slavonic *Faudal* from the Ruthenian *Taudal*). All this does not seem plausible.

If indeed the Church Slavonic translation was based on the Ruthenian text, a couple of inferences should be made. According to the manuscript description, the Ruthenian *Book of Taudal the Knight* in the Swidziński Miscellany is incomplete; it is missing a significant portion of the ending. The Church Slavonic version, in contrast, contains all twelve chapters. If we accept a Ruthenian version as a source then there likely existed another, complete Ruthenian copy which served as a source for the Church Slavonic *Edifying Story*. Like the Ruthenian *Book of Taudal*, the Church Slavonic translation should have also been carried out some time before 1492, when eschatological expectations were especially intense.

---

[40] It is possible that a Czech translator was involved in the translation of the Wiślica Statute of Kazimierz the Great (1347) from Latin into Ruthenian (Perwolf 1886, Florovskii 1947, 52–54.) See Chapter One.

Furthermore, if indeed the Church Slavonic translation was based on the Ruthenian text, a number of questions concerning the much debated status of the Ruthenian language as a literary vernacular and its relationship to Church Slavonic as a lingua sacra at the end of the fifteenth century inevitably come to mind. Regardless of whether the Church Slavonic *Edifying Story Told by Faudal* was translated from Ruthenian or from Czech, its source language was a vernacular. The very existence of two versions of the same Catholic text in Ruthenian and Church Slavonic speaks strongly in favor of the argument that Ruthenian bookmen possessed active literacy in Church Slavonic and that the use of Ruthenian in religious and devotional writings was a deliberate choice, whether stylistic or ideological.

## TEXT ADAPTATION

Like the Swidziński Miscellany, the manuscript which includes the Church Slavonic *Edifying Story Told by Faudal the Warrior* contains primarily works with eschatological content. The inclusion of the *Edifying Story Told by Faudal*, a story of a common mortal who suffered the torments of Purgatory, in an Orthodox eschatological miscellany might seem extraordinary but is not unexplainable, especially in the context of the approaching end of the seventh millennium. An account of the other world did not contradict official Orthodox doctrine but it demanded certain adjustments. This might explain why the translator was so careful to translate the *Visio Tundali* into Church Slavonic, and to strip it of its foreign features and irrelevant historical details.

With regard to the way this Catholic text was adapted into the Orthodox corpus, it is interesting to observe how the title of the text (and along with it perhaps also the genre and function) altered with its transmission from language to language and, consequently, from culture to culture. In Latin it originated in a canonical genre of the *visio*. When it entered the Ruthenian vernacular it underwent a certain degree of popularization, turning into a "книга," a book. However, when it returned to the sphere of the ecclesiastical lingua sacra, Church Slavonic, it acquired a new generic nuance, characteristic of Orthodox edificatory literature: it became a "повесть полезна," an edifying, instructive story. In addition, the Church Slavonic version introduced two new elements into the narrative. It switched to first-person narration, a feature not present in either the original Latin or Ruthenian versions. It also integrated Augustine's discourse *On the Three Lawful States* (ѿ пре҃х въ҃законенига҃х) into the end of the vision in the form of a short homily on the sin of fornication. This compositional frame accentuated the purpose of moral edification for the *Edifying Story Told by Faudal the Warrior*.

## CONCLUSION

As the Slavic versions of the *Visio Tundali* traveled east through time and space, we can only speculate and hypothesize about the nature of their relationship, the actual circumstances of their transmission, and the human intentions and events that stood behind them. This being said, an examination of the language, sources and textual history of the Ruthenian and Church Slavonic translations of the *Vsion of Tundal* suggests that both are associated with the same version of this vision, and that both could have entered the Ruthenian textual corpus with the mediation of the Prague Emmaus Glagolite monks.

The Church Slavonic *Edifying Story* was most likely translated in the fifteenth-century from the Ruthenian *Book of Taudal* (or, as is less likely, from a Czech or Latin version). The existence of Ruthenian and Church Slavonic versions of the *Visio Tundali* speaks in favor of the argument that Ruthenian churchmen possessed an active literacy in Church Slavonic and that the use of Ruthenian was a deliberate stylistic choice on the part of the translator.

## TRANSMISSION OF THE *VISIO TUNDALI* IN SLAVIC VERSIONS

**Latin *Visio Tundali***
Helinand de Froidmont, *Chronicon* (1211-1223)
Vincent de Beauvais, *Speculum Historiale* (1244)

**Czech** (hypothetical)
*Tundalovo/Taudalovo vidění*
*The Vision of Tundal*

**Croatian Glagolitic**
*Čtenie dobroga viteza Dundula*
*The Narration of the Good Knight Dundul*
Petris Miscellany (1468)

**Ruthenian** (hypothetical)

**Ruthenian**
к҇нига ѿ таоу́дале рыцари
*The Book of Taudal the Knight*
Swidziński Miscellany (early 16th c.)
Krasiński Collection
translated at Kleparz?

**(East Slavic) Church Slavonic**
повеⷭⷮ полезна сказаⷩ҇ ѐ фаоудалоⷨ воиноⷨ
*The Edifying Story Told by Faudal the Warrior*
BOZ 92 Miscellany (1495–1505)
Zamojski Collection
translated in Ruthenia?

## Chapter Four
## THE RUTHENIAN *TALE OF SIVILLA THE PROPHETESS*

The Ruthenian *Tale of Sivilla the Prophetess* (**сказаниѐ ѿ сивилле прⷪрчици**) was a part of the same sixteenth-century manuscript miscellany as the *Book of Taudal the Knight* (**кнга ѿ таоуⷮдале рыцари**): the Swidziński Miscellany of Lithuanian Chronicles #82 from the Krasiński Collection (ff. 119v–124v).[1] Therefore, it suffered the same fate: the manuscript was destroyed in a fire during WWII along with the greater part of the collection. Fortunately, Evfimii Karskii, who succinctly described this miscellany,[2] also published the complete text of the Ruthenian *Tale of Sivilla the Prophetess.*[3]

### GERMAN AND CZECH SOURCES

At present, the Ruthenian *Tale of Sivilla the Prophetess* is the only known East Slavic translation of this particular version of the *Sibylline Prophecy*, which is based on a fifteenth-century Czech source. It does not resemble any of the East Slavic translations found in Chronographs and other compilations.[4] The story line is composed of several legends and prophecies. It starts with the meeting of King Solomon and the prophetess Sivilla (Sibyl), sometimes associated with the Queen of Sheba. However, unlike the Queen of Sheba, Sivilla is called an astrologer (**звѣздарька**), learned in techniques of divination from the stars (**иже въ звѣзⷣахъ мнѡгый вещи в бѹдѫщиⷯ речаⷯ провидѣла**). Like the Queen of Sheba, the Ruthenian Sivilla is wise, beautiful and rich but one of her feet is that of a goose.[5] This goose-like foot, however, is miraculously cured after Sivilla refuses

---

[1] Pułaski 1915, 76–78.

[2] Karskii, 1894, 6–19.

[3] Karskii 1898, 2–10. In Karskii's words, "повесть печатается палеографически точно" [the publication of the legend is paleographically accurate].

[4] Karski 1898 provides a detailed description and bibliographic record of the legends and other Sibylline texts, associated with the Ruthenian *Tale of Sivilla the Prophetess*. On other versions of the *Sibylline Prophecies* in East Slavic tradition and the updated bibliography see an overview in Mil'kov 1999 and Pesensen 2007.

[5] In all apocrypha the Queen of Sheba is described with a defect in her feet. Usually, they are either deformed or covered with hair or fur. A goose-like foot is not common although it is also present in a Bulgarian legend, where Sibyl is allegedly born from an egg (Karskii 1898, 12–13). It seems that in German folklore Sibyls were also associated with birds.

to step on the Crucifixion Tree (пре҃ѕ адамово дрѣво ити), "the Tree of Adam," on which Jesus would later be crucified.[6] This miracle prompts many questions from the wise but skeptical King Solomon, which are patiently answered by Sivilla. She prophesizes the birth and teachings of Christ, the spread of Christianity and the fall of Judaism, the signs of the advent of the Antichrist, the appearance of the Last Emperor, fifteen indications of the end of the world, and the Second Coming of Christ to speak the Last Judgment.

When Karskii published the Ruthenian *Tale of Sivilla the Prophetess* he was not familiar with its sources. A Czech provenance of this text was first established by Alexander Brückner, who pointed out a possible Czech source in an early sixteenth-century Czech miscellany from the Ossoliński Collection in L'viv, calling the Ruthenian text a "wortliche Übersetzung."[7] Following Brückner, a Czech scholar, Věra Brynychová pointed to yet another version of the Czech *Proroctví Sibyllino* from the fifteenth-century Pinvičkův Miscellany.[8] She concluded that, although there is a significant similarity between all three texts, there must have existed another Czech redaction of the prophecy which could have been a source for both the Ruthenian and the other two Czech versions.

As it turns out, in Czech, too, the *Proroctví Sibyllino* was not an original work; it was most likely translated into Czech from a German poetic adaptation. The Czech version even shows some signs of rhyme and rhythmical structure. Although an immediate German protograph has yet to be discovered, several versions of the German *Sibyllenweissagung* show that it could have served as a source for the Czech text.[9] In her study of the German *Sibyllenweissagung*, Ingeborg Neske suggests that the German version was written sometime in the middle of the fourteenth century, although the earliest manuscript containing it dates back to 1400.[10] This German composition is, in its turn, a late medieval reworking of a Latin *Sibylla Tiburtina* into a narrative which has been referred to as "political theology under the mask of the prophecy."[11]

---

[6] The "Crucifixion Tree" was planted on the grave of Adam and later used as a bridge in Solomon's Temple. It is this bridge that Sivilla refuses to cross. Beyer 1987, 209–249 gives a very detailed account of association of the Queen of Sheba with Sibyl, and the legend of the Crucifixion Tree. He asserts that this connection becomes especially prominent in German texts.

[7] Brückner 1881.

[8] Brynychová 1927. This version was published by Ferdinand Menčík (Menčík 1879).

[9] Neske 1985 provides a detailed description of the textual history and transmission of the late medieval German *Sibyllenweissagung*.

[10] Neske 1985, 41–44.

[11] Rauch 1973, 138.

The Latin *Sibylla Tiburtina* talks about a number of rulers involved in the events leading up to the End of the World, the focus being, of course, on the Last Emperor. As time went by, this list was gradually amended and updated to refer to current kings and emperors. This aspect certainly contributed to the *Sibylla Tiburtina*'s political resonance. However, Anke Holdenried, who has recently published a comprehensive study of the manuscripts and interpretation of the Latin *Sibylla Tiburtina*, argues that the importance of this political resonance is probably somewhat exaggerated by modern historiography and that considering its political aspect as a key feature of this text takes too narrow a view. In addition to presenting a painstaking examination of about one hundred versions of the Latin *Sibylla Tiburtina*, Holdenried's work is valuable in that she demonstrates the importance of the manuscript context for interpreting medieval texts – especially those found in manuscript miscellanies – and for the study of their reception.[12]

## Dates of the Czech and Ruthenian Translations

It is hard to state with certainty when the German *Sibyllenweissagung* was introduced to the Czech environment. A description of the L'viv Ossoliński Miscellany in *Archive im Königreiche Galizien und Lodomerien* by Beda Franciscus Dudík dated it to the fifteenth century.[13] In addition to the *Proroctví Sibyllino* on ff. 55v–71 it also contains *Apolon, pověst romantičná* (*Apollo, a Romantic Story*) on ff. 1–55, and *Mníšek Bosáček* (*A Barefoot Monk*) on ff. 71v–101. The last text recounts that in the year 1449, a highly learned monk from the Order of Barefoot Monks (Franciscans?) came to Pope Clement's Court, suggesting the year 1449 as the terminus *post quem* for the compilation of the manuscript. However, individual texts could have been composed at an earlier date.

The texts in the Pinvičkův Miscellany (Czech National Museum Library, II F 8 (4 D 4)) are more numerous and provide a better idea of a possible compilation date:

Part I.
ff. 1–98. Kronika Dalimilova, *The Chronicle of Dalimil*, dated 1459;
ff. 98v–123. Nová rada, *The New Council*, dated 1459;
ff. 123v–127v. Skládání o podkoním a žáku, *A Story about a Stable-man and his Stdent*;

[12] Holdenried 2006.
[13] Dudík 1867, 183.

ff. 128–153. Apolon;
ff. 153–160. Walterus a Grizeldis;
ff. 160v–186v. Tandariáš, dated 1463;
f. 187. O zlobivé ženě, *About a mean woman*;
Part II.
ff. 188v–191. Kroniky české, *The Czech Chronicles*, for the years 893–1457;
ff. 192–207. Kronika česká, *The Czech Chronicle*, for the years 1378–1461;
ff. 210v–213. Proroctví Sibyllino, *The Sibylline Prophecy*.

In addition to the *Proroctví Sibyllino*, the Ossoliński and Pinvičkův miscellanies share another text, the *Tale of Apollo*; this suggests a possible connection between these miscellanies. In general, the contexts of both manuscripts are similar in that they contain primarily popular legends, tales and chronicle accounts.

In his catalogue of the National Museum manuscripts, František Bartoš dated the Pinvičkův Miscellany to 1459–1469. He determined the *ante quem* date in 1469 based on an inscription found on f. 213 at the end of the *Proroctví Sibyllino*, which he interpreted as "*Impletum a. d. 1409 et alias 69.*"[14] This inscription follows a brief, eight-line prophecy about the Eagle of Emperor Friedrich and most likely refers to it. Both entries are located at the end of the *Proroctví Sibyllino* and are written by the same hand. The Latin inscription most likely indicates the year when the prophecy about Friedrich was fulfilled (*impletum*). Whatever the meaning, the date itself in the manuscript is not "1409 et alias 69" as Bartoš provided in the catalogue. Its exact transcription is "*Impletum anno d(o)m(ini) 1000$^{o}$ etc. quadragesi(m)o nono et alias 49$^{o}$*" (Fulfilled / Completed in one thousand etc. fortieth ninth and in another way 49), suggesting a new date of 1(?)49.[15] It is unclear whether this date is related to the *Proroctví Sibyllino*.

The latest text in the Pinvičkův miscellany is dated 1463. Therefore, the two extant versions of the Czech *Proroctví Sibyllino*, one in a fifteenth or an early sixteenth-century miscellany from the L'viv Ossoliński Collection, and another in the Pinvičkův Miscellany, suggest only the *terminus ante quem* for the Czech translation – 1463. Similarly, it is difficult to establish a precise date for the Ruthenian translation and to establish its exact Czech source.

Although significant similarity exists between the two mentioned Czech versions and the Ruthenian translation, they notably deviate in several places. In

[14] Bartoš 1926, 89–90.

[15] 1000 and "etc" are written in special characters. Apparently, Bartoš read the Arabic numeral '49' as a combination of 'lx9' and interpreted the Latin numeral *quadragesimus* as *quadringentesimus*.

some cases the Ruthenian text contains a shorter rendering of more extensive Czech passages. Brynychová explained this by the fact that another Czech redaction of the prophecy must have existed, closer to the Ruthenian *Tale of Sivilla the Prophetess*.[16] There has most likely been at least one other redaction of the Czech text because the Ruthenian translation shows a combination of features from the Ossoliński and the Pinvičkův Miscellanies. However, a search through a number of catalogued versions of the Czech *Proroctví Sibyllino* has not yet revealed another such redaction.[17] While it is very likely that the source was a different version of the *Proroctví Sibyllino*, it is also possible that the Ruthenian translator simply summarized and modified several Czech passages in his Ruthenian translation. Such free, interpretational mode of translation was definitely not uncommon in the fifteenth century; it would not be surprising if we never find a direct source for the Ruthenian *Tale of Sivilla the Prophetess* because the translation could have been made in a "retelling" fashion.

Karskii's dating of the Ruthenian translation to shortly before 1492 is based on his interpretation of several historical facts mentioned in the *Tale of Sivilla the Prophetess* that supposedly occurred before the "end of the world," which was expected in the year 1492.[18] To support his argument that many translations in the Swidziński Miscellany are pre–1492, Karskii also referred to the opening sentence of the treatise *On the Last Times, On the Kingdom of Michael* (слово ѡ҆ последнем времени ѡ҆ михайловѣ црс҃твѣ). It reads: Єгдаж боудеть ѿ последнем времени. ѿ исходе. ҂з҃. тысмщь лѣт... [When it will be during the Last Times, at the end of the seventh millennium...], and speaks about the Last Times in the Future Tense. According to Karskii, the focus of several texts in this miscellany was a prediction of an "end" and he argued that they could be of interest to a miscellany compiler only before 1492.[19]

[16] Brynychová 1927.

[17] I have checked the following manuscripts: XVII A 24 and XVII D 18 from the Prague National Library and II E 60, II F 7, IV A 35, IV H 11, IV G 28a (same as V G 92), V G 88 from the Library of the Czech National Museum. I have not had an opportunity to look at the Strahov manuscript, A.T. VI 101, but it was known to Zíbrt, who published the Ossoliński text (Zíbrt 1910). Apparently, it retains a different version of the *Proroctví Sibyllino* than that in our manuscripts. There are also numerous print versions of the prophecy but they also do not seem to render the discussed version.

[18] The year 7000, according to the Orthodox ecclesiastical system of chronology.

[19] Karskii 1894, 17–18 and 1898, 17. Although the eschatological theme of the Ruthenian *Tale of Sivilla* indeed suggests that it could have been translated shortly before 1492, in my view, it would be too hasty to agree with Karskii's assumption that after 1492 the text would have lost its immediate appeal. Eschatological and apocalyptic themes have always attracted Orthodox believers and one finds as many post–1492 eschatological texts as pre–1492 ones.

Previously, when the *Tale of Sivilla the Prophetess* was dated to the sixteenth century by Karskii and to the second half of the fifteenth century by Brückner, it was not possible to offer an accurate interpretation of the historical events and figures mentioned in it. Dating its source text to the fourteenth century provides a more accurate explanation of its original historical context. In following the German and Czech versions, the Ruthenian *Tale of Sivilla* retains a clear anti-Catholic point of view. It predicts troubles and afflictions caused by both secular rulers and by the Church. Among the historical events prophesied by Sivilla is an over seven years war (вѧще ниᶾ҃ли за се̑дмь лѣтъ) between two kings, Ludwig and Friedrich, for the title of Holy Roman Emperor (ѿ римс̑кое цр҃ство). This probably refers to Ludwig IV the Bavarian (1287–1347) and Friedrich the Handsome of Austria (1286–1330). Indeed, the war between them lasted for a little more than seven years from 1314 to 1322, when Ludwig defeated and imprisoned Friedrich. Sivilla also predicted the rule of "the last" Emperor Charles, most likely referring to Charles IV (1316–1378).[20] Perhaps this circumstance was one of this text's main political attractions in Czech lands. On the whole, Sivilla's prophecies reflected anti-Catholic, protestant ideas by referencing the discord between papal priests and bishops and other priests, as well as their pursuit of power and wealth.

In addition to the prophecies regarding European kings and emperors, this version of the *Sibylline Prophecy* contains a prophetic account of fifteen indications of the Last Times that will take place in fifteen days preceding the End of the World and the Last Judgment.

## Of Comets, Stars and Dates

Now that we know about some intermediate versions of the *Tale of Sivilla the Prophetess*, we can scrutinize its adaptation. Various textual discrepancies between the German, Czech and Ruthenian versions show how this text continued to evolve by being reinterpreted and modified through subsequent translation and circulation.

---

[20] A number of prophetic texts about the future of Czech lands associated with the Sibylline prophetic tradition circulated both in manuscripts and early printed books. Such are, for example, various versions of the *Proroctví slepého mládence* (*The Prophecy of a Blind Youth*), also known as *Výtah z dvanácterého Sibyllinėho proroctví (An Excerpt from the Twelf Sibylline Prophecies), Piseň o zkáze Českého království pro polepšení života (A Song about the Downfall of the Czech Kingdom for the Improvement of Life)*, *Proroctví Michaldy, královny ze Sáby, třinácté Sibylly* (*The Prophecy of Michalda, the Queen of Sheba, the Thirteenth Sibyl*), etc. (Zíbrt 1902).

According to Sibyl in one of the original German versions, the signs of the coming of the Last Times would start with the appearance of a comet (a star with a tail) after the year 1300. This was more or less in line with historical reality: in September of 1301 Comet Halley appeared on the European sky, reaching its peak brightness on September 23.[21] The next date provided by Sybil for misfortune to afflict the Christian world was predicted to arrive sixty one years later, specifically in 1361. Quite understandably, the Czech and Ruthenian versions, which were translated in the fifteenth century, modify the date of the comet appearance by one hundred years, placing it in 1400 (although, the date could have been already modified in one of the later German sources as well).[22] They did not err by much. Indeed, on February 8, 1402 there appeared a very bright comet in the sky (named later D1) for about seventy days. In Europe, it was brightest on March 12 and was seen during daylight for eight days. Europeans were able to observe the comet by the naked eye until the middle of April, when it went out of sight.[23]

The second date for a comet in the Czech and Ruthenian versions was predicted not sixty one, as in the German original, but seventy one years later. Incidentally, this prophecy has also been confirmed by a naked eye observation in Europe on December 25, 1471. A very bright broom star (named later Y1) remained in the sky for fifty-nine days, until February 1472. On January 22 and 23 it was particularly close to Earth and moving very quickly.[24]

The following table shows corresponding examples with the dates from German, Czech and Ruthenian versions:

| **German *Sibyllenweissagung*** | **Czech *Proroctví Sibyllino*** | **Ruthenian сказаниѥ ѿ сивилле** |
|---|---|---|
| **1. [Czech and Ruthenian: When it will be] after 1300/1400 AD, at this time there will be a star in the sky as wide as an arch [Czech and Ruthenian: having a tail like that of a peacock].** | | |
| 1300:<br>*Vbir dreyczehen hundert iar nach Christi geburt yn der czit ein stern, eins pfohen czegels wyt, wurt man an dem hymel sehen.* | 1400:<br>*Když bude po čtrnácti stech letech po Kristově natození, v ty časy nastane jedna hvězda na nebi a bude mieti ocas jako pávový.* | 1400:<br>Єгда боудеⷮ по четырьнадесѧтиⷯ стеⷯ летеⷯ. по хⷭ҇вѣ нарожєнїи. в тыи часы настанеⷮ єдина звѣзда на нбⷭ҇ѣ. а хвостъ имоущи ꙗко набобъ. |

[21] This comet was also observed in China, Japan and Korea and numerous observers described it as a broom star comet (Yeomans 1991, 400).

[22] For example, the date in 1461 appears in the German *Sibyllenweissagung* from the fifteenth-century manuscript Cod 537 (1440) from the Bern City Library (Neske 1985, 56–58).

[23] Yeomans 1991, 405.

[24] Yeomans 1991, 409–410.

**2. After 61 [Czech and Ruthenian: 71] years there will be a lot of Christians [Czech and Ruthenian: clerics in the Christian world].**

| 1361: | 1471: | 1471: |
|---|---|---|
| *Vbir einvndsechczig iar Dy christen werdent pos gar.* | *po prvém a po sedmdesáti letech křest'anství bude plno kněžstva.* | По первоⷨ и по сеⷣми десѧти летеⷯ. хрⷭ҇тианъ̏ство боудеⷮ пол̏но кнѧⷤ҇ство. |

The modification of the second date (1471) is of some interest. One would expect the date of the second comet to be modified from 1361 to 1461, as was done in some later German versions. An obvious question arises: what was the motivation for tampering with the date of the prophecy? One possible explanation is that the Czech *Proroctví Sibyllino* was copied or translated after 1461 and the scribe had to modify the date to 1471 in order to put it in the prophetic future. In this case, the Czech translator or scribe, who "predicted" the appearance of a broom star on December 25, 1471, should be given credit for either a lucky guess or a great prophetic talent. Conversely, the Ruthenian *Tale of Sivilla the Prophetess* could have appeared some time between 1461 and 1492 (keeping in mind that these time limits are defined by the available manuscript evidence and its interpretation). The comet that appeared on the European sky in the winter of 1471–1472 could have attracted more attention and credibility to this prophetic text if the Ruthenian translator encountered it after 1471.

The names of the European rulers fighting for the title of Holy Roman Emperor had most likely also been reinterpreted to fit the fifteenth-century context. For example, the names of Ludwig and Friedrich could have been associated with the war between the King of France Louis XI and the Habsburg Emperor Friedrich III for the Kingdom of Burgundy. Indeed, this is exactly how Karskii, who was not aware of an earlier origin of this text, interpreted these names.[25] And perhaps this is how fifteenth-century Czech readers interpreted them as well.

While the Germans, and possibly Czechs, had an interest in the European political battlefield, Ruthenians were apparently far from being aware of these conflicts. Names did not tell them much; and that is why these passages relating to bellicose emperors are shortened already in Czech, and even more so in Ruthenian, versions. For example, one of the passages that is absent from the Ruthenian *Tale of Sivilla* but is retained in both Czech versions is the prophecy about King Friedrich, who will gather an army to embark on a crusade. After having gained the Lord's Tomb this King Friedrich will come to the Jerusalem

[25] Karskii 1898.

Tree, which has no leaves; he will put his shield on it and lie down under it. And then the tree will blossom and the good times will begin for Christians.

## Translator's Technique

In the absence of an established source text, it is difficult to form a definite opinion about the translation technique of the Ruthenian *Tale of Sivilla the Prophetess*. Therefore, we are left to judge the mode of translation based on the extant Czech versions. Since the *Tale of Sivilla* sometimes deviates from both Czech texts, I will only draw on Czech examples where the textual correspondence is complete or very close. For the sake of comparison I will further use Czech equivalents from the Ossoliński Miscellany, whose version stands closer to the Ruthenian translation.[26]

The comparison of passages with textual correspondence shows a close dependence of the Ruthenian text on Czech, sometimes even exhibiting a literal, word for word, translation. A fairly detailed comparison of several passages was made by Věra Brynychová.[27] Here I will only cite the opening phrase of the text to illustrate the relationship between the Ruthenian and the Czech versions:

| **Ruthenian** сказаниѥ ѿ сивиⷧле | **Czech** ***Proroctví Sibyllino*** |
|---|---|
| того чаⷭу за моудраго цр҇ѧ саломона. бѣѧше прⷪрчица ѕвѣздарькаименеⷨ сивиⷧла, а та бѣѧше веⷧми моудра. иже въ ѕвѣзⷣахъ многый вещи вбудѫщиⷯ речаⷯ провидѣла. преⷤ многыⷯ тысѧщь лѣⷮ. что сѧ вⷩ землѧⷯ стати маѐть. | *Toho času za múdrého krále Šalamúna bieše prorokyně hvězdářka, jménem Sybilla a ta bieše převelmi múdrá, že na hvězdách mnohé věci v budúcích časiech předzvěděla přez mnoho tisíce let, co se v zemiech státi má.* |

Some of the most noticeable traits of this translation technique are:

### Pseudo-Translations

The translator rendered Czech words as transcriptions with the same meaning in Ruthenian:

| | **Ruthenian** | **Czech** |
|---|---|---|
| **(S 9)** | къ поⷣобенъству | *ku podobenství* |
| **(S 65)** | потлачено | *potlačeno* |
| **(S 105)** | погоршеⷩе | *pohoršení* |
| **(S 189)** | вырченїє | *vyřčenie* |
| **(S 173)** | на панѧⷯ або паннаⷯ | *na paniech anebo na pannách* |

[26] Zíbrt 1910. Zíbrt published the text according to a transcription made by A. Rościszewski in 1840 (The Czech National Museum, I E 2).

[27] Brynychová 1927.

## Lexical Doublets

As in the Ruthenian *Song of Songs* and the *Book of Taudal*, there are also Ruthenian lexical doublets in the *Tale of Sivilla* that elucidate Czech lexemes. It seems that it was a common practice among scribes to supply a pseudo-translation with a Ruthenian equivalent to clarify it. Here are several examples of this trend:

| **(S 132–134) Czech** | **Ruthenian** |
|---|---|
| A tot' já tobě pravím, že když ten ciesařem bude, ten přiezni od kněží mieti nebude. | а̀ то ꙗ́ повѣдаю. и̇же тоⷮ е̇̏гда цесаⷬ боудеⷮ. тоⷮ прїа̀зни ѿ к҃нѕѧ и̇ дѫхо̏вныⷯ и̇мѧти не бȣдеⷮ. |
| And I'll tell you that when this one will be emperor he won't have sympathy from clerics. | And I'll tell you that when this one will be emperor he won't have sympathy from clerics and clergy. |
| **(S 190–192)** | |
| *budú súditi mužie i ženy, a to podle přiezni, ale ne podle spravedlivosti.* | боу̑дѫⷮ сȣдити моу̑жи и жены воⷧе при̑а̏зни. си рѣчь мъ̏зды раⷣꙵ. а не поⷧе пра̏вды. |
| ... will judge men and women by their fancy and not by justice | ... will judge men and women by their fancy, that is for reward, and not by justice. |
| **(S 245–246)** | |
| *Sedmý den, že skálé pukati se bude.* | сеⷧмый д҃нь горы и̇ ска̏лы поукатисѧ боу̑дѫⷮ. |
| On the seventh day, that rock will crack. | On the seventh day mountains and rocks will crack. |

## Mistranslations

There are a number of mistranslations in the *Tale of Sivilla* that suggest that the translator was a Ruthenian (non-native speaker of Czech). For example:

| **(S 127) Czech** | **Ruthenian** |
|---|---|
| *Avšak tomu se musí zdařiti.* | ѿбаче томоу̑ мȣси сѧ̑ зд̏разити |
| However, this has to happen. | However, this has to betray (?). |

The Czech *zdařiti* ('to happen, to occur') was reinterpreted as **зд̏разити**, under the influence of the Polish *zdradzić* ('to betray,' cf. the Czech *zraditi*). This misunderstanding might also have occurred because of unintentional letter transposition.

| **(S 87) Czech** | **Ruthenian** |
|---|---|
| *Tieži tebe zprav mě toho* | во̑прошаю тѧ того с̏пра̏вне |
| I ask you, tell me this. | I ask you about this accurately. |

The translator erroneously read the Czech *zprav mě* (meaning 'tell me') as *zprávně* (also spelled as *správně,* meaning 'correctly, accurately') and accordingly transcribed it in Ruthenian as **с̑пра̏вне**, 'correctly, accurately'.

Occasionally, the translator endeavored to introduce a Church Slavonic linguistic component, especially when there was a linguistic resemblance found in the Czech source text. In most cases this occurs in conjunctions and in such verbal forms as Aorists and Imperfects. However, it is also possible that the Church Slavonic dress is an addition of later copying.

For more examples of deviations and misinterpretations in the Ruthenian translation I defer to the work of Věra Brynychová. Based on the examples discussed above and the analysis in Brynychová's work we should conclude that the Ruthenian *Tale of Sivilla the Prophetess* was translated from one of the Czech versions of the *Proroctví Sibyllino* by a Ruthenian translator, whose knowledge of Czech could have been better.

## TEXT ADAPTATION

Several deviations and mistranslations in the Ruthenian *Tale of Sivilla the Prophetess* reflect the ignorance, or indifference, of the Ruthenian translator to issues related to European clothing and shoe fashion. In contrast, these issues seemed to be of particular importance to German and Czech readers. Among many manifestations of human corruption and pride Sivilla mentions non-observance by commoners of the difference in attire that distinguished them from the nobility. While the Czech version describes exact styles, the Ruthenian translation only retains a general idea of the difference.

| **(S 178–183) Czech** | **Ruthenian** |
|---|---|
| *A taky každý bude chtieti svú vuoli mieti.* | каждый боуде$^{т}$ хотети свою волю и҆мѣти. |
| *Jak chodí pán neb panoše, takéž chce* | како ходи$^{т}$ господинъ такъ хоще$^{т}$ и |
| *sedlák choditi jako jinoše.* | селѧнинъ ходити |
| *A jestliže pán ponese klobúk špičatý,* | носи$^{т}$ ли господинъ ѿдежȣ болѧрьскȣ. |
| *sedlák bude chtieti mieti takový,* | и҆ селѧнинъ хоще$^{т}$ и҆мети таковоу$^{ж}$, |
| *budelit' na pánu kukla bez cípa,* | носи$^{т}$ ли господинъ клобоукъ болѧрьскїй. |
| *musít' být na sedláku taková.* | и҆ селѧнинъ хоще$^{т}$ мети таковый же. |
| And also everyone will want to have his way. Just like an aristocrat or a younger noble is dressed, so a peasant wants to be dressed like young people. | Everyone will want to have his way. Just like an aristocrat is dressed, so a peasant wants to be dressed. |
| And if an aristocrat wears a pointed hat, a peasant would want to have the same, if an aristocrat has a hood without a tip, a peasant would want to have the same. | If an aristocrat wears a dress of a boyar,[28] a peasant too wants to have the same, if an aristocrat wears a hat of a boyar a peasant too wants to have the same one. |

[28] A 'boyar' is a member of the highest rank of nobility in Medieval Rus'.

The Ruthenian translator also did not quite understand the allusion to a new European fashion in shoes, which was decidedly censured both by Church and by secular officials:

| **(S 183–185) Czech** | **Ruthenian** |
|---|---|
| *Také nastanú třevíce s dlúhými špicemi* | такоⷤ настаноуⷮ и҆ ѿ҆бꙋви ди҇вны̑. |
| *a budú známy po rynku i po ulicech.* | бѫдоуⷮ зна҇менїӓ на то҇ржищи и҆ на ѹ̑лицаⷯ. |
| *A tak bude v pýše mnoho zámysluov,* | и тако впи҇шет҇ сѧ много замысловъ. |
| *že by múdrý to vida mohl* | и҆ же бы мо҇глъ мꙋ҇̈дрый то вѣдаⷮ |
| *z smysla vystúpiti.* | и̑ выйти и҆с҇ смы҇словъ. |
| Also there will come pointy shoes. And they will be worn (literally, known) at markets and on streets. | Also there will come strange shoes. There will be signs at markets and on streets. |
| And many schemes will be devised in pride, that a wise man, seeing that, could go crazy. | And many schemes will be written in (?), that a wise man could know that and go crazy. |

Since the abovementioned shoe fashion was unknown among Ruthenians, the translator tried to reinterpret this passage in a more comprehensible way, emphasizing the idea of a blasphemous custom rather than censuring a specific shoe style. He translated the Czech *třevíce s dlúhými špicemi* ('pointy shoes') as ѿ҆бꙋви ди҇вны ('strange shoes') and reinterpreted the Czech *známy* ('known') as зна҇менїӓ ('signs') to give it a more dramatic meaning. He also misunderstood the next sentence and reinterpreted the phrase *bude v pýše* ('will be in pride') as впи҇шет сѧ ('will be written in') and confused the Czech participle *vida* ('seeing') with the infinitive вѣдаⷮ ('to know').

## The *Sibylline Prophecies* and the Emmaus Monastery Frescoes

Given the lack of any explicit evidence, it cannot be definitively claimed that the translation of the Ruthenian *Tale of Sivilla the Prophetess* was associated with the sources of the Emmaus Glagolite monks. Its inclusion in the same manuscript with the Ruthenian *Book of Taudal the Knight* suggests, however, that the transmission of these two texts may be related. It is also probable that the Czech *Proroctví Sibylino* was translated at the time of Charles IV since it prophesizes the rule of Charles as the "last emperor." It predicts that Charles will end discord among other rulers and will reign over Christians until the End of Times.

Other circumstances point to even a closer link between the Emmaus Monastery *Na Slovanech* and the Sibylline prophetic tradition in Bohemia. One of the south wing's walls in the Emmaus Monastery ambit contains a fresco depicting prophecies of the Tiburtine Sibyl. This is the oldest fresco depiction of Sibyl in Bohemia, dating from about 1358–1362.[29] It is divided into two panels. The upper panel portrays the Virgin with the Christ Child standing on a crescent moon against a shining sun with two angels at her sides. In the lower panel the enthroned Sibyl points out the miracle of the Virgin to Emperor Octavian Augustus, positioned on her right.[30] Along the central axis of the composition there is a picture of the Temple of the World in a form of a Gothic cathedral. There are three women standing on the left of Sibyl and three men on the right of Emperor Augustus. The whole empty background space is filled with stars.[31] The neighboring murals complement this composition with images of various Sibylline prophecies about Christ, such as the Annunciation of Mary, the Birth of Christ, the Adoration of the Magi, the Mocking of Christ, and others.[32]

The development of the Sibylline prophetic tradition in Bohemia dates back to the fourteenth century. The beginnings of this theme are found in such works of Czech literature as the rhymed *Legend of St. Kateřina*, the Old Czech *Pasionál* (based on the *Legenda Aurea*), Thomáš Štítný's writings and folk songs. One of the reasons for the Sibylline prophecies' popularity was their interpretation of world history and their imperial rhetoric. It was precisely this set of themes that attracted the attention of Charles IV's ideological circle.

A Czech art historian, Karel Stejskal, has devoted several studies to Emmaus fresco murals and has come to the conclusion that the Sibylline fresco on the south wing wall is directly connected with Charles' ideological program. According to Stejskal, the themes for Emmaus frescoes were suggested by one of the humanists from Charles' court. As a likely candidate Stejskal names Charles' chancellor, Jan of Středa. Like the Emmaus Glagolites and Charles, Jan of Středa believed in Saint Jerome's Slavic origin and took great interest in Czech biblical translations.[33]

In particular, Stejskal discusses the association between Giovanni dei Marignolli's the *Cronica Bohemorum*, commissioned by Charles in the 1350s, and the Sibylline fresco of the Emmaus Monastery.[34] He argues that the depiction of

---

[29] Unfortunately, Emmaus murals were seriously damaged during a WWII fire and their study is now largely based on pre-war photographs. Recently, the frescoes have been partially restored and are now open to the public.

[30] The meeting between Sibyl and Emperor Augustus is described in the *Sibylla Tiburtina*.

[31] Stejskal 1968, 129. In his paper, Stejskal also includes a couple of images of the Sibylline fresco.

[32] Stejskal 1968, 131.

[33] Stejskal 1975, 116–117.

[34] Stejskal 1968, 130, Emler 1882, 492–614.

the Virgin clothed in the sun and the Tiburtine Sibyl pointing her out to Emperor Augustus in the Emmaus fresco is ideologically connected with the representation of the Czech people as "the people of the sun" in the Marignolli's chronicle:[35]

... *Slaui ... quasi solares vel luminosi vel magis gloriosi dicuntur.*
[...the Slavs ... are said to be as if of the sun or the most shining and most glorious.].[36]

In formulating his concept of the Slavs as "the people of the sun" Marignolli referred to Prophet Isaiah's "The City of the Sun" (*Unde Eliopolis civitas Solis in Ysaia*).[37] Written in the genre of prophetic historiography, Marignolli's chronicle substantiated the glorious origin of the Slavs and Bohemians according to Charles' aspirations.[38] Incidentally, Marignolli used the Sibylline prophecies freely throughout his work.[39]

One final observation remains to be mentioned. As in the Czech *Proroctví Sibyllino*, in the Ruthenian *Tale of Sivilla* Sibyl is called an astrologer (Czech *hvězdářka*, Ruthenian звѣздарька), an attribute not usually applied to Sibyls. It is noteworthy, then, that on the Emmaus fresco Sibyl is surrounded by starry skies, which emphasize her connection with cosmic powers and suggest that her divination comes from the stars.

Considering the association of the Sibylline tradition, particularly of the Tirbutine Sibyl's prophecies, with the Emmaus Monastery's murals it is possible that a Czech version of the text, from which the Ruthenian *Tale of Sivilla the Prophetess* was translated, could have originated in the Prague Emmaus Monastery and been in the possession of the Glagolite monks in Kleparz.

## CONCLUSION

The Ruthenian *Tale of Sivilla the Prophetess* (сказаниѥ̆ ѿ сивиллє прⷪрчици) was translated from Czech by a Ruthenian scribe, possibly after 1461 and most likely

---

35 Stejskal 1968, 137; Chadraba 1975, 129. The image of Virgin with the child in the sun and the Tiburtine Sibyl pointing her out to Augustus is also found in other paintings and works of art, for example, in Antoine Caron's *Augustus and the Tiburtine Sibyl* (1571), in an illumination (f. 22) of the fifteenth-century *Book of Hours* of the Duke of Berry, as well as in Petrarch's poem "beautiful virgin, clothed with the sun" (Canzone III, *Vergine bella che di sol vestita*).

36 Emler 1882, 522.

37 Isaiah 19:18. Emler 1882, 523.

38 Chadraba 1975, Cinke 1975.

39 Chadraba 1975, 127–128.

before 1492. This dating is based on a variety of considerations: (i) the Czech and Ruthenian manuscript evidence; (ii) historical events, names, and dates mentioned in the Czech and Ruthenian versions; (iii) the reasoning that the text, due to its eschatological content, could have been of interest to a Ruthenian Orthodox translator primarily before 1492, when the end of the world was expected. Despite various passages which were obscure in meaning, Ruthenian bookmen were obviously interested in this exotic text. According to Karskii, the manuscript bore signs of frequent use and diligent study: there were numerous inscriptions and comments in the margins and its leaves were worn from reading.[40]

The Czech *Proroctví Sibyllino* had been modeled on one of the poetic versions of the late medieval German *Sibyllenweissagung*, which was originally reworked from the Latin *Sibylla Tiburtina* in the middle or the second half of the fourteenth century and which by the fifteenth century had clear Protestant implications. The text circulated in Central Europe for over a century before it finally reached the Ruthenian milieu.

Now that we have more or less established the transmission of the German, Czech and Ruthenian Tiburtine Sibyl's prophecies, we can see how it was modified and modernized, and how scribes and translators manipulated names and dates and made certain other adjustments to address contemporary historical contexts and provide new functions for the text. The context of the Czech manuscripts suggests that this story was largely perceived as a legend and a historical work. However, the mode of its reinterpretation by the translator of the Ruthenian *Tale of Sivilla the Prophetess* shows that he first and foremost saw it as a devotional and theological text, which conveys a message about the corruption of true faith and social order, about the downfall of the wicked and the inevitable punishment – the End of the World and the Last Judgment. Unlike Central European readers, whose consciousness had been stirred by the Hussite wars and other disturbances of the fifteenth century, Ruthenians were not so disposed to perceive this text as a political treatise directed against secular and ecclesiastical authorities. Rather, in the Ruthenian Orthodox context its political tone was somewhat minimized and the devotional and theological aspects became more prominent. The translator of the Ruthenian *Tale of Sivilla the Prophetess* was not merely translating from the foreign Czech into his native Ruthenian, and from a Latin script into more familiar Cyrillic letters; he was also translating a Western Christian text into an Orthodox Ruthenian one.

---

[40] Karskii, 1894, 6–19.

## Chapter Five
# THE RUTHENIAN *BOOK OF TOVIT*

Immediately preceding the Ruthenian *Tale of Sivilla the Prophetess* in the Swidziński Miscellany, on ff. 77–91v, is a Ruthenian translation of the *Book of Tovit*, the книга товиѳъ (the spelling тобиѳъ in Pułaski 1915 with a "б" is most likely a mistake).[1] Evfimii Karskii published a short excerpt from the Ruthenian *Book of Tovit* in his description of the miscellany, which he regarded as having been written in a "remarkably pure Ruthenian dialect of the old time."[2] As in the case of the Ruthenian *Tale of Sivilla the Prophetess* (сказаниѥ́ ѿ сивил҃лє) and the Ruthenian *Book of Taudal the Knight* (кни҃га ѿ таѹ҆́далє рыцари) from the destroyed Swidziński Miscellany, Karskii's fragment is still the only evidence of this translation. This is also the only known Ruthenian translation from Czech of the *Book of Tovit*.

## CZECH SOURCE

Unfortunately, Karskii did not have access to the manuscripts of the Czech Bible and therefore was unable to form a more accurate opinion about the source of the Ruthenian *Book of Tovit.* He, therefore, mistakenly ascribed it to a group of Ruthenian translations that he assumed had been made from the Venetian edition of the Czech Bible (1506).[3] This assumption led him to two erroneous conclusions. He inaccurately dated the translation to the sixteenth century, and made incorrect assumptions about its authorship. In view of the fact that the Czech Venetian edition was used by Frantsishak Skaryna as one of the sources for his *Bibliia Rus'ka*, Karskii considered the Ruthenian *Book of Tovit* to belong to Skaryna himself or to be associated with his activity. The visible divergence between the

---

[1] Pułaski 1915. The Swidziński Miscellany of Lithuanian Chronicles #82 from the Krasiński Collection (ff. 77–91v).

[2] "...на замечательно чистом западнорусском наречии старого времени" (Karskii 1894, 15).

[3] Karskii 1921, 29–30. Hrushevs'kyi 1960, 119, following Karskii, confidently assumed that "залежність сеї збірки від чеського тексту 1506 р. не підлягае сумніву" [dependence of this collection on the Czech text of 1506 is without a doubt]. The Venetian edition of 1506 is a printed Bible which, along with the *Pražská Bible* of 1488 and *Kutnohorská Bible* of 1489, belongs to the fourth redaction of the Czech Bible.

translation and the text of the original he attributed to the creativity of the translator. There is no denying that Skaryna was a creative translator; still, it seems more probable that the differences between the Ruthenian *Book of Tovit* and the Venetian Czech Bible arose from the fact that the source of this translation was one of the earlier Czech Bibles of the second redaction. Below is a fragment from the Czech *Litoměřická Bible* (1429) given in parallel with Karskii's publication of a fragment from the Ruthenian *Book of Tovit*.[4] This shows its much closer (though not absolute) connection with the text of the Czech second biblical redaction:

| **Swidziński Miscellany** | **Czech *Litoměřická Bible* (1429)** |
|---|---|
| пригодило сѧ единого дн҃е | *přihodi ſe že ſwaty tobiaš gednoho* |
| иже товиѳъ погребалъ тѣла мр҃твыⷯ | *dne pochovauage tiela mrtwa* |
| и оутроудил сѧ велми . а пришеⷣ к домоу | *vſtal bieſe . a domow přiſed* |
| поⷣле стены верже себе ѿпочиноути и | *podle ſtieny ſebu wrhl y* |
| оуснoулъ. а в тоⷨ оуснꙋтий лайна сий рѣⷱ калъ | *vſnul a w tom vſnuti layna* |
| ластовица горкꙋ емꙋ зъ гнѣзда въ ѡчи | *wlaſtovicže horka gemu w oči z* |
| оупꙋстила . такъ же пакы оуснoулъ.[5] | *hniezda vpadnu tak že ynhod*[6] *oſlnv* |
| и оубо то покꙋшеніе | *Ale to pokuſenie* |
| на него бг҃ъ препоустилъ прото што бы | *proto boh byl nan přepuſtil . aby* |
| боудѫщиⷨ данъ былъ приклаⷣ его , | *buduciem dan byl přiklad geho* |
| трьпеливости ꙗко и ст҃ого иѡва . | *trpieliuoſti jako y ſswateho joba .* |
| оубо егдаⷤ ст҃ыⷩ иѡвъ ѿ своего детинъства | *Nebo když od ſweho dietinſtwa* |
| бг҃а сѧ боꙗше . | *wždy ſe boha bogieſe* |
| а приказаніе его полнѧше | *a přikazanie oſtřiehaſe .* |

[One day it happened that Tovit was burying bodies of the dead and got very tired. And he came to his house and lay down by the wall to rest and fell asleep. And in his sleep, a sparrow dropped warm excrement from a nest into his eyes, so that he fell asleep (in Czech: became blind). And this ordeal was sent to him by God to give future generations an example of his patience, like that of blessed Job because when blessed Job from his childhood was fearful of God and fulfilled his commands…]

The version in the Czech *Litoměřická Bible*, with a few variations, textologically resembles that found in the Czech Glagolitic Bible (1416).[7] The latter

---

[4] Karskii 1894, 15. The manuscript of the *Litoměřická Bible* has been lost. Its text is preserved in photocopies at the Czech Language Institute in Prague (Kyas 1997, 81).

[5] This is a mistranslation of the Czech *oſlnu* (oslnúti), 'became blind.'

[6] This word should read *ynhed*, cf. *yhned* in the *Boskovská Bible* (1415–1430) of the same redaction. It is noteworthy that the same textual variant (*ynhed* vs. *yhned*) is present in the Czech Glagolitic Bible of 1416: *tak in'hed' osl'nul'* (Pacnerová 2000, 165).

[7] Pacnerová 2000, 165.

was written in the Prague Emmaus Monastery, where the Croatian Glagoljaši were active, and where they could also have been involved in the translation and revision of the Czech Bible. The version of the Szaroszpatak Codex (the *Biblia królowej Zofii*) of 1455, mentioned earlier in relation to the Ruthenian *Song of Songs*, likewise shows significant textological similarity with the version in the *Litoměřická Bible*:

**Polish *Biblia królowej Zofii* (1455)**

*przigodzi ſyę genego dnya*
*pochowauaięc cyala martwa*
*yvſtal bil ado domv prziſzedw*
*podle ſcyani ſobę rzucyw yvſnę.*
*A w tem vſnyenyv gnoy iaſtkolyci*
*goręci emv woczy vpadnye*
*tak iſze ręcze oſzlnęl. Ale to pokuſzenye*
*przeto bog bil nayn przepuſcyl abi*
*będęcim bil dan prziklad gego*
*cyrpyedlywoſcy iako y ſwętego Joba.*
*Bo gdiſz odſwego dzecynſtwa zawſzdy*
*ſyę boga bal aprzikazanya gego otrzegal...*

**Czech *Bible Litoměřická* (1429)**

*přihodi ſe že ſwaty tobiaš gednoho*
*dne pochovauage tiela mrtwa*
*vſtal bieſe . a domow přiſed*
*podle ſtieny ſebu wrhl y vſnul*
*a w tom vſnuti layna wlaſtovičže*
*horka gemu w oči z hniezda vpadnu*
*tak že y hned oſlnv . Ale to pokuſenie*
*proto boh byl nan přepuſtil . aby*
*buduciem dan byl přiklad geho*
*trpieliuoſti jako y ſswateho joba .*
*Nebo když od ſweho dietinſtwa wždy*
*ſe boha bogieſe a přikazanie oſtřiehaſe*

Establishing the second redaction of the Czech Bible as a source allows us to date the Ruthenian translation of the *Book of Tovit* to no later than the second half of the fifteenth century and perhaps even earlier.

## Language of Translation

For a better idea of the extent to which the Ruthenian language of the *Book of Tovit* is different from Church Slavonic, it suffices to compare it to the same fragment from the *Ostrih Bible* of 1581, which, although also influenced by a Czech source, still retains the Church Slavonic idiom more consistently:

**Swidziński Miscellany**

пригодило сѧ единого дн҃е иже товиѳъ
погребалъ тѣла мр҃твыⷯ и ѹтроѹдил сѧ
велми . а пришеⷣ к домоѹ поⷣле стены верже
себе ѿпочиноѹти и ѹсноѹлъ .
а в тоⷨ ѹснꙋтий лайна сий рѣⷱ калъ
ластовица горкꙋ емꙋ зъ гнѣзда въ ѡчи
ѹпꙋстила . такъ же пакы ѹсноѹлъ . и

***Ostrih Bible* (1581)**

Слꙋчи́ же сѧ нѣкоего дн҃е ѹтрꙋжеⷩ ѿ
гро́ба градѧ̀,
прїиде до до́мꙋ своего,
и возлѧже близь стѣны̀ и ѹспѐ,
и спѧ́щꙋ емꙋ падѐ гно́и
теплъ на ѻ́чи его ѿ гнѣзда̀
ла́стовича . и бысть слѣпъ .

| | |
|---|---|
| оу҆бо то покꙋшенїє҆ на него бг҃ъ препоу҆стилъ | сїє же и҆скꙋше́нїє ѿ бг҃а слꙋчи́сѧ є҆мꙋ . |
| прото што бы боу҆джщиⷨ данъ былъ | да́ же послѣⷣнимъ лю́демъ да́стьсѧ |
| приклаⷣ е҆го , тръпеливости | ѻ҆браⷥ терпѣнїѧ є҆го, ꙗ҆ко и҆ пра́веⷣнаго |
| ꙗ҆ко и҆ ст҃ого и҆ѡ҆ва . оубо егдаⷤ ст҃ыи и҆ѡ҆въ | ї҆ѻва . и҆же ѿ младе́нчества своє҆го вьсегда̀ |
| ѿ своє҆го детинъства бг҃а сѧ боꙗ҆ше . а҆ | бг҃а боѧ́сѧ и҆ за́повѣди є҆го съхранѧа |
| приказанїє҆ е҆го полнѧше | |

Similar to the Ruthenian *Song of Songs* and the *Tale of Sivilla the Prophetess*, the text of the Ruthenian *Book of Tovit*, as far as can be judged from the fragment, is a faithful translation that adheres closely to its Czech source. The following words and constructions from the Ruthenian *Book of Tovit* clearly replicate Czech patterns and differ from the Church Slavonic equivalents:

| Czech | Ruthenian | Church Slavonic | English |
|---|---|---|---|
| *přihodi ſe* | пригодило сѧ | Слꙋчи же сѧ | it happened |
| *vſnuti* | оу҆снꙋтий | спѧ́щꙋ є҆мꙋ | while sleeping |
| *layna* | лайна | гно́и | excrement |
| *oſlnu* | оу҆снoу҆лъ | бы́сть слѣпъ | became blind |
| *proto... aby* | прото што бы | да́ же | in order to |
| *pokuſenie* | покꙋшенїє҆ | и҆скꙋше́нїє | temptation |
| *trpieliuoſti* | тръпеливости | терпѣнїѧ | endurance |
| *dietinſtwa* | детинъства | младе́нчества | childhood |

As we have seen in the Ruthenian *Song of Songs*, the Ruthenian *Book of Tovit* exhibits marks of the "Orthodox language" in that, for example, it converts the Czech names *Tobiaš* and *Job* into the Orthodox Church Slavonic товиѳъ, *Tovit*, and и҆ѡ҆въ, *Iov*, with a "v". Товитос is yet another form of *Tovit* which appears in the incipit "Товитосъ бимше съ поколѣнїѧ..." published by Pułaski in his catalogue description.[8] However, it is impossible to say whether this last name change was a decision made by the translator or a later development introduced by a copier. The translator was most likely a Ruthenian, as is evidenced by at least one mistranslation, based on sound similarity: the Ruthenian оу҆снoу҆лъ ('fell asleep') for the Czech *oſlnu* ('became blind).

[8] Pułaski 1915.

## Chapter Six
## RUTHENICA BOHEMICA: LINGUISTIC FEATURES IN RUTHENIAN TRANSLATIONS FROM CZECH

Original ecclesiastical texts predating the rise of polemical literature at the end of the sixteenth century are scarce; therefore, most Ruthenian texts from the fifteenth and sixteenth centuries are translations. These Ruthenian translations display features of the source languages: lexical and morphological traits, as well as syntactic structures uncharacteristic of East Slavic. Unfortunately, of all Ruthenian texts translations and their language have been examined least methodically. Although philologists in the nineteenth and the first half of the twentieth centuries devoted much attention to studying and publishing Ruthenian translations, their methods were very descriptive and non-systematic, and their examination usually focused on establishing a source language without thoroughly analyzing the translation technique or providing a systemic analysis of the language. Among significant recent contributions are studies of Ruthenian translations from Hebrew,[1] Polish,[2] and Latin.[3] A number of descriptions of individual Ruthenian texts and corpora of texts have also been put together, such as Kuraszkiewicz's analysis of Galician-Volhynian documents, Stang's work on the fifteenth and sixteenth-century chancery language, Gröschel's study of Vyshens'kyi's language, and Pugh's monograph on the language of Smotryts'kyi, to mention only a few.[4] While these and other studies focus primarily on the chancery language and the language and style of individual authors, numerous anonymous texts in manuscript miscellanies, such as translations from Czech discussed in this study, have not yet received sufficient scholarly and particularly linguistic attention.

In this chapter I will give an overview of common Ruthenian linguistic features based on the data drawn from the discussed texts. At the same time, I will highlight features that are specific to translations from Czech, especially

---

[1] Altbauer 1992, Taube 1993, 1995a, 1995b, 1997, 2004, 2005a, 2005b, and his forthcoming study of *The Logika of the Judaizers*.

[2] Zoltán 2004.

[3] Fałowski 2003.

[4] For example, Kuraszkiewicz 1934, Stang 1935 and 1939, Gröschel 1972, Pugh 1985 and 1996. With respect to this I should perhaps mention an impressive corpus of studies devoted to the language of translations of Frantsishak Skaryna. Although his *Bibliia Rus'ka* contains many Ruthenian features, on the whole it is not an example of Ruthenian vernacular.

when they occur more than once. Undoubtedly, the list below is far from complete and should in no way be considered an exhaustive inventory of Ruthenian language features. It functions as a mini-grammar of Ruthenica Bohemica – the Ruthenian translations from Czech.

## GENERAL OVERVIEW

### 1. PHONOLOGY / ORTHOGRAPHY

Fifteenth and sixteenth-century Ruthenian texts do not present much evidence for the study of spoken language. The orthography does not consistently show phonological developments known to exist in the vernacular language of that period. Most likely, only those vernacular linguistic traits that were a part of an educated person's pronunciation would have been reflected in the text more or less consistently. One should also keep in mind that the existence of certain orthographic practices could have favored a particular spelling no matter what the actual pronunciation of the scribe was. Thus, the examination of phonology in Ruthenian translations from Czech is primarily concerned with the description of orthography.

The orthography in all four Ruthenian texts shows a mixture of East Slavic and Church Slavonic features. A certain number of West Slavic phonological features are represented in individual lexemes which are not the result of an internal phonological development, but of a morphological and lexical interference. Therefore, they will be discussed in the corresponding sections. Common East Slavic features include the presence of ž and č in place of **dj*, **tj* and pleophony. Yet other East Slavic traits in different proportions represent features known to exist in fifteenth-century Ukrainian and/or Belarusian dialects.

The features listed below are common to all four Ruthenian texts. Since these phonological developments are comprehensively described in numerous textbooks and research articles on the history of Belarusian, Ukrainian and Russian, I provide only a basic description and short reference, emphasizing territorial origin.[5]

**1.1. The coalescence of *e and *i:** The loss of distinction between *ě* and *i* is expressed graphically by fluctuation of letters и and ѣ. This change originated in Bukovyna, Pokuttia and Transcarpathia (South Ukrainian dialects), then expand-

[5] For a more detailed discussion of these features on South and West Russian, Belarusian and Ukrainian territories including an overview of the bibliography, see Shevelov 1979, Wexler 1977, Borkovskii and Kuznetsov 1963, Uspenskii 2002.

ed north until it stopped reaching Polissian dialects. It is attested in texts starting from the late thirteenth century.[6]

**1.2. The coalescence of etymological *e and *ě:** The loss of distinction between *ě* and *e* in both stressed and unstressed positions is expressed graphically by fluctuation of letters є and ѣ.[7] This change occurred in the Northeast Belarusian (and partly in Southwestern) dialects and is dated to the second half of the thirteenth century. It is attested in texts starting from the thirteenth and fourteenth centuries.[8] In the "Polish" 1595 edition of the Lithuanian Statute of 1588, which principally consisted of a transliteration in Latin characters, ѣ is consistently rendered as *ie,* where *i* indicates softness of the preceding consonant.[9]

**1.3. The coalescence of etymological *y and *i.** The coalescence of *i* and *y*, expressed graphically by fluctuation of letters и and ы. The process of coalescence consisted of a more or less parallel change of *i* and *y* into a high-mid front-mid vowel *ẏ*. The records of these changes are dated to the late thirteenth or early fourteenth century. By the mid-fifteenth century the area of coalescence of *i* and *y* in Ukrainian dialects was complete.[10] In the "Polish" 1595 edition of the Lithuanian Statute of 1588 ы is consistently rendered as *ÿ*, whereas и is rendered by both *i* and *ÿ*, mostly depending on the quality of the preceding consonant (the only visible fluctuation seems to be after *t*, otherwise *ÿ* is used after hard consonants, including *c* and *r*, and *i* after those that can be soft).

**1.4. Dispalatalization of *r'***, expressed graphically in the confusion of и and ы after р. This feature must be considered in conjunction with the coalescence of /y/ and /i/.

**1.5. The rise of *o* < *e* after postdentals.** The rise of *o* < *e* after hushing sounds (postdentals) provided there was no front vowel in the following syllable in both stressed and unstressed position (Kyiv-Palesse (Polissia) dialects).[11] This change occurred before the eleventh century in most Belarusian dialects under two conditions: in a stressed position and followed by a non-palatalized consonant, in Ukrainian dialects independent of stress.[12] The hardening of the originally soft hushings and affricates, rendered by usage of ы in place of /i/, and ѻ in place of /e/ should be viewed in conjunction with this development.

---

[6] Shevelov 1979, 425–428.

[7] On differentiation of *e and *ě in bookish pronunciation, see Uspenskii 2002, 163–173.

[8] Wexler 1977, 120–123.

[9] Miakishev 2001, 185.

[10] Shevelov 1979, 379–385, 422–423.

[11] Wexler 1977, 96.

[12] Wexler 1977, 111–112.

**1.6. The change of bilabial *w* into *u*:** The alternation *v : u* in prepositions and prefixes before the consonant, rendered graphically by the fluctuation of spelling with в and ѹ. The alternation *v : u* in prepositions and prefixes before the consonant most probably reflects the sonant quality of bilabial *w*. Belarusian and Ukrainian dialects inherited the Common Slavic bilabial *w*. As a consequence of the fall of *jers* it changed to *v* in prevocalic position in Belarusian dialects and to non-syllabic *u* before consonants. The *v* > *u* change (confusion of letters в and ѹ) is attested in thirteenth century texts originating in Belarus territory.[13] In Ukrainian, following the fall of *jers* the word-initial *v–* and *jer* also developed into *u–*. Shevelov dates this change to after 1150 although reliable records begin to appear only by about 1260.[14] It is also possible that the same graphic fluctuation can reflect fricative bilabial β.

**1.7. Spirantization of the velar stop *g* (through the stage of γ) into fricative *h*.**[15] The orthography reflects this by rendering the sound *h* with the letter г in borrowings and by a special digraph кг for the sound [*g*] in foreign words.

**1.8. Spelling with vocalization of the type *ъ* > *o*, *ь* > *e* and an additional ъ or apostrophe after sonant.** About half of the occurrences of *jers* with sonants in interconsonantal position reflect spelling with vocalization of the type *ъ* > *o*, *ь* > *e* and an additional ъ or apostrophe after sonant. The phonetic interpretations of this spelling are controversial. One of the phonetic explanations of spelling with an additional *jer* or apostrophe was offered by Aleksandr Potebnia. He called it the *second pleophony*, a phenomenon that developed in the North Russian (Novgorod) dialect.[16] It is possible that in Ruthenia there was no phonetic justification for this spelling, and that it was introduced there by Northern Russian scribes as an orthographic fashion.

**1.9. Umlaut *'a* > *e* after palatalized consonants (postdentals) and as a secondary phenomenon *a* > *e*.** This change occurred in Eastern and Central Polissia, South-West Ukrainian dialects (Bukovyna, Pokuttia, Hutsul, Dniester and Sjan), Western Polissia and Pidliashia. It did not spread to South-Eastern dialects and Carpathia. The change, although encompassing a large Ukrainian territory, was not accepted into Standard Ukrainian. The isogloss is very close to the Polish – Lithuanian frontier before 1569. This fact suggests that ***'a*** umlaut must have

---

[13] Wexler 1977, 140–141.

[14] Shevelov 1979, 294–301.

[15] The bibliography about this change is numerous and cannot be fully cited here. See, for example, Trubetzkoy 1987, 169–172; Durnovo 1969, 180; Uspenskii 2002, 155–159.

[16] The extensive discussion of the possible phonetic interpretations of this spelling is presented in Shevelov 1979, 286–293.

taken place some time before the Lublin Union and by 1569 became inoperative. More or less reliable examples are attested starting from the fourteenth century and their number increases in the fifteenth century.[17] Umlaut *a* > *e* after palatalized consonants is rendered by substitution of the letter є for ѧ and ꙗ.

**1.10. The rise of *u* < *o* in verbs in *–ova–* by analogy with the Present Tense stem *–uj–*.** The rise of *u* < *o* in пережюванїю (*The Song of Songs* 7:9) occurred by analogy with the Present Tense stem *žuju*. Such forms are found in Eastern Belarus, mostly around Homel'.[18]

**1.11. *Akan'e*:** delabialization of unstressed *o and loss of distinction between unstressed *o and *a. In writing, *akan'e* is attested only starting from the mid-fourteenth century in records originating in Novgorod, Pskov, Muscovy and other regions.[19] Scholars disagree on the causes and chronology of the rise of *akan'e*. It is generally regarded as being a consequence of the fall of *jers*, strong dynamic stress, or of a Baltic substratum.[20]

**1.12. *Cokan'e*:** loss of distinction between affricates *c and *č.[21] *Cokan'e* is found mostly in North-West Russian dialects (Novgorod, Pskov, Smolensk, Polatsk, Tver') and in North Belarusian dialects, for example in thirteenth and fourteenth century Polatsk texts but not in texts from the fifteenth century. It is also found in the Sebež and Nevel' districts and East of Vitebsk and North of Smolensk[22] and is observed in scattered villages in the Berestja region.[23]

**1.13. The preservation of palatalized postdentals in spelling.** The preservation of palatalized postdentals is expressed by the consistent use of ю ['u] and ꙗ ['a] after postdentals. Most likely it was an orthographic rule.

**1.14. The rise of *y* < ъ in a weak position after interconsonantal *r*.** This change occurred by the fifteenth century, mostly in Belarusian dialects, but is also found in neighboring Ukrainian dialects.[24]

**1.15. Dispalatalization of word-final labials.** This is a common change in Ukrainian and Belarusian dialects. It occurred after the fall of *jers* (around mid-

[17] Shevelov 1979, 541–548.

[18] Wexler 1977, 175.

[19] Zalizniak 1995, 60 and 453; Sobolevskii 1907, 77; Borkovskii and Kuznetsov 1963, 141–148.

[20] Borkovskii and Kuznetsov 1963, 143; Wexler 1977, 78–88; Shevelov 1979, 86–88 and 513–515 ("new *a*").

[21] On *cokan'e* as a Circum-Baltic feature, see Čekmonas 2001, 341–346.

[22] Wexler 1977, 109–110.

[23] Shevelov 1979, 739.

[24] Wexler 1977, 164.

twelfth century) but is attested only in the fourteenth century.[25]

**1.16. *L*-epentheticum.** (Since the use of *l*–epentheticum is morphologically conditioned, it is discussed in 2.6.)

**1.17. Loss of initial *ji–.** This feature is discussed in Lexicon (4.1.) since its existence in Ruthenian is connected with lexical transfer rather than with phonological development. The same is true concerning West Slavic non-pleophonic forms of Czech or Polish type.

## 2. Morphology

### 2.1. Noun

**2.1.1. Nominative masculine plural in –ове and –еве along with –и.** Endings in *–ové* and *–evé* as markers of animacy, although subject to certain rules, are still alive in Czech and Polish whereas their counterparts in East Slavic are no longer productive and their spread was most probably caused by West Slavic influence.[26] This feature was also characteristic of Meletii Smotryts'kyi's language.[27]

**2.1.2. Genitive plural**

Genitive plural ending –ѹ (instead of –овъ) reflects vowel contraction that occurred in West Slavic.

**2.1.3. Lack of expression of animacy.**

Accusative case is used instead of Genitive (as in Czech) to indicate animate direct objects.

**2.1.4.** Transcription of proper names according to West Slavic patterns.

### 2.2. Adjective

**2.2.1.** Contracted adjectives которыж in place of которыиж (as in West Slavic).

**2.2.2. Methods of comparison and intensification:**

**Comparative**: Comparative forms are formed according to rules in West Slavic.

**Superlative**: Superlative forms "na(j) + comparative" were not characteristic of Old East Slavic, which used the construction "pre + positive adjective," and emerged most probably as a result of Polish influence.[28]

### 2.3. Pronoun

First person singular pronoun *ja* is spelled with either ѧ or ꙗ.

- Demonstrative: fluctuation between тот and тыи.

---

[25] Wexler 1977, 142–144, Shevelov 1979, 360–363.

[26] The plural endings *–ove* and *–eve* were characteristic of many Belarusian and Ukrainian dialects but ceased to be productive (Bulyka 1988, 67).

[27] Pugh 1996, 72.

[28] Fałowski 1984.

- Relative: fluctuation between **которыи, иже (то)** and **ишто**.
- Indefinite (some, any, –ever, other, many): pronouns with –**колвекъ**.
- Distributive: **кождыи**.

## 2.4. Adverb

Adverbs in –**е** along with East Slavic adverbs in –**о**. Adverbs in –**ѣ** are also characteristic of Church Slavonic, a fact that could have influenced their transfer from Czech into Ruthenian.[29]

## 2.5. Verb

### 2.5.1. Present Tense

- occurrence of third person singular and plural forms without –**ть** (West Slavic feature) along with East Slavic forms;
- first person singular ending in *–m* (West Slavic);
- first person plural ending in *–mo*.

### 2.5.2. Past Tenses

- Perfect with auxiliary (**ймѣлъ єсть товарища**);
- Czech Plusquamperfectum (**възвратилсѧ есть былъ**);
- absence of Aorists where Aorists are not present in Czech but presence of Aorists where they are.

### 2.5.3. Compound and Periphrastic Future

Along with Present Tense forms of perfective verbs with the meaning of Future Tense, there are West Slavic influenced forms of Compound and Periphrastic Future:

- forms of the auxiliary **быти** with Past Participle in *-l* ;
- forms of the verb **ймѣти** with Infinitive designating predestined future event.

### 2.5.4. Optative

Optative is expressed by the word **радъ** with auxiliary and Past Participle in *–l* following the Czech pattern.

### 2.5.5. Imperative

Ruthenian texts are characterized by truncated forms of Imperative characteristic of West Slavic.

### 2.5.6. The verb 'to be'

First person singular Present Tense forms of the verb 'to be' **єсмь** and **єсми** are used interchangeably.

### 2.5.7. The verb 'to have'

The verb **ймѣти** is used:

- to express the modal meaning of predestined future or obligation;

[29] On the history of these forms, see Sigalov 1995.

- to express possession (see 3.6.).

**2.6. Passive Participle**

There are a number of Passive Participles formed without *l*–epentheticum, a West Slavic feature.

## 3. Syntax

**3.1.** The use of conjunctions **абы** and **прото(же)**.
**3.2.** Separate position (usually after the first stressed word in a sentence) of the reflexive particle **сѧ**.
**3.3.** The use of demonstrative (deictic) pronoun **тот**, **та**, **то** with or without a noun as referential expression.
**3.4.** The use of the conjunction **а** meaning 'and' in compound sentences.
**3.5.** Fluctuation in the expression of relative clauses with conjunctions **ишто**, **иже то** and **которыи**, 'which.'
**3.6.** In addition to the modal meaning of predestined future and obligation, the verb **ѝмѣти** can denote possession. In the terms proposed by Alexander Isačenko, who divided all Slavic languages into "have" and "be" languages, Ruthenian is a "have" language, that is, it uses the verb 'to have' to denote possession.[30]

## 4. Lexicon

In addition to cases of borrowing and loan-translation, some of the West Slavic phonological and morphological features could have come into Ruthenian as a result of lexical transfer. Another mechanism that could, at least partially, explain this phenomenon is a mechanism of relexification, formulated by Paul Wexler in a number of his works regarding Jewish languages.[31] According to Wexler, relexification in a language is "a process whereby speakers systematically replace their native vocabulary by the lexicon of another language, or more precisely by the "phonetic strings" from another language, since the semantic and syntactic parameters of the latter are not usually taken over."[32] Although Ruthenian's syntactic level is as contaminated by the language-intruder's syntax as its lexicon, we can certainly agree that some processes in Ruthenian are similar to those of relexified languages.

---

[30] Isačenko 1974.
[31] Wexler 2002 and 2006; Horvath and Wexler 1997.
[32] Wexler 2006, xiv.

**4.1. Fall of initial *ji*–:** This trait, although usually presented as a phonological development, is discussed here in the context of a lexical West Slavic component. Shevelov has demonstrated that the loss of the initial *ji-* has nothing to do with the loss of *jers* and that it is only attested in two lexemes: the verb *iměti* (*měti*) and the preposition/prefix *iz* (*z*), as well as composite words containing it. In both cases it is plausible to suppose Polish influence (although Shevelov himself does not strongly support this assumption).[33] Taking into consideration Czech influence and the existence of other words with initial и (for example играцемъ or ишто for Czech *žto*), it is possible to regard this as lexical interference, rather than phonological change.

**4.2. Czech-type non-pleophonic forms.** The non-pleophonic forms are influenced by Czech. Their usage was supported by the existence of non-pleophonic forms in Church Slavonic and Polish. The regular occurrence of non-pleophonic forms of the Czech type can be explained by the fact that they are identical to Church Slavonic and thus could have been preferred for stylistic reasons.

**4.3. Particles ж(е) то and то.** The use of the particles *–žto* and *to* is a stylistic trait of Old Czech. Its influence in the Ruthenian translations is reflected in the comparable frequency of occurrence of ж(е) то and тот то.

**4.4.** Some morphological features such as, for example, methods of comparison and intensification, may also be a result of lexical transfer or relexification.

---

[33] Shevelov 1979, 268–272.

## THE RUTHENIAN *SONG OF SONGS* LINGUISTIC ANALYSIS

In 1861, the Ruthenian *Song of Songs* was published by N. M. Kostomarov in the periodical *Osnova* as the *Old South Russian Translation of the Song of Songs with Concluding Remarks about Love.*[34] The fact that it was translated from Czech was accepted by all of the scholars who had looked at this text.[35] However, the disagreement concerning the language of translation (a disagreement of which the scholars themselves were apparently unaware) is noteworthy, and reflects the complexity of the language situation in fifteenth and sixteenth-century Ruthenia. Kostomarov called this translation South Russian, referring to the language of the population of the territory of present-day Ukraine. Vladimirov mentioned this text twice in his works but did not characterize its language, referring only to the definition proposed by Kostomarov.[36] Sobolevskii in his review of Vladimirov's monograph about Skaryna called the Ruthenian *Song of Songs* a translation into Belarusian, but did not explain why.[37] Karskii shared this opinion, including the text of the *Song of Songs* in the corpus of the Belarusian language for his *Belorusy.*[38] Subsequently, Florovskii devoted a chapter to it in his book about the influence of the Czech Bible in the history of Russian culture.[39] Although he called it *The Song of Songs in a Ukrainian Translation of the Fifteenth Century*, he further defined its language as Belarusian-Ukrainian. These fluctuations are not surprising, particularly given the lack of a consensus in East Slavic scholarship about both the criteria for the delimitation of Ukrainian from Belarusian documents of that period and the question of whether this delimitation is necessary at all.

Unfortunately, Kostomarov's edition of the Ruthenian *Song of Songs* is not suitable for linguistic analysis since it contains a significant number of errors

[34] Kostomarov 1861, 49-64.

[35] Alekseev 1980, 7 and 1983, 285; Florovskii 1939, 141 and [1946] 1988, 232–242; Golovatskii 1865, 235–236; Perwolf 1874, 255; Sobolevskii 1888, 323 and 1910, 197–198; Thomson 1998, 881–882; Vladimirov [1888] 1989, 340–342.

[36] Vladimirov [1888] 1989, 340–342.

[37] Sobolevskii 1888, 323.

[38] Karskii 1955.

[39] Florovskii 1946, 232–242.

and inaccuracies, already pointed out by Vladimirov.[40] However, it is most surprising that scholars, nevertheless, continued to form their opinions about the Ruthenian *Song of Songs* on the basis of the published text in *Osnova* (instead of the original manuscript); it even appears as one of the sources for the *Istorychnyi slovnyk ukraïns'koho iazyka* (The Historical Ukrainian Dictionary).[41] The following pages present a linguistic examination of the Ruthenian *Song of Songs* based on the edition offered in Appendix I. The examples are cited with an indication of their location in the text (chapter : verse). For the sake of comparison, variants are drawn from the following contemporaneous translations of the *Song of Songs*: "Skaryna" – a translation of the *Song of Songs* in Skaryna's *Bibliia Rus'ka* (beginning of the sixteenth century) inspired by Church Slavonic and Czech versions, and "Vilno262" – a fifteenth-century Ruthenian translation of the *Song of Songs* from Hebrew in a manuscript from the Library of the Lithuanian Academy of Sciences in Vilnius (# 262). The language of Vilno262 was not directly influenced by Church Slavonic as in the case of Skaryna's translation, but shows very strong dependence on Hebrew and, to a certain extent, reflects Ruthenian vernacular usage.

## 1. Phonology / Orthography

The orthography reflects the phonetic background of the text as composed of linguistic features known to exist in both fifteenth-century Belarusian and Ukrainian dialects. This allows us to speak of the phonological representation of the Ruthenian *Song of Songs* as supradialectal *koine*.

**1.1. Loss of distinction between phonemes *ě* and *e* in both stressed and unstressed position**. There seems to be no systematic distribution of **ѣ** and **є**. The cases of fluctuation are as follows:

- **ѣ** instead of **є** :

**дцѣри** (1:4) along with **дщєри** (2:7, 3:10, 3:11, 5:8, 5:16, 6:8), **дщєро** (7:1), **д҆чєрь** (7:4) and **дщєрьми** (2:2); **знамѣнати** (1:5); **пасѣшь** (1:6); **цѣрькви** (1:7 rubric); **пасѣть** (6:3); **пєрсѣи** (7:3); **ѡгородѣмжє** (8:9).

- **є** in place of **ѣ** :

**по стадє**[х] (1:6); **к нєвѣстє** (1:7, 4:1, 5:9, 8:4, 8:5, 8:11 rubric) along with **нєвѣстѣ** (6:4, 8:12 rubric); **ѐздьцо**[м] (1:8); **оу возє**[х] (1:8); **прєбывати** (1:12); **дрєвїємъ** (2:3); **квєтїємъ** (2:5) along with **квѣтьѧ** (7:12); **лєвїца** (2:6, 8:3); **сєрнє** (2:9);

[40] Vladimirov [1888] 1989, 340–342. Vladimirov compared it with the manuscript and published the first two chapters of the *Song of Songs* with corrections in the Appendix.

[41] Tymchenko 1930.

сквозе (2:9); поспешиͨ (2:10); ѻбрезываніа (2:12); ӑпатекарева (3:6) along with ӑпатѣкъ (4:16); насилнеишиͯ (3:7); древа (3:9); вежа (4:4, 7:4); млеко (4:11); стенниͥ (4:11) along with стѣнникъ (5:1); древомъ (4:14); провеите (4:16); ѐжь (5:1); ѐлъ (5:1); ѐжьте (5:1); намилеишїи (5:1); выповедꙋючи (5:4 rubric); сквозе (5:4); прейскꙋшеноу (5:5); х͠ве (5:9, 6:1, 8:5, 8:11 rubric); ѿповедаеть (5:10 rubric) along with ѿповѣдаѐть (6:2, 7:1 rubric); ӑпатекаревъ (5:13); пресладко (5:16); жалобне (7:1 rubric); требꙋючи (7:2); намилеишаѧ (7:6); наилепшее (7:9) along with налѣпшее (5:11); селеͯ (7:11); заквеͭли (7:12) along with сквитла (7:12); поцеловала (8:1) along with цѣлꙋи (1:1); сестре (8:8); преͣо (8:12); набж͠не беͥ престани (8:13 rubric); вѣрьне (8:13 rubric); козе (8:14).

**1.2. Differentiation between phonemes *i* and *y*.** The differentiation between phonemes ***i*** and ***y*** is graphically rendered by a consistent use of the etymological и and ы. Dispalatalization of *r'* is expressed in the confusion of и and ы after р: товарышоͥ (1:6); стрыженыͯ (4:2); крыны (6:3); along with кьриноͯ (4:5); зрить (7:4); приподоблаючї ю (6:4 rubric).

**1.3. The rise of *o* < *e* after postdentals.**

- *o* < *e*:

чорна (1:4); жонами (1:7); ѐздьцоͫ (1:8); пришолъ (2:8); ѿшоͣ (2:11, 5:6, 6:0); нашои (2:12 twice); оужо (2:12); ѡвоцомъ (4:13); жьжонъ (5:9); жонъ (6:1, 6:8); жоны (6:8); перепꙋцоныи (7:1 rubric); к жолобомъ (7:5); книжокъ (8:1 rubric); ѡвоцоͥ (8:12);

- but otherwise always же:

always женихꙋ (in rubric); стороже (1:5, 8:11); пришелъ (2:12); печеркаͯ (2:14); сторожеве (3:3, 5:7); дщери (2:7, 3:10, 3:11, 5:8, 5:16, 6:8, 8:4); дщеро (7:1); ложе (3:7); вечерѧдло (3:9); стрыженыͯ (4:2); черленыи (4:3); пꙋшечными (4:4); поченъши (4:8); затверженыи (4:15); прейскꙋшеноу (5:5); червеныи (5:10); чело (5:11); черны (5:12); посажены (5:13); оуглажены (5:14); зрѧженаѧ (6:4, 6:10); оуглаженаѧ (7:2); пшеничныи (7:2); ѡбложеныи (7:2); дчерь множества (7:4); наилепшее (7:9); желаючи (8:1 rubric); несъвершени (8:8 rubric); нш͠еи (8:8); нейзрѣченное (8:14 rubric).

**1.4. The alternation of *v* and *u* in prepositions and prefixes before a consonant. The change of bilabial *w* into *u*, rendered graphically by the fluctuation of spelling between оу and в.**

- Letter оу in prefixes and prepositions before a consonant (21 occurrences):

оувел (1:3); оу винницаͯ (1:5, 1:13); оу возеͯ (1:8); оу ѣдлѣ (1:11); оу нашои (2:12); оувелъ (2:4); оустꙋпаеть (3:6); оунꙋтрь (4:3); оудномъ (4:9); оузъѧвили (5:8); оу заградаͯ (6:2); пооустоваючи (6:10); оу вобꙋви (7:1); оу зевоне (7:4); оу

**броны** (7:4); **ѹ҆ роскоша**^х^ (7:6); **ѹ҆ст8плю** (7:8); **ѹ҆ бронахъ** (7:13); **ѹ҆ст8паёть** (8:5); **ѹ҆ винограде̑**^х^ (8:13).

- Letter **в** in prefixes and prepositions before a consonant (35 occurrences):

**в добровонности** (1:3); **в тобѣ** (1:3); **въ мнѣ** (2:4); **въста**^н^ (2:10, 2:13, 4:16); **вь земли** (2:12); **в дире**^х^ **скалны**^х^ **а҆ в печерка**^х^ (2:14); **в невѣсты** (3:1 rubric); **в** **ночи** (3:1); **встан8** (3:2); **встала** (5:5); **вьстанмо** (7:12); **в церьква**^х^ (3:3 rubric); **въвед8** (3:4); **вн8трь** (4:1); **възгладненїемъ** (4:9); **взѧли** (5:7); **възъжаданы** (5:16); **взывали** (6:9); **в бѣда**^х^ **а҆ в напастѣ**^х^ **и҆ в пок8сохъ** (6:13 rubric); **в невѣ** (8:1 rubric); **възлегши** (8:5); **в вѣрѣ** (8:8 rubric); **влаимо**^ж^ (8:9); **въ дн҃и и҆ в ночи** (8:13 rubric); **въ ѱ҃лмѣхъ и҆ в пѣ**^с^**хъ и҆ в пѣнїа**^х^ (8:13 rubric); **въ всемъ** (8:13 rubric); **в горнеѐ цр**^с^**тво** (8:14 rubric).

**1.5. Spirantization of velar stop *g* (through the intermediate stage of γ) into fricative *h*.**[42]

- spirantized *h* is rendered by **г**: **гермонъ** (4:8), cf. Czech *hermon*.
- *g* is rendered by digraph **кг**: **ѐкгадди** (1:13), cf. Czech *engady*; **мандракгоры** (7:13), cf. Czech *mandragory*. The spelling of **ѐкгадди** with **кг** (and without **н**) is also attested in the text of the *Song of Songs* from the Vilno262 codex.

**1.6. Spelling with vocalization of the type ъ > *o*, ь > *e* and an additional ъ or apostrophe after a sonant.** The examples of the vocalized *jers* with sonants in interconsonantal position are as follows:

- **горълич҃ка** (1:9); **перси** (1:1, 7:12, 8:1); **горъличинъ** (2:12); **дерьжачи** (3:8); **распростеръль** (3:10); **перъси** (4:10); **затверженыи** (4:15); **твердо** (8:6); **порканы** (8:9); ^не^**съвершен** (8:8 rubric).
- **персеи** (1:3, 7:7, 8:8); **персѣи** (7:3); **перси** (7:8); **тернїемъ** (2:2); **держала** (3:4); **поскверны** (4:7); **зернѧты**^х^ (4:13); **первыми** (4:14); **непоскверненаѧ** (5:2); **толк8чего** (5:2); **перв8ю** (5:13); **полныѧ** (5:14).

**1.7. Umlaut '*a* > *e* after palatalized consonants and, as a secondary phenomenon, *a* > *e*:**

- after *j*: **прїетелко** (1:8, 1:14, 2:10) instead of **прїѧтелко**, **моеѐ** (2:7) instead of **моѧѧ** (unstressed position).
- after postdentals: **жедала** (2:3) instead of **жѧдала** (stressed position).[43]
- as a secondary development *a* > *e*: **бе**^р^**вѣ** (1:5) instead of **ба**^р^**вѣ**; **ремени** (8:6) instead of **рамени**.

---

[42] The bibliography about this change is numerous and cannot be fully cited here. See, for example, Trubetzkoy 1987, 169–172; Durnovo 1969, 180.

[43] However, this form may be also a result of influence by the Old Polish variant *żędać* along with *żądać*.

**1.8. A*kan'e***: да, 'and,' instead of до, 'up to': и҆ поведꙋ до домꙋ мт҃ри моє́и . а҆ да покойка ро$^{ди}$тельници (8:2).

**1.9. C*okan'e***: ци (3:1) instead of чи.

**1.10. The preservation of palatalized postdentals in spelling.** The preservation of palatalized postdentals is expressed by the consistent use of ю ['u] and ѧ ['a] after the postdentals. It is possible that it was an orthographic rule: прочютити (2:2, 3:5); скачючи (2:8); чює$^{т}$ (5:2); тѣшѧчї ю (7:1 rubric); поχвачю (7:8); пережюванїю (7:9).

**1.11. The rise of *y* from ъ in a weak position after the interconsonantal *r*.** Although there is only one occurrence of the rise of *y* from ъ in a weak position after the interconsonantal *r* (задрыжало (5:4)), there are no examples of a different development of this sequence.

**1.12. The rise of *u* < *o* in verbs in *–ova–* by analogy with the Present Tense stem *–uj–*.** The rise of *u* from *o* in the verbal noun пережюванїю (7:9) occurs by analogy with the Present Tense stem *žuju*, "I chew."

## 2. Morphology

The morphological analysis of the Ruthenian *Song of Songs* shows the linguistic interference of West Slavic, particularly Czech elements. The occurrence of West Slavic morphological features is inconsistent; these features are found in variation with their East Slavic equivalents:

### 2.1. Noun

**(i)** Nominative case plural ending *–(o/e)ve*, cf. Czech *–ove*:
стороже́ве (3:3, 5:7), cf. Czech *ſtrażnij*; тѣневе (2:17, 4:6), cf. Czech *ſtienowe*; кӱ́прове (4:13), cf. Czech *Cyprowe*; столпове (5:15), cf. Czech *ſlupowe*; зꙋбове (6:6), cf. Czech *zubowe* along with зꙋбы (4:2); свѧ҃зкове (7:1), cf. Cz *ſwazowe*; гронове (7:8), cf. Czech *hroznowe*.

**(ii)** Vocative case singular ending of a-stem nouns *–o* (cf. Czech *–o*):
дщеро (7:1), cf. Czech *dcero*, also in Skaryna.

### 2.2. Adjective

There are a few cases of contracted forms of adjectives (only masculine singular forms are considered since in other instances it is hard to determine whether the form is a contracted long-form adjective or a short adjective):
ѿи красны є̇си ты милыи мои витѧжныи (1:15); а҆ ве$^{с}$ възъжаданы (5:16); по$^{до}$бны є$^{с}$ милыи мои серне (2:9); поиди милы мои (8:14).

### 2.3. Pronoun

**(i)** First person singular pronoun *ja* is spelled with either ıа or ѧ.

**(ii)** Genitive and Accusative cases of personal and reflexive pronouns ending in –ѣ is most likely influenced by analogy with the Dative and Locative forms:

- Genitive мене̑ (1:5, 5:2), себѣ (5:3);
- Accusative тебѣ (1:2, 1:3, 8:5) along with тобѣ (1:8) and тебе (6:13); себѣ (1:7).

**(iii)** Fluctuation between Accusative case forms of the third person feminine of the personal pronoun ю (6:8 twice, 6:13 rubric, 7:1 rubric, 8:1) and ѐє (6:7, 7:8 twice, 8:7; 8:14 rubric).

### 2.4. Verb

**(i)** First person singular Present forms of the verb 'to be' ѐсмь and ѐсми are used interchangeably:

- ѐсмь (1:4, 1:5 twice, 1:8, 2:3, 3:1, 5:5, 6:11, 7:13, 8:10);
- ѐсми (3:1, 3:2 twice, 3:4 and 5:1 three times, 5:3 twice, 5:6 four times, 6:12, 7:8, 8:10).

**(ii)** First person plural verbal ending in the Present in *–**mo***:

оучинимо (1:10); выидимо (7:11); вьстаи̂мо (7:12); ѡ̀смотремо (7:12); влаимо͛ (8:9) but оу҆чинимъ (8:8); ѡ̀городѣм͛ же (8:8).

**(iii)** Truncated forms of the Imperative:

- поᴬ (4:8 three times), подь (5:1), formed from поити, cf. Czech *pod*; оу҆ка͛ (1:6); въста͛ (2:10); въстань (2:13); оу҆ка͛ (2:14); неврать сѧ (2:17); въстань (4:16); навротьⷭ҇ навроть сѧ (6:13); поло͛ (8:6);
- along with full forms: поиди (2:10; 2:13, 7:11, 8:14); поспешиⷭ҇ (2:10); бꙋди (2:17); выидете (*e* from *ě*) (3:11); прїиди (5:1); ѿтвори (5:2); ѿврати (6:5).

**(iv)** Compound Past Tense verb forms are not as frequent in East Slavic as in West Slavic; in the Ruthenian *Song of Songs* they are a result of Czech influence:

| | | |
|---|---|---|
| **(1:11)** | Ruthenian | коли єⷭ҇ былъ цр҃ь оу ѣдлѣ |
| | Czech | *Kdyż g(es)t byl kral w gedle ſwem* |
| **(5:6)** | Ruthenian | а̀ле ѡ̀нъ сѧ оу҆же быᴧ оу҆хилилъ ѿшолъ |
| | Czech | *ale on ſie bie˙ſe vchylil a za˙ſel* |
| **(8:11)** | Ruthenian | вин̆ница была єⷭ҇ покоиномꙋ котораѧ͛ то маєть люди |
| | Czech | *Vinnice byla g(es)t pokoynemu w tee kterażt ma lidi* |

**(v)** The text of the Ruthenian *Song of Songs* is characterized by the absence of Aorists. The Czech source text retains almost none. The process of the disappearance of Aorists was characteristic of fifteenth-century Czech. In contrast, there are many Aorists in, for instance, the Vilno262 translation of the *Song of Songs*.

## 3. SYNTAX

**3.1.** The use of conjunctions ӑбы and прото. The conjunction ӑбы appears in the Ruthenian *Song of Songs* in the same grammatical construction as in the Czech text. This construction consists of the conjunction ӑбы merged with an auxiliary verb and a main verb in the form of a Past Participle in *–l*. It is consistently used in the Ruthenian *Song of Songs*, as opposed to the Skaryna, which sometimes retains the Church Slavonic syntax.

**(2:7, 3:5, 8:4)**

| | |
|---|---|
| Ruthenian | ӑбысте не боудили ӑни прочютити казали милоѐ моѐѐ |
| Czech | *aby ſte nebudili . ani procititi kazali zmilele .* |
| Skaryna | да не ѻ҃бꙋдите ӥни прочꙋтити кажете любоѐ моѐѧ |

**(5:5)**

| | |
|---|---|
| Ruthenian | в҃стала ѐсмь ӑбыⷯ ѿтворила миломȣ моѐмоу |
| Czech | *Wſtala ſem abych otewřiela milemu memu* |
| Skaryna | въстала ѐсмь дабыхъ ѿворила любомꙋ моѐмꙋ |

**(6:5)**

| | |
|---|---|
| Ruthenian | ѿврати оѻчи твои ѿмене бо тыи соуть ми оу҆чинили ӑбыⷯ оулѣте҃ |
| Czech | *Otwrat oczi twogi ote mne . neb ty gſu mi abych vletiel vcinili* |
| Skaryna | ѿврати ѻ҃чи твое ѿмене ӕко предⷩими ѐсмь залетелъ |

The conjunction прото(жь) is also found in the Vilno262. Anderš regards it as a direct borrowing from Czech into Ukrainian.[44]

**(1:2)**

| | |
|---|---|
| Ruthenian | прото молоⷣци миловали сȣть тебѣ |
| Czech | *proto mladicie milowali ſu tie .* |
| Vilno262 | протожь молодици полюбили тебе |

**3.2.** The use of the particles жто, usually after the conjunction которыи results from imitating the Czech source since the use of the particles *–žto* is a stylistic trait of Old Czech.

**(2:15)**

| | |
|---|---|
| Ruthenian | зымаите наⷨ лисенѧта малаѧ которыижто казѧⷮ ви҃нници |
| Czech | *Zlapayte li ſencie maličke nam . kterežto kazie vinicie .* |

---

[44] Anderš 1976, 65.

**(4:4)**
Ruthenian ıа́ко вежа дв҃два шіа твоѧ котораѧⷤто єⷭ҇ оу́дѣлана з дѣлы пꙋшечными
Czech *Yako vieżie dauidowa ˙ſige twa . kterażto g(es)t vdielana s alkeři.*
**(6:5)**
Ruthenian волосы твои ıа́ко стадо козъ. котороеⷤто сѧ оу́казало з галаа́дъ.
Czech *Wlaſowe twogi yako ſtada kozie kterażto ſu ſie vkazaly z galaad.*

**3.3.** The reflexive particle сѧ is frequently, almost consistently, separated from the verb. Although the separate use of the reflexive particle in pre-position was not unfamiliar to East Slavic, in the Ruthenian *Song of Songs* the position of сѧ regularly copies the Czech pattern in the source text (it follows the first stressed word in a sentence):

**(2:17)**
Ruthenian докоуⷧ҇ сѧ дн҃ь не наклониⷮ а̀ не оу́хилѧтьⷭ҇ тѣневе .
Czech *donidż ſie den nenakloni . a neuchylee ſie ſtienowe .*
**(4:1)**
Ruthenian кромѣ того што сѧ внꙋтрь таѧть
Czech *kromie toho czoż ſie wnitrz tagi*
**(5:6)**
Ruthenian а̀ле ѡ̀нъ сѧ оу́же быⷧ҇ оу́хилилъ ѿшолъ
Czech *ale on ſie bie˙ſe vchylil a za˙ſel*

**3.4.** Literal translations of many Czech syntactical constructions reproduce the same word order. For instance:

**(2:7)**
Ruthenian заклинаю ваⷭ҇ дщери ѐрⷭ҇лмкїа . череⷭ҇ ѻлени а̀ серны полныи . а̀бысте не боудили а̀ни прочютити казали милое̇ мое̇е̇ . докꙋль сама въсхочеть
Czech *Zaklinam was dcery geruzalemſke ſkrzie ſrny y geleny polſke*[45] *. aby ˙ſte nebudili . ani procititi kazali zmilele . donidżt ſama chce .*
**(5:7)**
Ruthenian знашли мѧ сꙋть сторожеве которыиⷤто сꙋть ѡ̀бхоживали мѣсто . били мѧ соуть й ранили . й в̏зѧли ми плащь мои сторожеве мꙋ҃ра
Czech *Nalezli ſu mie ſtrażnij kteřiż obchaziegij mieſto . bili ſu mie y ranili ſu mie . wzieli ſu mi plaſt moy ſtrażnij zdij .*

## 4. Lexicon

Some of the peculiarities in the use of the lexicon have been briefly mentioned in the discussion of the translator's technique. In this section I will analyze sev-

[45] *polni* in other Czech Bibles of the same redaction (*Nymburská, Lobkovická, Talmberská* Bibles).

eral of the most important lexemes related to the interpretation of this biblical book.

### 4.1. Love

There are two terms in the Ruthenian *Song of Songs* that correspond to the English 'love'. They reflect the distribution of terms in the Czech text that follows the Vulgate translation where those terms seem to have different shades of meaning. The word милость (Czech *milost*, Latin *amor*) stands for 'love, affection,' whereas любовь (Czech *laska*, Latin *charitas*) may be understood as 'regard, esteem, affection, benevolence, love.' For verbal forms, only the root мил– is used.

<u>Noun</u>: любоⷡ, cf. Czech *laſku*, Latin *charitatem* (2:4); люб̏ви, cf. Czech *laſky*, Latin *charitatem* (8:7); мл҃ⷭти и любовноє̇, cf. Czech *laſky*, Latin *charitate* (3:10); мл҃ⷭти, cf. Czech *miloſt*, Latin *amore* (2:5, 5:8); милѡ҃ⷭ, cf. Czech *miloſt*, Latin *dilectio* (8:6); but also любь,[46] cf. Czech *milowanie*, Latin *dilectione* (8:7) along with милованїє (rubric 8:14).

<u>Verb</u>: миловали, cf. Czech *milowali*, Latin *dilexerunt* (1:2); милоуют, cf. Czech *milugij*, Latin *diligunt* (1:3); милꙋеть, cf. Czech *miluge*, Latin *diligit* (1:6, 3:1, 3:2, 3:3, 3:4); cf. Skaryna возлюбиша, возлюбѧть, милуеть, Vilno262 любиⷮ.

The rubrics (text that divides speeches into a dialogue; most of them are absent in the Czech source) reveal the same usage. The fact that любовь and милость are often linked by conjunctions suggests that they probably have different meanings and reproduce the same distribution as in the biblical portion: млѡ҃ⷭ а̀ любовь (7:11); великою любовїю а̀ горѧчею м҃ⷭтью (8:1), и̂ мл҃ⷭти бж҃їа и̂ любьви (8:14).

### 4.2. Beloved

There are two variants for the female 'beloved,' Czech *přietelnicie, přietelkynye*: прїєтелко (three times) and милаѧ (six times). The latter seems to be a feminine counterpart to the masculine form of 'beloved' милыи, which copies the Czech *mily*.

<u>Female</u>: прїєтелко, cf. Czech *přietelnicie* (1:8, 1:14); милаѧ, cf. Czech *přietelnicie* (2:2, 2:13, 4:1, 4:7, 6:3); милаѧ, cf. Czech *přietelkynye* (5:2); прїєтелко моа милаѧ, cf. Czech *přietelnicie* (2:10); cf. Skaryna прїѧтелко, Vilno262 подрꙋго .

<u>Male</u>: милыи, cf. Czech *mily* (1:12, 1:13, 1:15, 2:3, 2:9, 2:10, 2:16, 2:17, 5:1, 5:4, 5:9, 5:10, 6:1, 6:2, 6:3, 7:11, 8:14); милого, cf. Czech *mileho* (2:8, 5:2, 5:8); миломꙋ, cf. Czech *milemu* (5:5, 5:6); милыи . любимыи, cf. Czech *mily ... a ...*

---

[46] The scribe probably forgot to put a *tilda* over the word.

*přietel* (5:16); милом8, cf. Czech *milemu* (6:3, 7:9, 7:10); cf. Skaryna любыи, Vilno262 милостникъ, любовникъ.

### 4.3. Vineyard

вин҆ница, cf. Czech *vinnice*, a direct borrowing from Czech; cf. Skaryna вин҆ница, вин҆ницє, виноградъ, Vilno262 виницю or винограды.

### 4.4. Garden

Czech *zahrada* is "translated" as заграда:[47] cf. Czech *do zahrady* (5:1, 6:2, 6:11), ѹ҆ заградаˣ, cf. Czech *w zahradach* (6:2); as ѡ҆городокъ (4:12; 4:16) or as ѡ҆горóдъ: до ѡ҆горóда (5:1); and as винограды: ѹ҆ виноградѣˣ, cf. Czech *w zahradach* (8:13).

These fluctuations in translation show that this word might have been perceived as foreign and was probably influenced by the Czech source text, cf. Skaryna заграда, Vilno262 огородъ.

### 4.5. Mother

The text of the Ruthenian *Song of Songs* consistently follows the pattern of the Czech text with regard to the translation of the word 'mother': м҃три for Czech. *matře* (1:5), *mateře* (3:4, 8:2), and *mateři* (6:9); м҃ти for Czech *matie* (3:11); м҃тки for Czech *matky* (8:1) and м҃тка for Czech *matka* (8:5). Vilno262 in most cases uses the word матка.

### 4.6. Daughter

There are three kinds of translation of Czech *dcery*: Church Slavonic дщери (2:7, 3:10, 3:11, 5:8, 5:16, 6:9, 8:4), East Slavic дочки (3:5), a hybrid д҃черь (7:4), and Czech influenced variants д҃цѣри (1:4) and дщеро (7:1).

### 4.7. Borrowings from Czech

One of the most noticeable borrowings is ѹ ѣдлѣ, cf. Czech *w gedle* (1:11). In the Czech text translated from the Vulgate, *gedlo (jedlo)* renders the Latin *accubitio*, 'a lying or reclining at meals, at table.' Jan Gebauer[48] does not record this word. It probably means something close to 'eating room' (in other Czech redactions of the Bible this word is translated as *v pokogi*). It was borrowed into the Ruthenian *Song of Songs* along with its unclear meaning. Some other borrowings are: и҆зрѧ҃ди҃лъ, cf. Czech *zřiedil* (2:4); правица, cf. Czech *prauicie* (2:6); погорки, cf. Czech *pahorky* (2:8); превалъ, cf. Czech *přewal* (2:11); тварь, cf. Czech *twař* (2:14); ѹ҆хилѧть҃с, cf. Czech *neuchylee ſie* (2:17); невратьсѧ, cf. Czech *nawrat ſie* (2:17); а҆патекарева, cf. Czech *apatekařowa* (3:6); вечерѧдло, cf. Czech *Wečzeradlo* (3:9); в кор8нѣ, короѹновала, cf. Czech *w korunye, koruno-*

---

[47] It is interesting that this word also appears in the *Laodicean Epistle* (Taube 1995b).

[48] Gebauer 1970.

*wala* (3:11); оу҆ломокъ, cf. Czech *vlomek* (4:3); не схилатьса, cf. Czech *ſie ... a neſchyle* (4:6); коруновала, cf. Czech *korunowana* (4:8); выборныи, cf. Czech *wyborny* (5:10; 5:15); ѿ а҆патекаревъ, cf. Czech *od apatekařow* (5:13); тварность, cf. Czech *twarnoſt* (5:15); са є҆ⷭ҇ оу҆хилилъ, cf. Czech *ſie g(es)t vchylil* (6:1); постава, cf. Czech *poſtawa* (7:7).

**4.8.** In the opinion of Shevelov the use of the adverb докуль may be regarded as a characteristic Belarusian language feature, in contrast to the Ukrainian use of the forms доколе and доколѧ.[49]

**4.9.** In general, the text of the Ruthenian *Song of Songs* contains almost no Church Slavonic lexicon, grammatical forms, or spelling.

## CONCLUSION

The linguistic analysis of the Ruthenian *Song of Songs* shows a mixture of East Slavic and Czech (West Slavic) linguistic features and makes the dependence of the Ruthenian translation on a Czech source evident. Language mixing in this case is not only due to close translation but could also be considered a stylistic act. The text of the Ruthenian *Song of Songs* in Moscow Synod Collection #558 manuscript is, most likely, an apograph removed from the original by several decades. Nonetheless, it has retained a heavily Bohemized idiom, which apparently did not disturb copyists. Almost no traces of an attempt to Slavonicize the text during later copying can be detected, suggesting that the language was probably considered natural by the Ruthenian scribe.

[49] Shevelov 1979, 400.

# The Ruthenian *Book of Taudal the Knight* Linguistic Analysis

## 1. Phonology / Orthography

As in the Ruthenian *Song of Songs*, the orthography in the Ruthenian *Book of Taudal the Knight* does not represent phonological vernacular features consistently and reflects traits known to exist in both Belarusian and/or Ukrainian fifteenth-century dialects. General East Slavic features in the text include the presence of ž and č in place of **dj*, **tj* (нарожєнїӓ (T 1))[50] or pleophony (чєрє҃с (T 42, 53, 61, S 39, 145)). The phonological base of this Ruthenian text is also, therefore, a supradialectal koine.

**1.1. The loss of distinction between phonemes *ě* and *i*, expressed graphically by fluctuation of letters и and ѣ:**
повѣдилъ (T 59, 61), instead of повѣдѣлъ; ѿповѣдѣла, примогаше (T 25), instead of прѣмогашє vs. прємогалъ (T 26).

**1.2. The loss of distinction between *ě* and *e* in both stressed and unstressed positions, expressed graphically by fluctuation of letters є and ѣ.** Fluctuations are mostly in the endings and prefixes and only occasionally in the stems. The cases of fluctuation are as follows:

- **Prefix:** прє– instead of прѣ–:

прєглоѵбокїи (T 53), прєширокїи (T 67), прєдрагими (T 70);

- **Ending in Dative/Locative:** по роцє (T 17), рєцє (T 49), в рꙋцє (T 58), на свѣтє (T 76), ѡ трєхъ розєхъ (T 41);
- **Ending - Adverb:** вєсєлє (T 75), добрє (T 83), but поволнѣ (T 33);
- **Root:** –вѣд–/–вєд–: повѣдати (T 12, S 22), повѣда (T 44), повѣдилъ (T 59, 61); рєки (T 48), рєцє (T 49); вєтръ (T 39);
- **Verbal stem vowel:**

дозрєти (T 47) along with ѹзрѣли (T 63) and ѹзрѣ (T 70).

**1.3. Dispalatalization of *r'*** is expressed graphically in the confusion of и and ъı after ρ, related to the coalescence of /y/ and /i/ in one phoneme. Otherwise the differentiation between phonemes *i* and *y* is graphically rendered by a consistent

[50] A number next to the letter "T" indicates a line number in Appendix II.

use of the etymological **и** and **ы**: **тисѧчаго тридцатого** (T 1), **покривала** (T 25), **покривалом** (T 27), **покривале** (T 28) along with **покрывало** (T 30).

**1.4. The change of bilabial *w* into *u* in prepositions and prefixes before the consonant, rendered graphically by the fluctuation of spelling ѹ and в.**

- Letter **ѹ** in prefixes and prepositions before consonant (3 occurrences):

**ѹвращахж** (T 43), **ѹ даль** (T 53); **ѹпадаше** (T 46);

- Letter **в** in prefixes and prepositions before consonant (15 occurrences):

**в томъ** (T 4), **въ добытыхъ** (T 14), **в ритеръствѣ** (T 15); **вътръгахоѹ** (T 43); **в тыи** (T 43); **въ моѹкы** (T 44); **в неи** (T 49), **в шириноѹ** (T 53), **в ризы** (T 58, 77), **в томъ** (T 65, 66), **въ всю** (T 77), **въ нб$^{с}$номъ** (T 80), **въ силѣ** (T 83).

**1.5. The rise of *o* < *e* after postdentals.** The rise of *o* < *e* after hushing sounds (postdentals) provided there was no front vowel in the following syllable in both stressed and unstressed position:

**ничого** (T 10), **горѧщого** (T 23), **прошолъ** (T 56), **прешолъ** (T 59).

**1.6. The rise of *akan'e* (delabialization of unstressed o):** **в манастыри** (T 6), **апѧть** (T 31), **таваришовъ** (T 14) along with **товариша** (T 15).

## 2. MORPHOLOGY

The morphological analysis of the Ruthenian *Book of Taudal the Knight* shows both linguistic interference of West Slavic elements and their variation with East Slavic equivalents:[51]

### 2.1. NOUN

**(i) Declension:**

- **Nominative plural in –ове and –еве :** **дивове** (T 49);
- **Genitive plural ending:**

vowel contraction: **[ѿцовъ а] бра$^{т}$и** (T 33) instead of **братии**, cf. Czech *bratří*; **[таваришовъ и] приıателе** (T 14) instead of **приıателеи**, cf. Czech *přietelé*; **[много] доуши [грѣшны$^{х}$]** (T 28) along with **доушь** (T 48, 55), Czech *duší*;

**(ii) Proper names:**[52]

**єѵгенїюсъ** (T 4, 5), **таоудалоусъ**, **таоудалю$^{с}$** (T 16, 75) along with **таоудалъ** (T 9), **ѡ таоудале**, cf. Church Slavonic **фаоудалъ**.

---

[51] Several of the linguistic features discussed below as West Slavic are also found in some East Slavic dialects. However, their presence in the discussed texts is most likely of West Slavic origin.

[52] In Czech, proper names of Latin origin retain the Latin ending *–us* (*–usz* in Polish) in Nominative and drop it in oblique cases.

**2.2. ADJECTIVE**

**(i) Superlative:** наигорше (T 29), cf. Czech *najhorší*; наидраⷤшаⷮ (T 71), наꙵдраⷤши (T 73), cf. Czech *najdražší*; наперveи (T 58), cf. Czech *najprve*.

**(ii) Contracted adjectives:**[53] тоⷮ домъ былъ преширокїи а ѡкржглы (T 68), cf. Czech *okrúhlý*.

**2.3. ADVERBS in –е along with East Slavic adverbs in –о:**

веселе (T 75), добре (T 83), поволнѣ (T 33), along with силно (T 39), cf. Czech *silně*, дареⷨно (T 33), cf. Czech *daremně*.

**2.4. NUMERAL**

една лавичька (T 51), еⷣно слн҃це (T 67), cf. Czech and Polish *jedna, jedno*.

**2.5. VERB**

**(i) Present Tense:**

- **Third person singular and plural without –ть :**

словоѹ (T 5), слове (T 6) along with the majority of forms in –ть.

**(ii) Past Tenses:**

- **Compound Past Tense (cf. Czech Plusquamperfectum):**[54]

възвратилсѧ есть былъ до рима з влаⷯ (T 5); ишто бѧше джша тръпѣла всѣхъ моѹкъ (T 26); смрад иже премоглъ былъ вси моѹкы (T 50), cf. Imperfect in Church Slavonic превосходѧ (CS 45);[55] есть доѹша была перво видѣла (T 51).

- **Perfect with auxiliary:**[56]

ꙗкоже есть евгенїюсъ папежемъ былъ воленъ (T 4); былъ есть единъ моѹⷤ родомъ (T 8); выдалъ есть что мѣлъ (T 14), cf. Imperfect in Church Slavonic всѧ ѐлика ѝмѧше (CS 14); и любимого ѝмѣлъ ѐсть товарища (T 15); было есть полно катовъ (T 40); есть быⷧ его краль на свѣте (T 76).

**(iii) Passive Participles without *l*–epentheticum:**

збавена (T 60), cf. Czech *zbavená*, P *zbawiona*, приготована (T 33), cf. Czech *přihotovaná*, along with приправлена (T 71).

The above record is not an exhaustive list of all of the West Slavic morphological features present in the texts. Some of the traits prevail over corresponding East Slavic features, such as adverbs in –е, Nominative plural in –ове and –еве; others are present in variation with East Slavic forms, such as Passive Partici-

---

[53] Only masculine singular forms are considered since, in other instances, it is hard to determine whether the form is a contracted long-form adjective or a short adjective.

[54] Compound Past Tense verbal forms are not characteristic of East Slavic but are quite common in Czech.

[55] "CS" indicates examples from the Church Slavonic *Edifying Story Told by Faudal the Warrior* (повеⷭⷮ полезна сиа̀ сказаⷩ ѐ фаоѹдалоⷨ воиноⷨ) published in Appendix II.

[56] These forms are more consistently used in fifteenth-century Czech than in East Slavic.

ples without *l*–epentheticum. This variation is an indication that the presence of West Slavic morphological features is due to grammatical interference.

## 3. SYNTAX

**3.1. The use of the verb йм҇ѣти to express possession (Ruthenian is a “have” language):** валкоу мѣлъ (T 3), ‘he had a war.’

**3.2. Demonstrative (deictic) pronoun as referential expression:**

- **Referential expression I (solo):**

и любимого йм҇ѣлъ ѐсть товарища$_i$ […] тотъ$_i$ ємоу былъ долже$^{н}$ три кони (T 15), ‘and he had a best friend$_i$ […] he$_i$ owed him three horses;’
ни$^{ж}$ли єдинъ закȏнникъ$_i$ презвитеръ$_i$ , тотъ$_i$ єго прошолъ безъ шкоды (T 56–57), ‘than a monk$_i$ presbyter$_i$, he$_i$ crossed it [bridge] without incident.’

- **Referential expression II (with noun):** то$^{т}$ (то) / тот же то[57]

пото$^{м}$ пріидоша ќгорѣ$_i$ […] и на тои$_i$ же то горѣ$_i$ было есть полно катовъ (T 36, 40), ‘then they came to a mountain [...] and on this mountain there were a lot of executioners;’ пріидоша до глоубокого долоу$_i$ […] то$^{т}$$_i$ то долъ$_i$ горды$^{х}$ есть моужеи пышныхъ (T 46, 62), ‘they came to a deep abyss [...] this abyss is for proud and arrogant men;’ мостокъ$_i$ чере$^{с}$ долъ […] стого$^{ж}$$_i$ то мостъка$_i$ таоудалова доуша видѣла много доушь (T 52, 55), ‘a little bridge across the abyss [...] from this bridge the soul of Taudal saw many souls.’
Although the usage of тот as a referential expression is listed here as a syntactical feature, the overall frequency of usage of this pronoun in Ruthenian, directly influenced by Czech (and indirectly by Polish), suggests that this feature was acquired lexically (see further discussion in Lexicon).

**3.3. Prepositions and their government:**[58]

- **до, ‘to, into’ with Genitive, vs. Church Slavonic в(о) with Accusative:**
по тои тѧ моуце поведоу до большихъ (T 34); и пріидоша до долоу (T 22, 46), cf. придохомъ же в ровъ (CS 41); възвратилсѧ есть былъ до рима з вла$^{х}$ (T 5), до цр҇кви таке$^{ж}$ неходѧше (T 12), cf. во цр҇ковъ же на мл҇тв8 не входѧ (CS 13); along with **в(о) with Accusative**: а в тотъ долъ грозныи [...] идѧхоу много доуши (T 27);
- **по, ‘after,’ with Locative:** по тои моуце (T 34), по хвили (T 43), по роце (T 17);
- **пре$^{д}$ , ‘to’ (with Accusative, signifying direction):** поиде множествїє ихъ до

[57] Frequent use of *tot (že to)* is characteristic of Czech.

[58] The following prepositions and/or their usage are characteristic of West Slavic and are not common in East Slavic.

того домꙋ з дары своими **пре^д** кралѧ (T 73–74), cf. къ цр҃ю (CS 66);

- **скрозе** 'through' with Accusative: **скрозе** то покрывало цѣдıахоу тїи грѣшныа доуши, иıако воскъ **скрозе** пла^т цедѧтъ (T 30–31), cf. **сквозѣ** (CS 26);
- **про, 'for, because of' with Accusative:** ишто есть валькоу **про** ерл҃имъ мѣлъ (T 3), **про** великыи страхъ (T 45);
- **с, 'from, of' with Genitive (cf. Czech and Polish *z*) along with ис:**

**с** того мѣста былъ есть единъ моу^ж родомъ (T 8), **с** того **со** всего еще бѧше наигорше (T 29).

**3.4. Conjunctions in subordinate clauses:**

- **object clauses with иже бы and же 'that' (Polish że, żeby and Czech *že, žeby*) vs. Church Slavonic ıако:**

а в то^м домоу такаа бѧше свѣлость же не гл҃ю иже бы е^дно сл҃нце свѣтило (T 66–67), cf. не ıако ѿ единого сл҃нца . но ıако многыѧ сл҃нца (CS 59–60);
и довнима^л иже бы иное вѣще хвалы въ нб^сномъ цр^ствїи не было (T 79–80), cf. мнѣти ми ıако си^х болше и нѣ^с хвалы в небесно^м цр^стви (CS 72).

- **characterizing relative clauses with ишто, иже то and которыи 'which' (Czech *žto*):**

ишто есть валькоу про ерл҃имъ мѣлъ (T 3), ишто словоу гамїа (T 5), along with **иже то:** иже то слове глозоналъ (T 6); along with **которыи:** а иныи^м тымъ, которыиже даре^мно поволнѣ враж^доуют дѣло^м (T 33–34).

**3.5. Coordination: conjunction а meaning 'and' (typical of Czech and Old Polish) along with и :**

- а

пото^м прїидоша к горѣ велми великои а прелишь къ грознои. а тоу бѧше поу^т велми оузкыи (T 36); пото^м доуша таоудалова про великыи страхъ а грозоу оупадаше за агг҃ло^м идоущи. прїидоша до глоубокого долоу нечистого а велми темного, его^ж великости не могла дш҃а дозрети а едно слышала звоукъ реки пловоущꙋю серою а рыдание доушь в тои реце (T 45–49);

- и

ними^жто доуши давѧхоу, которыи хотѣли чере^с тоу горѫ проити . и вътръгахоу ихъ в тыи моукы а по хвили оувращахѫ ихъ въ ѡгонь и ѡпѧть засѧ въ моукы (T 42–44).

## 4. Lexicon

The *Book of Taudal the Knight* contains a considerable West Slavic lexical component. The fact that many Czech words which entered the Ruthenian translation also existed in Polish aided Czech lexical interference. The following is a selective list of lexemes arranged by parts of speech:

**4.1. Noun**

валкоу (T 3), cf. Czech *válka*, Polish *walka*; вражебниковъ (T 32), враждельникъ (T 35), cf. Czech *vražedlník*, Polish *wražda*, *wražebny*; грозоу (T 56), cf. Czech *hruoza*, Polish *groza*; гоу$^{д}$цомъ (T 13), cf. Czech *hudec*, cf. CS брацающи$^{м}$; законникъ (T 56), в ризы зако$^{н}$скы (T 58), cf. Czech *zakonník*, Polish *zakonnik*; cf. CS во мнишескои ѡдежи; зволенъцоу (T 54), cf. Czech *zvolenec*, Polish *zwolennik*; въ панви (T 29), cf. Czech and Polish *panev*; папе$^{ж}$ (T 5), папежемъ (T 4), cf. Czech *papež*, Polish *papeż*; пистцо$^{м}$ (T 13), поставци (T 70), cf. Czech *postavec*; [ѡ] реча$^{х}$ (T 20), cf. Czech *řeč*, Polish *rzecz* ‘thing’; рокоу, роце (T 17), cf. Czech and Polish *rok* along with лѣта, лѣто, лѣте (T 1, 2, 3, 4, 6); [в] ритеръствѣ (T 15), cf. Czech *rytieřstvo*, Polish *rycerstwo*, cf. CS ѿ вои$^{н}$; [безъ] оуразоу (T 61), cf. Polish *uraz*, *bez urazu*, хвили (T 43), cf. Czech *chvíle*, P *chwila*, шкоды (T 57), cf. Czech *škody*, Polish *szkody*.

**4.2. Adjective**

вале$^{ч}$ного (T 2), cf. Czech *valečný*, Polish *waleczny*; витѧ$^{ж}$ныи (T 10), cf. Czech, Polish *wiciężny*, and CS крѣпо$^{к}$; жа$^{д}$ное (T 22), жадъномоу (T 54), cf. Czech *žadný*, Polish *żadny*; пышныхъ (T 62), cf. Czech *pyšný*, Polish *pyszny* and CS грды$^{х}$; словоутного родоу (T 9), cf. Czech *slovutný*, Polish *sławętny*.

**4.3. Verb**

–вѣд–: повѣдати (T 12), повѣда (T 44), повѣдилъ (T 59, 61); довнима$^{л}$ (T 79), cf. CS мнѣти ми; здало бы$^{с}$ (T 80), cf. Czech *zdati se*; моусить (T 60), cf. Czech *musiti*, Polish *musić*, CS имаиши; премоглъ [былъ] (T 50), cf. Czech *přemoci*, Polish *przemóc*, привиталъ (T 18), cf. Polish *przywitować* and CS приемъ; словоу (T 5), слове (T 6), cf. Czech *slúti*, Polish *słuć*, оуживати (T 83), cf. Czech *užívati*, Polish *używać*, ‘use.’

**4.4. Past Passive Participle**

[былъ] воленъ (T 4), cf. Czech *voliti*, Polish *wolić*, ‘chosen,’ приправлена (T 71), cf. Czech *připraviti*, ‘prepared,’ оутворена (T 68), cf. Czech *utvořiti*, Polish *utworzyciel*, ‘made, created.’

**4.5. Adverb**

велми (T 9, 23, 23, 36, 37, 38, 39, 41, 47, 50, 52, 74), cf. Czech *velmi*, Polish *wielmi*, досы$^{т}$ (T 80), cf. Czech *dosyt*, Polish *dosyć*, посполоу (T 21), cf. Czech and Polish *pospolu*, прелишь (T 11, 22, 36, 38), cf. Czech *přieliš*, Polish *przylisz*, таке$^{ж}$ (T 12), cf. Czech *také*, Polish *takie*, along with тако (T 4), cf. Polish *tako*, засѧ (T 44), cf. Czech *zasě*, Polish *zasię*, ника$^{м}$ (T 19), cf. Czech and Polish *nikam*.

### 4.6. Particle

The use of the particles *–žto* and *to* is a stylistic trait of Old Czech. Its influence in the Ruthenian translations is reflected in the comparable frequency of the occurrence of ж(е) то and тот то:

- ж(е) то:

и на тои же то горѣ (T 40), ними^ж то доуши давахоу (T 42), с того^ж то мостъка (T 55);

- demonstrative pronoun with то:

боудешь збавена тое то муки (T 60), то^т то долъ (T 62), на то^м то свѣте (T 72).

### 4.7. Conjunction

тоу пакъ (T 51), cf. Czech *pak.*

### 4.8. Fall of initial *ji–*:[59]

- **мѣти – имѣти 'to have' (cf. Czech *měti*, Polish *mieć*):** мѣлъ (T 3, 14, 14);
- **з – из 'from' (cf. Czech and Polish *z*):** з вла^х (T 5), з мръхи (T 50);

It is also present in such words as зволенъцоу (T 54), cf. Czech *zvolenec*, Polish *zwolennik*, збавена (T 60), cf. Czech *zbaviti*, Polish *zbawić*.

### 4.9. Czech-type non-pleophonic forms:

драгаго (T 68, 69), злата (T 68, 69), златыи (T 70), златыхъ (T 79), кра^л (T 72), краль (T 76), краля (T 74), крале^м (T 76, 81), наидра^жша^т (T 71), повлаць (T 69), пре^д (T 13, 75, 81, 74), напре^д (T 60), превелъ (T 61), предрагими (T 70), преити (T 54), прешолъ (T 59), премоглъ [былъ] (T 50), страны (T 37, 39).

### 4.10. Glosses

In his commentary to the edition of fragments from the *Book of Taudal*, Brückner mentions the existence of marginal glosses added by readers of the manuscript. These glosses, another form of linguistic variation (paratext), are usually provided for words of West Slavic origin:

кипѣ for ѡзеро врѣло, cf. Czech *vřěti*, 'to boil'; гостинница for его^ж господы, cf. Czech *hospoda*, 'inn'; болесть for про великꙋю мдлобꙋ, cf. Czech *mdloba*.

## Conclusion

Similar to the language of the Ruthenian *Song of Songs*, the linguistic variation of West Slavic and East Slavic features in the Ruthenian *Book of Taudal the Knight* indicates linguistic interference and mixing as well as a close dependence

[59] This feature is listed as lexical since its occurrence in Ruthenian is a result of a lexical transfer rather than of independent phonological development.

on a Czech source. While the orthography reflects a mixture of Belarusian and Ukrainian features and remains primarily East Slavic, the lexicon, syntax and, to a lesser extent, morphology contain a significant Czech (West Slavic) component. Although the Czech *Vision of Tundal* has not yet been discovered, the linguistic analysis of the Ruthenian translation makes it evident that it did exist.

# THE RUTHENIAN *TALE OF SIVILLA THE PROPHETESS* LINGUISTIC ANALYSIS

The Ruthenian *Tale of Sivilla the Prophetess* contains some Church Slavonic components, as well as orthographic features that are usually interpreted as a result of the "second South Slavic influence." This fact may be explained either by the personal linguistic preferences and techniques of the translator, who may have been better trained in Church Slavonic than the other translators, or by a later Slavonization of this text during circulation and copying.

## 1. PHONOLOGY / ORTHOGRAPHY

As in other Ruthenian translations, phonological vernacular features are not represented consistently and are common to both Belarusian and Ukrainian dialects.

**1.1. Loss of distinction between phonemes *ě* and i, expressed graphically by fluctuation of letters и and ѣ:**

ѿповѣдила (S 40),[60] along with повѣдѣлъ, ѿповѣдѣла.

**1.2. Loss of distinction between *ě* and *e* in both stressed and unstressed positions, expressed graphically by fluctuation of letters е and ѣ.** There seems to be no systematic distribution of ѣ and е in the *Tale of Sivilla the Prophetess*, whereas in the Ruthenian *Book of Taudal* the fluctuations are mostly in the endings and prefixes and only occasionally in the stems. The cases of fluctuation are as follows:

- **Prefix:**

пре– instead of прѣ–: превели^кихъ (S 163), предивнꙋ (S 172);

- **Ending in Dative/Locative**:

ѡ красе, саломоновѣ (S 13) but о красотѣ (S 24), сивилле (S 32, 37, 195), въ вѣне (S 206), по ѡбѣде на цареве дворе (S 37), в ѡкрꙋгле (S 48), на нбе (S 48) but на нбѣ (S 93), ѡ хе а христиане^х (S 76), на небесе^х (S 58), в людє^х (S 164), прикладе^х (S 111), в деле^х (S 209), все^м (S 63), мне (S 50);

- **Ending – Adverb:**

миле (S 20), первеє (S 27), добре (S 30, 85), нне (S 50), справне (S 87), целе (S 88), нерадне (S 103), силне (S 128), радеє (S 224), зле (S 230);

[60] A number next to the letter "S" indicates a line number in the *Tale of Sivilla* in Appendix V.

- **Root:**

–вѣд–/–вед–: поведати (S 90), otherwise only ѣ: вѣдати (S 23, 46), повѣ^ж^ (S 38), вѣси (S 52), вѣдали (S 206), повѣдай (S 45), повѣдаю (S 47, 132), повѣдано (S 24), повѣдающи (S 16), звѣдала (S 26), сподвѣдай (S 196), исповѣдано (S 155), ѿповѣдила (S 40), ѿповѣдала (S 47), оувѣдалъ (S 15); –вѣр–/–вер–: вѣрь (S 73), вѣрити (S 44, 77, 86), невѣрность (S 187), along with верити (S 70), верети (S 60), вери^ш^ (S 72), веришь (S 81), оу вере (S 216, 217), въ вере (S 229), недоверенъ (S 221); ѿвѣща (S 21, 53); ѣсти (S 27); древо (S 30, 39, 245), древе (S 42); знаменати (S 95), знаменаи (S 107); время (S 163); места (S 205), месте (S 215); потребꙋ (S 212); пре^ж^ (S 6); прелести (S 97); редъкїй (S 140);

- **Verbal stem vowel:**

оусмотре (S 73), хоте^л^ (S 46), хотети (S 104, 107, 120, 178, 203); тръпети (S 153).

**1.3. The rise of *o* < *e* after postdentals.** The rise of *o* < *e* after hushing sounds (postdentals) provided there was no front vowel in the following syllable in both stressed and unstressed positions:

ещо (S 196), затрачо^м^ (S 123), ѡщищова^ти^ (S 114).

**1.4. The change of bilabial *w* into *u* in prepositions and prefixes before the consonant, rendered graphically by the fluctuation of spelling оу and в.**

- Letter оу in prefixes and prepositions before consonant (five occurrences):

оуспоминати (S 140), оу великꙋю нꙋжꙋ (S 157), оу вере (S 216, 217), оу скарбы (S 204);

- Letter в in prefixes and prepositions before consonant (four occurrences):

въ хоудобꙋ (S 157), во великꙋю ганьбꙋ (S 160), невго^л^нꙋ (S 173), въ вере (S 229).

**1.5. The umlaut *'a* > *e* after palatalized consonants (postdentals) and, as a secondary phenomenon, *a* > *e*.** Umlaut *a* > *e* after palatalized consonants is rendered by the substitution of the letter е for ѧ and ꙗ:

жедати (S 203, 212) instead of жѧдати, cf. Polish *żędać*;[61] тресенїе (S 97) and трестисѧ (S 247); оумолче (S 75) formed from оумълчати, cf. Czech *umlčě*.[62]

**1.6. *Cokan'e*: loss of distinction between affricates:**

ѡщищова^ти^ (S 114), цервове (S 161).

**1.7. The rise of *y* < ъ in a weak position after interconsonantal *r* :**

нестривалый (S 218), cf. Czech *nesetrvalý*.

---

[61] This form may also be the result of influence by the Old Polish variant *żędać* along with *żądać*.

[62] This form may have been influenced by the Czech Aorist form *umlčě* (*umlčěti*).

**1.8. The dispalatalization of word-final labials:**
к̏ровъ (S 145) 'blood.'
**1.9. Church Slavonic (South Slavic) Features**:

- reflexes of **tj* as щ in participles, for example:

ч҄тоущїй и҆ молѧщїйсѧ (S 63), и҆моущи (S 94), рекꙋще (S 146), добываю҆щи (S 170), текоущїй (S 242), along with боудꙋчи (S 221); and conjugated forms of the verb хотѣти: хощꙋ (S 22, 26, ), хоще[т] (S 90, 179, 181, etc.).

- Church Slavonic orthographic rendering of syllabic sonorants:

дръжати (S 85), т̏ръпети (S 153), along with мр̏твы[х] (S 233, 250, 259), пер̏выи (S 236, 250).

## 2. Morphology

Linguistic interference of West Slavic elements is also present on the morphological level, exhibited by the following features and their variation with East Slavic equivalents:[63]

### 2.1. Noun

- **Nominative plural in –ове and –еве along with –и:**

жидове (S 82), дивове (S 95), цареве (S 137), грѣхове (S 167), цер̏вове (S 161), along with моры, глади (S 96), ц҃ри (S 125);

- **Genitive plural ending:**

–овъ vs. –оу: ѿцоу (S 119) instead of ѿцовъ, cf. Czech *otců*; lack of animacy (Accusative case plural as in Czech and Polish): боудж[т] соудити <u>моужи и жены</u> (S 190), cf. Czech *súditi budú muže i ženy*.

- **Vocative case:**

сивилло (S 38, 45, 76, etc.).

- **Proper name:**

The use of Саломонъ instead of the expected Соломонъ is rather influenced by Czech *Šalamún* than is a case of akan'e.

### 2.2. Adjective

**(i) Comparative:** Чи[м] старшїй а҆ ты[м] <u>горшїй</u> (S 165), 'worse', in place of the expected хоужїи, cf. Czech *horší*; радеѐ (S 224), cf. Czech *raději*;
**(ii) Contracted adjectives:**[64] которы[ж] (S 43), cf. Czech *který*.

---

[63] Several of the linguistic features discussed here as West Slavic are also found in some East Slavic dialects. However, their appearance in the Ruthenian *Tale of Sivilla* is of West Slavic provenance.

[64] Only masculine singular forms are considered since, in other instances, it is hard to determine whether the form is a contracted long-form adjective or a short adjective.

**2.3. ADVERBS in –є along with East Slavic adverbs in –ѻ:**

добре (S 30, 85), зле (S 230), миле (S 20), справне (S 87), целе (S 88), силне (S 128), cf. Czech *silně*, but ровно (S 239), cf. Czech *rovně*.

**2.4. VERB**

**(i) Present Tense:**

- **Third person singular and plural without –ть :**

ажь сѧ имъ зле стане (S 230), сѧ то стане (S 233), along with [сѧ] станет (S 234, 235, 235, 237, 238, 240, 242); дїаволꙋ достанꙋ (S 231).

- **First person singular ending in –*m*:**

видим (S 48), cf. Czech *vidím*, присѧгам (S 146, 146), cf. Czech *přisáhám*, вемъ (S 54, 90), вѣм (S 101), cf. Czech *viem* along with повѣдаю (S 47, 132), cf. Czech *povědě*.

- **Reflexive forms:**

Reflexive verb стати сѧ (in different forms in S 5, 29, 32, 74, 101, 195, 198, 230, 233, 234, 235, 238, 240, 242) as in Czech *stát se*, Polish *stać się* along with стати (S 194, 207, 236, 237) without a reflexive marker as in East Slavic.

**(ii) Past Tenses:**

- **Perfect with auxiliary:**[65] сивилле гꙋсиѧ нога есть была ѹздравена (S 32–33).
- **Czech Aorist form:** црь ѹмолче того часꙋ (S 75), cf. Czech *umlčěti* vs. Church Slavonic ѹмльчати.

The use of Aorists and Imperfects was already quite uncharacteristic of the fifteenth-century East Slavic vernacular but is often found in fifteenth-century Czech literary language. Since there are signs of intentional Slavonization in the Ruthenian *Tale of Sivilla*, the use of Aorists and Imperfects was also caused by the desire of the translator (or a later copier) to introduce a Church Slavonic stylistic touch. Other examples include:

бѣѧше (S 1, 3, 7, 35), cf. Czech *bieše*; смоущаше (S 10), cf. Czech *stydieše*; ѿвѣща (S 21, 53), cf. Czech *odpovědě*; глаше (S 71), cf. Czech *pravieše*; ѹмолче (S 75), cf. Czech *umlče*.

**(iii) Future Tenses:**

Along with Present Tense forms of perfective verbs with the meaning of Future Tense, there are the following grammatical forms in the Future Tense:

- **Compound Future**: **auxiliary быти with Infinitive:**

а егдаж сѧ боудет хрстиѧнъство множити . тогда ваши люди жидовъскїи боудоут гинꙋти (S 82–84), 'and when Christianity will be spreading, then your Jewish people will be perishing.'

[65] This form is more consistently used in fifteenth-century Czech than in East Slavic.

- **Compound Future: auxiliary выти with Past Participle in *–l* :**

въ десѧ̑тый дн҃ь ҄ктоко҄лве бꙋдеть ҄где сѧ̑ съкрыл (S 248–249), cf. Czech *desátý den, že kdož se kolivěk byl kde ukryl.*

- **Periphrastic Future: inflected form of ймѣти used with Infinitive with the meaning of a predestined future event:**

что сѧ̑ ҄вземлѧх стати маѐть (S 6), cf. Czech *co se v zemiech státi má*, 'what is to happen in the world;' иже сѧ̑ маеть дитѧ̑ … народити (S 40–41), cf. Czech *že se má dietě naroditi*, 'that a child is to be born;' а маѐть оумрти на том ҄древе (S 42), cf. Czech *a to má na tom dřevě potom umřieti*, 'and must die on this tree;' а то сѧ̑ ҄все мает стати (S 74), cf. Czech *a to se všechno státi má*, 'and all this is to happen;' какъ до҄лго свѣт маѐть с҄тоѧ̑ти (S 88), cf. Czech *kterak dlúho svět má státi*, 'how long will the world exist;' вѣм что сѧ̑ маѐть ҄стати (S 101), cf. Czech *věm, co se státi má*, 'I know what will happen.'

**(iv) Optative: радъ with auxiliary and Past Participle in *–l*:**

й рада бых то за ҄правдꙋ ҄звѣдала (S 25–26), cf. Czech *ráda bych to za pravdu zvěděla*, 'I would like to know it;' ради бы вѣдали (S 205–206), cf. Czech *rádi by viděli*, 'they would like to know' along with хотел бых того радъ вѣдати (S 46), cf. Czech *chtěl bych, by mi ji pověděla*, 'I would like to know.'

**(v) Imperative**: повѣж (S 38), cf. Czech *pověz*, along with повѣдай (S 45).

**(vi) Passive Participles without *l*–epentheticum:**[66]

оуздравена (S 33), cf. Czech *uzdravená*, Polish *uzdrowiona*, along with зъ҄ѣавлены (S 50).

## 3. Syntax

### 3.1. Modal meaning of the verb ймѣти:

- **of predestined future (see above);**
- **of obligation:** а тїй кой бы мели земли боронити (S 111), Czech *a ti, jenž by měli země bránit* 'and those who should defend the land;' иже с ним ѐсти ймѣла (S 28-29), Czech *jenž s ním jiesti měla*, 'that should have eaten with him;' имам верити (S 86), Czech *já mám tomu věřiti*, 'I ought to believe.'
- **to express possession (Ruthenian is a "have" language):**

ногꙋ … мѣла (S 9), 'she had a leg.'

### 3.2. Demonstrative (deictic) pronoun as referential expression:

- **Referential expression I (solo):**

[66] Participial forms without *l*–epentheticum are characteristic of West Slavic.

бѣаше пр͠рчица$_i$ ѕвѣздарька$_i$ имене^м сивилла, а та$_i$ бѣаше велми моудра (S 2–3), cf. Czech *bieše prorokyně*$_i$ *hvězdářka*$_i$, *jménem Sybilla a ta*$_i$ *bieše převelmi múdrá*, 'there was a prophetess$_i$ astrologer$_i$ by the name of Sibylla and she$_i$ was very wise;' в тый часы настане^т єдина звѣзда$_i$ на нб҃ѣ. [...] а та$_i$ боудe^т знаменати... (S 95), cf. Czech *v ty časy nastane jedna hvězda*$_i$ *na nebi* [...] *a ta*$_i$ *bude znamenati* ..., 'at this time there will rise a star$_i$ in the sky [...] and this star$_i$ will signify...;'

- **Referential expression II (with noun):** то^т (то) / тот же то[67]

а та бѣаше велми моудра$_i$ [...] та$_i$ єй моу^дрость$_i$ є^с ѿ бг҃а дана (S 3, 6),[68] 'and she was very wise [...] this wisdom of hers was from God.'

Although the usage of *tot* as a referential expression is listed here as a syntactical feature, the overall frequency of the usage of this pronoun in Ruthenian, directly influenced by Czech (and indirectly by Polish), suggests that it was acquired lexically.

### 3.3. Prepositions and their Government:[69]

- **во^дле / по^дле, 'according to' with Genitive (cf. Czech *vedlé*, *podlé*, Polish *wedle*, *podle* with Genitive):**[70] боудж^т сѹдити моужи и жены во^дле приязни ... а не по^дле правды (S 191–192);
- **за, 'during, in the time of' with Genitive:** за моудраго цр҃ѧ саломона (S 1);
- **w, 'for' with Accusative:** воевати ѡ ри^мское цр^ство (S 127);
- **по, 'after' with Locative:** ажь было и по ѡбѣде (S 36–37), боуде^т по четырнадесѧти^х сте^х лете^х (S 91–92), по х^свѣ нарожєнїи (S 92), по перво^м и по седми десѧти лете^х (S 101–102), по єго смр҃ти (S 135);
- **пре^с**, along with **черезъ:** и приго^дилосѧ [...] пре^с адамово древо ити [...] и не хотѣла єсть черезъ єго ити (S 30–31);
- **c and зъ, 'from, of' with Genitive (cf. Czech and Polish *z*) along with ис:** иже сѧ маеть дитѧ ис тебе на то^т то свѣ^т наро^ди^ти зъ дв҃ы (S 40–41), cf. Czech *že se má dietě naroditi* ***jistě*** [71] *na tento svět z panny*; выити ис смысловъ (S 186), cf. Czech *z smysla vystúpiti*.

### 3.4. Conjunctions in Subordinate Clauses:

- **purpose clauses with абы 'in order to/that ...' (cf. Czech and Polish *aby*):**

---

[67] Frequent use of *tot (že to)* is characteristic of Czech.

[68] The attested Czech texts do not coincide with the Ruthenian translation in this sentence.

[69] The following prepositions and/or their usage are characteristic of West Slavic and are not common in East Slavic.

[70] For the detailed discussion of these prepositions, see Hruca 1976.

[71] The Ruthenian ис тебе, 'from you,' is a mistranslation of the Czech adverb *jistě*, 'certainly.'

ѧбы изволилъ вѣдати (S 22–23), то проꙋто ѧбы искоꙋси свои оу вере (S 216), ѧбы в тоⷨ прирожеⷩи кагалъсѧ ѧ мел съкрꙋшеніє срⷣца (S 222), ѧбы затрачоⷩ чл҃къ не быⷧ но радеѐ избавленъ (S 223), ради бы вѣдали бы все было въ иⷯ вѣне (S 205–206).

- **object clauses with иже бы and же 'that' (Polish że, żeby and Czech *že, žeby*):** ижe бы моглъ мꙋдрый то вѣдаⷮ (S 185–186).
- **прото and а протоⷤ, 'for that reason' (Czech *proto, protože*):**

и прото ижеⷭ жаⷣнаа правда скоро не станеть (S 193), то прото ѧбы искоꙋси свои оу вере (S 216), и протоⷤ люⷣи не боꙋдоуⷮ ихъ въ чти мети (S 105).

**3.5. Coordination: conjunction а meaning 'and' (cf. Czech and Old Polish usage) along with и :**

- а

боємъ збито боꙋдеⷮ а оу великꙋю нꙋжꙋ и въ хоꙋдобꙋ много иⷯ оупадеⷮ . много съжьжено а побиєно боꙋдеⷮ много мечеⷨ а звлаштиє господарьство погыбнеⷮ а воинъство (S 156-160);

- и

и знаєма бѣѧше . и бѧше красна . а богата (S 6–7), боꙋдеⷮ чл҃къ. и истинный б҃ъ. а боꙋдеⷮ іс҃ хс҃ назваⷩ. (S 56).

**3.6. Position of the Reflexive Particle сѧ.** In most cases the reflexive particle appears after the first stressed word as in Czech:

что сѧ в землаⷯ стати маєть (S 6), cf. Czech *co se v zemiech státi má*; иже сѧ маєть дитѧ нароⷣити (S 40–41), cf. Czech *že se má dietě naroditi*; а то сѧ все маєⷮ стати (S 74), cf. Czech *a to se všechno státi má.*

A comparison with the Czech *Proroctví Sibyllino* shows that in cases where сѧ does not appear in the second place in the Ruthenian translation, the same holds true for Czech. For example: а в тоⷮ чаⷭ сталъ сѧ єсть дивъ ѿ бг҃а (S 32), cf. Czech *tu ihned od Boha stal se div veliký*; дрꙋгы дн҃ь дивъ сѧ станетъ (S 237), cf. Czech *druhý den div se stane.*

## 4. Lexicon

Along with Church Slavonic features the text contains a considerable West Slavic lexical component either of Czech or Polish origin. The following is a selective list of lexemes arranged by parts of speech:

### 4.1. Noun

вады (S 155), cf. Czech *váda*, Polish *wada*, гаⷩбы, ганьбꙋ (S 104, 160), cf. Czech *hanba*, Polish *gańba*, грозы (S 249), cf. Czech *hruoza*, Polish *groza*, замоꙋтокъ

(S 143), cf. Czech *zámutek*, Polish *zamęt*, зв҃лаштиѥ (S 159), звлаш҃тный (S 235), cf. Czech *zvlášti*, *zvláščě*, *zvláščni*, Polish *zwłaszcza*, ѕвѣздарька (S 2) instead of ѕвѣздочьтьца, cf. Czech *hvězdářka*, Polish *gwiazdarz*, зл҃одей (S 113), cf. Czech *zloděj*, Polish *złodziej*, зр҃ады (S 154), cf. Czech and Polish *zrada*, кл҃обоукъ (S 181), cf. Czech *klobúk*, Polish *kłobuk*, ѡ красе (S 13) along with ѡ красотѣ (S 24), cf. Czech *krása*, Polish *krasa*, лȣпежи (S 154), cf. Czech *lúpeži*, мѣ҃ста (S 205), мор҃ди (S 154), cf. Czech and Polish *mord*, мор҃дери (S 112), cf. Czech and Polish *morderz*, моць (S 121), cf. Czech and Polish *moc*, в том ѡ҃крȣгле (S 48-49), cf. Czech *okršlek*, *okrúhle*, Polish *okrągło*, панѧ[X], пан҃на[X] (S 173), cf. Czech and Polish *pani* and *panna*, папежи (S 200), cf. Czech *papež*, Polish *papeż*, погор҃шенїѥ (S 211), cf. Czech *pohoršenie*, Polish *pogorszenie*, поз[д]виженїѥ (S 210), cf. Czech *pozdviženie*, полеп҃шенїѥ (S 164), cf. Czech *polepšenie*, Polish *polepszenie*, пот҃воры (S 240), cf. Czech *potwora* and Polish *potwór*, потребȣ (S 212), cf. Czech *potřeba*, Polish *potrzeba*, прик҃ладе[X] (S 110), cf. Czech *příklad*, Polish *przykład*, п҃сота (S 143), cf. Czech and Polish *psota*, пыхы (S 169), пыхи (S 210), cf. Czech and Polish *pycha*, в … реча[X] (S 4), cf. Czech *řeč*, Polish *rzecz* 'thing,' свар (S 200), cf. Czech *svár*, Polish *swar*, сп҃рав҃не (S 87), cf. Czech *sprav mě*, *spravně*, оудоли (S 248), cf. Czech *údolí*, оуставе[н]їѧ (S 58), cf. Czech *ustavenie*, Polish *ustawienie*, фальши (S 154), фал҃шенїѥ (S 98), фальшьнос҃ть (S 187), cf. Czech *faleš*, *falešnost*, Polish *fałsz*, часы (S 79, 93, 108, 187), cf. Czech *časy*, Polish *czasy* 'time,' шкоды (S 151), cf. Czech *škody*, Polish *szkody*.

**4.2. ADJECTIVE**

вале[ч]ного (T 2), cf. Czech *valečný*, Polish *waleczny*, жа[д]наѧ (S 194), жа[д]ного (S 66), cf. Czech *žadný*, Polish *żadny*, нестривалый (S 218), cf. Czech *nesetrvalý*, рȣгава (S 68), cf. Czech *rúhavá*, с҃талый (S 217, 218), cf. Czech *stalý*, Polish *stały*.

**4.3. PRONOUN**

- Indefinite pronoun with кол҃ве(къ), cf. Czech *kolvěk*, Polish *kolwiek*: ачькол҃векъ (S 77), к҃то кол҃ве (S 248), ѩкоко[л]ве (S 137).

**4.4. VERB**

- **'to say, tell, respond'**: зв҃ѣдала (S 26), cf. Czech *zvěděla*, ѿповѣдила (S 40), ѿповѣдала (S 47) along with ѿвѣща (S 53), cf. Czech (*od*)*pověde*. Other forms are повѣдай (S 45), повѣдаю (S 132), сподвѣдай (S 196).
- **other verbs**

–гин–/–гыбн–: гинȣти (S 84), загине[т] (S 187), погыноу[т] (S 256, 257) along with погыбне[т] (S 159) cf. Czech *hynúti*, *zahyne*; забиѥть (S 123), cf. Czech *zabie*, моусишь (S 27), мȣси (S 127), cf. Czech *musiti*, Polish *musić*, сѧ… наро[ди]ти (S 41, 52), cf. Czech *se...naroditi*, сѧ [на то] ѡ҃братити (S 69), cf. Czech *se...*

*obratiti*, 'convert;' ѿм[е]длею[т] (S 199), cf. Czech *zemdlejí*, Polish *omgleć*, *omdleć*, подѧковала (S 20), cf. Czech *poděkovala*, Polish *podziękować*, п҆рацовала (S 21), cf. Czech *se…trudila*, Polish *pracować się*, п҆рестали (S 118), cf. Czech *přestala*, Polish *przestać*, пригоди[ло] сѧ̑ (S 29), cf. Czech *přihodi se*, Polish *przygodzić się*, поукати сѧ (S 246), cf. Czech *pukati se*, Polish *pukać się*, с҆лоу̑ти (S 131) along with с҆лыти (S 137), с҆падне[т] (S 238), cf. Czech *spadne*, Polish *spaść*, не оу̑канеть (S 237), cf. Czech *neukane*, Polish *ukanąć*, ховати (S 113, 121), сѧ̑… ховати (S 104), cf. Czech *chovati se*, Polish *chować się* 'behave.'

**4.5. PAST PASSIVE PARTICIPLE**

затрачо[н] (S 223), cf. Czech *zatracen*, 'lost.'

**4.6. ADVERB:**

те[ж] (S 11) cf. Polish *też*, се[м] (S 21), cf. Czech *sem*, зде и҆ и҆н҆де (S 122), cf. Czech and Polish *zde i jinde*.

**4.7. PARTICLE**

The use of the particles *–žto* and *to* is a stylistic trait of Old Czech. Its influence in the Ruthenian translations is reflected in the comparable frequency of occurrence of ж(е) то and тот то:

- ж(е) то: ıако[ж] то (S 11, 33);
- Demonstrative pronoun with то: на то[т]то свѣ[т] (S 41).

**4.8. CONJUNCTION**

абъı 'in order to/that…' (S 22, 216, 222, 223), cf. Czech and Polish *aby*; а҆бо (S 164, 170, 173, 195), cf. Czech *anebo*, Polish *abo*, а҆жь (S 36, 80, 230), cf. Czech *až*, Polish *aże*, а҆ни (S 36, 66, 69, 177), а҆ни[ж] (S 106), cf. Czech *aniž*, Polish *aniż*, пакъ (S 228), cf. Czech and Polish *pak*, прото (S 193, 216), а прото[ж] (S 10, 105), cf. Czech *proto*, *protože*. Church Slavonic: понеже (S 16, 211), cf. Czech *nebo*; егда (S 27, 30, 78, etc.), cf. Czech *když*; ѿ҆баче (S 78, 127, 138), cf. Czech *(a)však*; вѧще (S 126, 136, 203), cf. Czech *viece*.

**4.9. Fall of initial *ji–*:**[72]

- **мѣти - и҆мѣти 'to have' (cf. Czech *měti*, Polish *mieć*):**

мѣти (S 67), мети (S 106, 182, 212), along with и҆мѣти (S 121, 134, 178), и҆мети (S 177, 181), ме[л] (S 223), along with и҆мѣлъ е҆сть; мѣла (S 9) along with и҆мѣла (S 29), мѣло (S 70), мели (S 111); има[м] (S 86), мае҆ть (S 6, 40, 42, 52, 74, 88, 90, 101, 196, 198);

- **з - из 'from' (cf. Czech and Polish *z*):**

з ноуже (S 43). It is also present in such words as з҆рады (S 154), cf. Czech and

[72] This feature is listed in Lexicon since its occurrence in Ruthenian is a result of a lexical transfer rather than of independent phonological development.

Polish *zrady*, з̏вѣдала (S 26), cf. Czech *zvěděla*, Polish *zwiedzieć*, с̏кажено (S 70, 109), cf. Czech *zkaženo*.

**4.10. Czech-type non-pleophonic forms**

The use of Czech non-pleophonic forms could have been assisted by their resemblance to Church Slavonic forms which suited the stylistic attitude of the translator: глади (S 96) along with голоᴬ (S 150), д̏рево (S 30, 39, 245), з̏лато (S 255), напреᴬ (S 196), преᴬ (S 233), п̏ре̏стали (S 118).

## CONCLUSION

As in the other Ruthenian texts, the *Song of Songs* and the *Book of Taudal the Knight*, the linguistic analysis of the *Tale of Sivilla the Prophetess* shows a mixture of West and East Slavic features, which occurs on all linguistic levels. In all three texts, the presence of the West Slavic element is more noticeable in the syntax and lexicon. It is to a lesser degree present in the morphology, whereas its occurrence on the phonological level is primarily due to lexical transfer.

The textual comparison of the Ruthenian *Tale of Sivilla the Prophetess* with the two extant Czech versions of this text shows that it is a very close translation from Czech. There is an insubstantial but, nevertheless, visible Church Slavonic linguistic component in the language of the translation that either results from the translator's desire to enrich his style, or is due to a Slavonization of the translation in the course of subsequent copying.

# Chapter Seven
# ANATOMY OF RUTHENIAN: LINGUISTIC SHIFT AND LITERACY CONTACT

Unfortunately, historical linguists and philologists cannot benefit from making use of informants to confirm their scholarly conjectures. Instead, they are left with the less reliable options of theorizing and hypothesizing. Even with these, it may not be possible to establish actual motivations and mechanisms of Ruthenian language formation as it occurred some time around the fifteenth century. Nonetheless, an attempt can be made to reconstruct the beginnings of Ruthenian as a written language by utilizing both what we know about the writing habits and attitudes in the fifteenth and sixteenth-century Grand Duchy of Lithuania, and what we can infer from extant texts.

## LINGUISTIC VARIATION. EAST SLAVIC – POLISH (WEST SLAVIC) VARIATION

The main difficulty in defining and analyzing written Ruthenian has always arisen from the fact that this language of writing was never standardized at the time of its existence, and that it was used in a large number of diverse texts with diverse functions displaying considerable linguistic variation.[1] If we look closely, though, we will discover that linguistic variation in Ruthenian texts is not entirely chaotic and inexplicable, and further that while the extent to which various linguistic features are present varies from one text to another, the essence of these features remains relatively consistent. Let us then consider the nature of linguistic variation in Ruthenian and identify its different layers. Once these layers are recognized, the seemingly motley language of Ruthenian texts may prove less perplexing.

One aspect of variation in Ruthenian, generally agreed on but still worthy of reconsideration, is the co-existence of East Slavic and Polish – or rather West Slavic – linguistic features.[2] Although the presence of the Polish component in

[1] Under "linguistic variation" I understand the existence of more than one variant for designating a single linguistic phenomenon.

[2] It is accurate to speak more generally about West Slavic (rather than separately about Polish and Czech) because in the fifteenth and sixteenth centuries literary Polish was to a great degree inspired and influenced by Czech, and the indirect influence of Czech also shows to some extent in Ruthenian.

Ruthenian is traditionally treated as an example of lexical borrowing, East Slavic – Polish variation is consistently present on all linguistic levels (except phonology / orthography). This fact raises an important theoretical question about the linguistic nature of written Ruthenian and necessitates a new critical and conceptual approach to this language, a task to which I hope to contribute in this chapter.

## ORTHOGRAPHIC VARIATION: THE DIALECTAL BASE

Another aspect of linguistic variation in Ruthenian is essentially orthographic and consists in the rather free fluctuation of Ukrainian and Belarusian linguistic features. Unfortunately, this circumstance has defined the traditional approach to Ruthenian texts, the object of which has been to identify and delimit Ukrainian and Belarusian records. Such an approach considers Ruthenian texts from the point of view of the modern division of languages. They are divided into Old Belarusian and Old Ukrainian according to their phonological traits. It is true that histories of Belarusian and Ukrainian must be based on data attested in texts from ethnically Belarusian and Ukrainian territories, yet it is not necessary and may not even be functional to label fifteenth-century Ruthenian texts as either Belarusian or Ukrainian. After all, the standardization and normalization of modern literary Belarusian and Ukrainian are relatively recent events.[3] Modern Ukrainian literary language came into being at the beginning of the nineteenth century, while the emergence of literary Belarusian came about even later, at the end of the nineteenth and beginning of the twentieth century.[4] Besides, language standardization was based primarily on political and administrative decisions, in which certain dialects of Belarusian and Ukrainian were chosen as a basis for the literary language.[5]

Various attempts have been made to establish a principle for the separation of Ukrainian historical documents from Belarusian. For example, Shevelov has proposed guidelines for delimiting Ukrainian records from Belarusian on the basis of phonological traits.[6] His main criteria are (i) confusion of the letters *e* and *ě* (a Belarusian feature) and (ii) confusion of the letters *i* and *y* (a Ukrainian

[3] By standardization I mean the choice of a language standard from among different varieties; by normalization I mean a prescriptive approach to language description.

[4] McMillin 1980, Shevelov 1980, Pritsak 1984, Strumins'kyj 1984.

[5] Central dialects for Belarusian (McMillin 1980, 113) and Southeast dialects for Ukrainian (Shevelov 1980, 152).

[6] Shevelov 1979, 398–402.

feature). However, practically no Ruthenian texts display either exclusively Belarusian or Ukrainian linguistic traits. As Shevelov himself stated: "As a rule, the Early Middle Ukrainian period bequeathed virtually no texts which could be characterized as straight Ukrainian."[7] On the other hand, determining the dialectal base of Ruthenian texts of the medieval period is problematic because these texts do not reflect the actual state of the spoken language. We should not forget that phonological characteristics are disguised behind various orthographic practices.

As is typical for the medieval period, Ruthenian bookmen had no concept of a normalized literary language. They formed literary practices by custom, not prescription, and even then the exemplification was mostly concerned with orthography. Although orthography was conservative in absorbing local (Belarusian and Ukrainian) phonetic features, nonetheless, some local traits crept into writing. At the same time, the lack of a standardized language and intensified attention to orthography allowed for a relatively unrestricted flow of a new lexical, morphological and syntactical element into written language, which arose mostly from contact with Polish. Recopying caused further variation in language. Scribes were often active in locations other than their place of training or birth, and they imported their own phonetic features into local writings. Although all chanceries were involved in elaborating linguistic practices of the administrative language, the princely chancery in Vilnius had greater authority and influence. As a result, an orthography that reflected Belarusian linguistic features acquired greater social prestige at a certain time and was preferred by scribes regardless of their native pronunciation.[8]

The abovementioned circumstances are complicated by another fact. While the modern definition of Belarusian and Ukrainian is supported by the existence of literary standardized languages, the language of the Belarusian-Ukrainian territory in the fifteenth and sixteenth centuries, having no codified norm, represented a dialectal continuum (especially in Palesse / Polissia).[9] Thus, texts might display vernacular linguistic traits characteristic of Belarusian or Ukrainian development in different proportions at different times depending on the individual manuscript.

Because most texts contain both Ukrainian and Belarusian linguistic traits, the same sources are used in Shevelov's *A Historical Phonology of the Ukrain-*

[7] Shevelov 1979, 398.

[8] This may be the reason why the documents originating in ethnic Ukrainian territories contain Belarusian phonological features.

[9] Shevelov 1979, 399.

*ian Language*[10] and Wexler's *A Historical Phonology of the Belorussian Language*.[11] Among them are such well-known sources as translations of Bielski and Stryjkowski's chronicles, Filalet's *Apokrysis*, *Apostol of Krekhiv*, Berynda's *Lexicon*, and works of Zizanii.

Conversely, if we turn to those studies that claim to follow the territorial principle, we will see that they are less than consistent, and even contradict their own tenets. For example, the introduction to *The Old Ukrainian Dictionary of the Fourteenth and Fifteenth Centuries* states that its choice of Ukrainian sources is based on territorial divisions, not linguistic considerations.[12] However, if we look at the list of the sources, we find that a great number of records come from Vilnius, Trakai, and Grodno, not at all ethnically Ukrainian territories.

The phonological principle, though necessary and appropriate for the diachronic analysis of Ukrainian and Belarusian phonological systems, is methodologically inappropriate for the synchronic linguistic categorization of fifteenth- and sixteenth-century Ruthenian texts. After all, it is important to keep in mind that though individual Belarusian and Ukrainian linguistic features appear occasionally in Ruthenian texts, orthography in general was rather disrespectful to local phonetic features. The reason for this linguistic attitude was aptly expressed by Paul Wexler:

> The formal fixation of an orthography is a good illustration of the superdialectal function of the written norm. Standardized orthographies usually fail to reflect the phonetic realities of the spoken word not because of the conservative character of orthography vis-à-vis the spoken language which is in a constant state of change, but also because orthographies are more efficient when they have cross-dialectal application.[13]

Stefan Pugh, for example, in his study of Meletii Smotryts'kyi's literary language, pointed out that although Smotryts'kyi's dialectal base (constrained by orthography) can be characterized as Ruthenian-Ukrainian, his morphology is noticeably Ruthenian-Belarusian.[14]

---

[10] Shevelov 1979.

[11] Wexler 1977.

[12] "Питання розмежування українських і білоруських пам'яток писемності XV–XVII ст. у цьому словнику спиралося не на мовний, а на територіальний принцап." [The question of delimitating fifteenth and sixteenth-century Ukrainian and Belarusian documents in this dictionary has been approached geographically, not linguistically.] (Humets'ka 1977, 9)

[13] Wexler 1971, 336.

[14] Pugh 1985.

This desire to delineate and separate became a serious impediment to the comprehensive linguistic characterization of Ruthenian. It completely ignores the fact that the co-existence of Ukrainian and Belarusian traits in one and the same text was a reality of literary Ruthenian, and should be accepted as a characteristic feature of this language. Moreover, speaking in socio-historical terms, predecessors of both Ukrainians and Belarusians lived in one state and shared a religious creed, forming a common political and cultural community. They even identified themselves as members of the same speech community, which they called *iazyk rus'ki*.

## STYLISTIC VARIATION: BAKHTINIAN *SPEECH GENRES* (FUNCTIONAL STYLES)

An additional kind of linguistic heterogeneity, while not unique to Ruthenian, played an important role in its development and use. In scholarly literature, the term Ruthenian refers to any of several varieties, which are sometimes treated as separate languages. The first in this list is Chancery Ruthenian, the administrative language of the Grand Duchy of Lithuania, a language of statutes, state documents, and Lithuanian chronicles. Chancery Ruthenian is fairly well described in a number of works and is supported by several historical dictionaries.[15] What is also considered a more or less separate variety is the language of religious polemical literature, which developed at the end of the sixteenth century and continued to be used in seventeenth-century religious disputes. Although no general account has been produced, there are studies of the language of individual Ruthenian authors that describe their idiolects (such as the language of Smotryts'kyi, Vyshens'kyi, and Galiatovs'kyi).[16] The existence of popular ecclesiastical prose and biblical translations written in the Ruthenian vernacular has been largely overlooked, with the exception of Skaryna's biblical translations, on which an extensive literature has been produced. This is due to a tradition that considers the language of ecclesiastical genres to be a Ruthenian variant of Church Slavonic or a Hybrid Ruthenian Church Slavonic, even though there are texts with almost no Church Slavonic features.[17] Although the above-mentioned varieties are now and then referred to as Ruthenian, there has been no

---

[15] Karskii 1894 and 1962, Ptashitskii 1887, Stang 1935 and 1939, Humets'ka 1977.

[16] Pugh 1985 and 1996, Frick 1985, Gröschel 1972, Witkowski 1969, etc.

[17] Robert Mathiesen even distinguishes between Ruthenian Middle Church Slavonic – among the Orthodox Slavs in the fourteenth and fifteenth centuries – and Ruthenian Catholic Late Church Slavonic – among the Catholic Slavs in the sixteenth and seventeenth centuries (Mathiesen 1984, 470).

attempt to compare them and derive a systematic description of the language(s) they represent. Yet until such a description is produced, the term Ruthenian will remain an ambiguously defined linguistic concept.

Even a cursory overview of these varieties makes it clear that such a division is based principally on differences in the function of the texts, differences which also exist in all modern languages. It is obvious that the language of business documents, polemical treatises, epistles, religious meditations, and popular ecclesiastical literature (with its quasi-aesthetic elements) must be stylistically differentiated. Consequently, linguistic variation in Ruthenian also derives from the stylistic choices a writer must make, choices that depend on the text's purpose as well as on the individual preference of the writer or the scribe. It is precisely this kind of linguistic variation that Bakhtin delineated in his concept of speech genres and corresponding styles. He described speech genres through the definition of an utterance:

> Language is realized in the form of individual concrete utterances (oral and written) by participants in the various areas of human activity. These utterances reflect the specific conditions and goals of each such area not only through their content (thematic) and linguistic style, that is, the selection of the lexical, phraseological, and grammatical resources of the language, but above all through their compositional structure. All three of these aspects – thematic content, style, and compositional structure – are inseparably linked to the *whole* of the utterance and are equally determined by the specific nature of the particular sphere of communication. Each separate utterance is individual, of course, but each sphere in which language is used develops its own *relatively stable types* of these utterances. These we may call *speech genres*.[18]

Thus, speech genres are typical forms of utterances and should be classified in terms of spheres of human activity. Bakhtin called attention to the extreme heterogeneity of speech genres and emphasized that their study should be connected with the study of styles, especially when historical change is in question:

> It is especially harmful to separate style from genre when elaborating historical problems. Historical changes in language styles are inseparably linked to changes in speech genres. Literary language is a complex, dynamic system of linguistic styles.[19]

Speakers' specific linguistic choices are a stylistic act, be it a particular lexeme, a particular grammatical form, a particular syntactic structure, or a particular

---

[18] Bakhtin 1986, 60.
[19] Bakhtin 1986, 65.

language. In this regard, the intrusion of Polish into Ruthenian may also be considered a stylistic act.

Closely related to the linguistic characteristics of style in Ruthenian are several extra-linguistic factors. These include the level of language competence and language habits of individuals, in particular, their social and aesthetic attitudes toward the use of various languages, and tolerance with regard to mixing languages or to "incorrect language." Such factors as a speaker's facility of verbal expression, his manner of learning, and relative proficiency in each language, even if at times difficult to account for, should also be considered where possible.

One of the factors that assisted the development of Ruthenian styles was the influence of humanistic ideas that came from the West and affected language attitudes in the Polish-Lithuanian Commonwealth. These ideas led to the secularization of written language and its gradual emancipation from the Church Slavonic canon in certain spheres. Circumstances became favorable for using language to express individuality. It goes without saying that not all genres allow for expression of the author's personality and style to the same degree:

> Various genres can reveal various layers and facets of the individual personality, and individual style can be found in various interrelations with the national language (общенародный язык). The very problem of the national (общенародное) and the individual (индивидуальное) in language is basically the problem of the utterance (after all, only here, in the utterance, is the national language embodied in individual form).[20]

Speech genres that require a standard form (a canon) would have a larger amount of shared features, features that represent collective linguistic activity (what Bakhtin calls "общенародное"). The chancery language, for example, was more or less uniform and full of phraseological formulas, whereas the language of popular ecclesiastical literature, such as saints' lives, visions, and edificatory prose, was relatively free from linguistic conventions. Accordingly, the style of ecclesiastical prose contains a higher proportion of the individual to the collective in language use. It is here that the influence of Polish in written Ruthenian was most evident, since the social and cultural prestige of Polish as a literary language served as a means of elevating style and allowed the infiltration of an even greater number of Polonisms than were already present in the spoken language.

---

[20] Bakhtin 1986, 63.

## LANGUAGE CONTACT AND LITERACY CONTACT

Reflecting on the genesis of Ruthenian, one cannot but ask a naive question: how did it come about that Ruthenian, as attested by written records of the fifteenth and sixteenth centuries, was so similar to Polish and so distant from the Muscovite language? It is true that Belarusian and Ukrainian dialects, which constituted the dialectal base of Ruthenian,[21] were already essentially different from the Great Russian (Muscovite) dialects, and were continuously diverging.[22] It is also true that language contact between Belarusian and Ukrainian dialects and Polish brought about language interference and language mixing, especially in borderland dialects. However, these provide only partial explanation. A more complete answer to the above question may be found only by examining the relationship between conventions of literacy and vernacular language use in the practice of Ruthenian bookmen as well as the socio-historical and cultural contexts of language contact in the Grand Duchy and the Polish-Lithuanian Commonwealth during this period.

The contact of Ruthenian communities with a socially and culturally dominant Polish milieu gradually produced a shift in their language, which contributed to the genesis of their written vernacular. Still, language contact in itself does not necessarily bring about language mixing and language shift. If the speakers of different languages remain in steady contact, retaining well-defined and established social roles, language shift may not occur. Language shift occurs under particular political, social, and economic circumstances, those that, on the one hand, increase interaction among speakers of different languages, and on the other, decrease the inclination to maintain linguistic distinctions. Research in social psychology gave rise to the communication accommodation theory (CAT), which has been effectively employed in analyzing cross-ethnic and cross-cultural communication.[23] It suggests that speakers modify their speech by adapting to the speech of others in order to reduce social differences. Language in this situation partakes in the relationship between power and culture. If the whole group feels a need, often unconscious, for social integration, its linguistic behavior may cause speech convergence.[24]

---

[21] Belarusian (and West Russian) and Ukrainian (and South Russian) dialects.

[22] Shevelov 1979.

[23] It is also known as speech accommodation theory (SAT) developed by a group of scholars headed by Howard Giles (Giles 1977; Giles and Smith 1979; Giles, Coupland and Coupland 1991).

[24] Giles, Coupland and Coupland 1991, 18–19.

In all probability, such a need was perceived by the East Slavic speakers of the Grand Duchy of Lithuania. It is quite revealing that among Ruthenians, the idea of an ecclesiastical union between Catholic and Orthodox believers was relatively favorably received in the fifteenth century, as compared to its absolute repudiation in Muscovy. Language shift in Ruthenia reflected this cultural climate: it is not surprising that the political and confessional flexibility of the Ruthenians likewise manifested itself in a linguistic flexibility, or a linguistic allegiance – an inclination to imitate a cultured Polish idiom resulted in the convergence of linguistic structures of East and West Slavic in the language of Ruthenians.

Given this context, let us try to comprehend a medieval literate mind and consider what happened when a scribe trained in a particular written language tried to implement what he knew about writing in this language into one with no literacy. Once a Ruthenian bookman departed from Church Slavonic towards the vernacular, he departed the field of strict literacy and entered the sphere of orality. This situation required that he use literary techniques developed in other "literate" languages. Obviously, he needed a model for imitation, and in the case of Ruthenian he found such a model in Polish literary language, and to a lesser degree in Church Slavonic.[25] This dependence on Polish or any other literary language's assistance is especially apparent in Ruthenian translations. In particular, translations from other cognate Slavic languages (Czech and Polish) opened a channel for literacy contact.

As I have already stated in the Introduction, Ruthenian literacy is a result of the relationship between the vernacular and the literary language. This is best seen in the following formula:

> **WRITTEN/LITERARY RUTHENIAN = VERNACULAR + LITERACY,**
> where
> **VERNACULAR** = Belarusian + Ukrainian spoken dialects + spoken Polish
> **LITERACY** = the knowledge of Church Slavonic + Polish literary languages

Consequently, as far as Ruthenian writing is concerned we deal with two kinds of literacy: Cyrillic literacy – a result of vernacularization of Church Slavonic – and Polish literacy – a product of internal development of the Polish literary language. These two kinds of literacy, when brought in contact, began interacting with each other, giving rise to Ruthenian literacy.

---

[25] The degree of dependence on either Polish or Church Slavonic was governed by the scribe's ideological and cultural orientation (see Introduction).

In Ruthenian-Polish linguistic and literacy contact we observe a similar pattern as was noted by Górnicki and Sandecki for the Czech and Polish relationship in the sixteenth century (see Chapter One). In both instances a more elaborate and culturally prestigious language functioned as a model for its less advanced genetically related neighbor. At the same time, while the status of Polish as a language of political and social prestige made it a serious rival of the written language of the Ruthenians, the importance of Cyrillic script as a symbol of Ruthenian Orthodox identity[26] was crucial to the cultivation and preservation of the independent status of written Ruthenian, which could have otherwise been absorbed by Polish completely. In general, to understand the cultural and political scene of Lithuanian Rus' lands, one must emphasize the significance of script in validating the contact between languages and confessions.[27] The choice of a script played a crucial role in cultural and textual transmission from Roman Catholic and Protestant lands into Orthodox Ruthenia. Speaking in structuralist linguistic terms, Cyrillic script became a distinctive feature of Ruthenian, thereby violating unshakable conventions that view notation systems as secondary and extra-linguistic.

Thus, two distinguishable but interrelated processes could be supposed to underlie the creation of Ruthenian texts. One is a systematic linguistic process of language contact between the speakers of Belarusian/Ukrainian dialects and the Poles, which resulted in language interference, mixing, and koineization; the other – the process of literacy contact, which introduced literacy interference from Polish and Church Slavonic into the language of emerging Ruthenian writings.

## From "Imperfect Learning" to Substratum Interference

The presence of a West Slavic linguistic component in the Ruthenian texts is traditionally explained by borrowing from Polish.[28] However, if it were indeed a process of systematic borrowing, what would be the reason for it in a language that already possessed its own equivalents? A borrowing usually fills a gap in a linguistic system, that is, it either creates a signifier for a concept not previously

[26] Ruthenian, first a language of the Orthodox Eastern Slavs, later became also a language of the Uniates.

[27] Mieses 1919.

[28] 'Borrowing' belongs to linguistic terms that may be used both in a broad and in a very narrow sense. It is the application of this term in a narrow sense that I do not advocate concerning the formation of Ruthenian.

represented (signified), or it allows an already signified concept to gain a new stylistic meaning. Such was not the case with Ruthenian: Polish and East Slavic equivalents exist side by side in one and the same Ruthenian texts. Rather, the infusion of a Polish component into Ruthenian should be explained by interference and language mixing. Linguistic interference is a rearrangement of already existing patterns, a reorganization of oppositions in a system, and the presence of variation is one of its main indicators. It marks a transitional state between the existence of two independent linguistic systems and the establishment of a third one, which emerges as a result of the confluence of elements from the two mixing languages.[29]

Generally, language contact theory distinguishes a dichotomy between borrowing and substratum interference (or shift-induced interference).[30] These two processes refer to different contact situations and produce different results. Borrowing interference occurs when a second language in a variety of ways and contexts influences the speakers' native language. Substratum interference, in contrast, occurs as a result of the imperfect learning of a target language, i.e. when the speakers' native language influences the way they use a target language. In this sense "imperfect learning" can be understood as covering a whole spectrum of inadequate usage of a target language. Additionally, in a situation of substratum interference "a shifting population is socio-politically subordinate to the people whose language they are shifting to."[31] In borrowing situations, interference is said to be stronger in lexicon and much weaker in syntax and phonology, whereas substratum interference mostly involves transferal of syntax and phonology.

Interpreting the term substratum interference broadly, it is possible to argue that the route to the genesis of Ruthenian lay through imperfect language transmission, which occurred as a result of the inadequate use of a target language. In the case of Ruthenian, "imperfect learning" implies stylistic imitation or the replication of Polish by Ruthenians, which occurs quite easily in contact between cognate languages.[32] This agrees with the formula of imperfect language transmission, proposed by Thomason and Kaufman, which states:

---

[29] Linguistic interference is a 'deviation from the norms of either language' (Weinreich 1968, 1).

[30] For detailed discussion and bibliography, see Thomason 2001.

[31] Thomason 2001, 75.

[32] On a naive level of observation this could be compared to the case of immigrants who intentionally demonstrate the extent of integration into a target language by phonetic accommodation, extensive borrowing, code-switching, and using calques in their native language.

If a whole population acquires a new language within possibly as little as a single lifetime, therefore necessarily other than by parental or peer-group enculturation, the linguistic system which results may have massive interference from the structure(s) of the language(s) originally spoken by the group. If this population is not integrated into the group that provided it with a new language, this deviant form of speech may crystallize into a new language.[33]

In the process of interference there is always a "giving" side and a "taking" side, but in the case of Ruthenian the direction is not an obvious one. Despite the seemingly apparent fact that Polish exerted influence on Eastern Slavic, it is possible to reverse the perspective and argue that the actual process of formation of Ruthenian as a language of writing had been the opposite: the interference came from East Slavic and affected the Polish, or rather Polonized, language that Ruthenians chose to use in writing. The more successful the process of replication or mastering of Polish by Ruthenians was, the less influence (if the word 'influence' could be used here) East Slavic exerted on it. If we hark back to the linguistic behavior of Ruthenian authors categorized by Ševčenko, we can view it from this perspective: the more favorably disposed the authors were to Polish culture, the more advanced their language learning was, and therefore, the more their literary language resembled Polish.

An example of minor substratum interference – the result either of good learning or thorough replication – appears in the usage of the Polish language by Meletii Smotryts'kyi and other Ruthenian authors,[34] which David Frick has elegantly termed "Polonica Orthodoxe."[35] Frick has shown that the interplay between Ruthenian and Polish in Smotryts'kyi's language was intentional. Emphasizing the behavioral component in Smotryts'kyi's linguistic preferences, he has suggested that "this was an appropriation of the Polish language for Orthodox purposes, an establishment of an Orthodox Polish rhetoric and sacred philology to compete with the Protestant, and especially, Catholic variants."[36]

As far as Ruthenian translations from Polish are concerned, striking examples of substratum interference and language accommodation are exhibited in such texts as the fifteenth-century *Povest' o trekh koroliakh-volkhvakh* (*The Legend of Three Kings*), the pseudonymous Khrystofor Filalet's *Apokrysis* (1597

---

[33] Thomason and Kaufman 1988, 10. Kaufman and Thomason emphasize the influence of social factors on contact-induce language change, largely ignoring linguistic constraints, although Thomason expresses more reservation on the subject (Thomason, 2001).

[34] On the usage of Polish by other Ruthenian authors, see Moszyńska 1998, Karpluk 1997, Kędelska 1993, Drzazgowski 1991, Łużny 1966.

[35] Frick 1995, 181-205.

[36] Frick 1995, 183.

in Polish, 1598 in Ruthenian), and the *Khronika* of Maciej Stryjkowski (1582 in Polish, mid-seventeenth century in Ruthenian). These and other translations appear to be the same as Polish text transcribed in Cyrillic characters, but in fact are not completely so. The language is characterized by a generally Polish syntax and lexicon, but for the most part an East Slavic morphology and phonological dress. Although these texts were composed at a later stage in the development of Ruthenian, they clearly indicate how interference had operated in the past. The Ruthenian translations from Czech analyzed in the previous chapters date from a relatively early period of Ruthenian, i.e. the middle and second half of the fifteenth century, and therefore furnish a good object for inquiry into the earlier stages of Ruthenian.

The model of the substratum interference can be, therefore, presented in the following chart, where NL – native language; TL – target language; RL – resulting language:

**TABLE 1. NL (EAST SLAVIC: BELARUSIAN AND UKRAINIAN DIALECTS) AND TL (POLISH)**

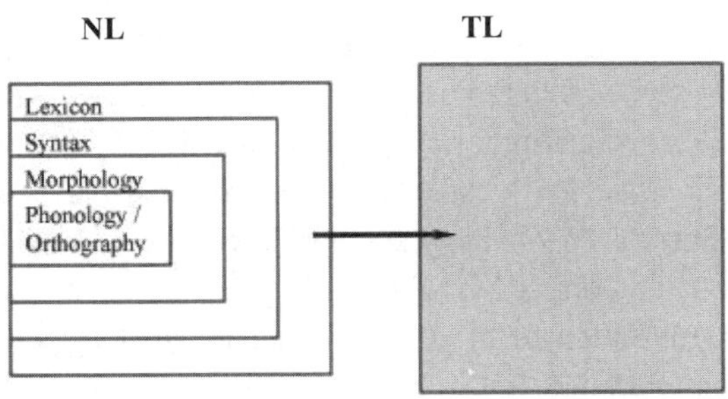


**TABLE 2. NL AND TL IN CONTACT**

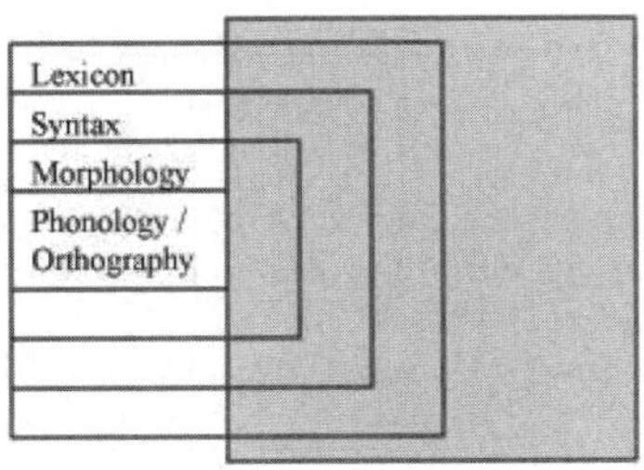

TABLE 3. RL (RUTHENIAN)

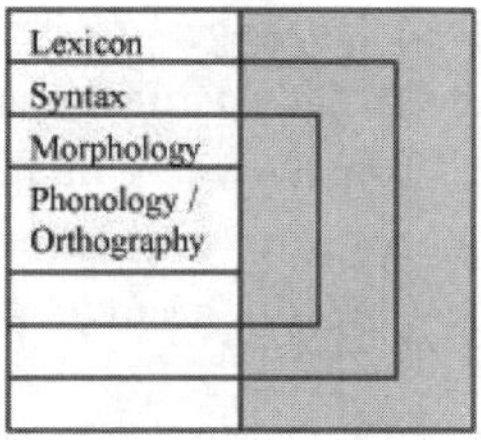


The theory of shift-induced interference has been constructed around spoken languages, which is why it cannot be applied to Ruthenian as a language of writing without modification. Therefore, we should view phonology as conditioned by orthographic practices. Incidentally, it is quite possible that, had the Ruthenians not desired to maintain their national identity, the Cyrillic alphabet that was especially instrumental in this endeavor could have easily given way to Latin characters and Ruthenian could have been gradually subsumed into Polish.[37]

## FROM SUBSTRATUM INTERFERENCE TO LANGUAGE MIXING

The Austrian scholar Hugo Schuchardt first substantiated the linguistic possibility of a mixed language at the end of the nineteenth century.[38] He proved that changes in language structure may result from economy of speech activity, and that they do not necessarily depend on internal systemic developments. Schuchardt's work prompted a new turn in the study of language contact. The concept of language contact, introduced by André Martinet[39] and then developed in a classic work by Uriel Weinreich,[40] covers a wide range of issues (both linguistic and extra-linguistic) connected with the process of formation of mixed languages. Research in the field of contact linguistics has produced both theoretical principles and case studies, and continues to be the focus of scholarly attention.[41]

[37] In fact, that happened later when *latinka* was proposed as a substitute alphabet. We can only hypothesize whether it demonstrated a less keenly felt need for preserving national identity.

[38] Schuchardt [1884] 1971.

[39] Martinet 1952.

[40] Weinreich 1968 (first edition in 1953).

[41] For example, Thomason and Kaufman 1988, van Coetsem 1988 and 2000, Ivir and Kalogjera 1991, Wölk and De Houwer 1977, Thomason 2001.

Amongst the various options for the realization of interlinguistic communication (mechanical borrowing, interference, code-switching), linguistic interference is largely responsible for the development of mixed languages. Generally, the motivation for the emergence of a mixed language is the establishment of mutual understanding between communities in sustained contact when the resulting mixed language allows easy communication without resort to translation. In those languages that have not undergone stabilization the resulting language mixture is manifested in variation on all linguistic levels.

The co-existence of Polish and East Slavic dialects (Belarusian and Ukrainian) in the Grand Duchy, both in the everyday and cultural spheres, created a situation of bilingualism.[42] In the sphere of writing it would be even more accurate to speak about multilingualism since the already existing situation of vernacular Ruthenian – learned Church Slavonic bilingualism was complicated by the influence of Polish as an alternative language of writing. The situation of bilingualism and/or multilingualism is a pre-condition of language mixing, which is an outcome of substratum interference. Indeed, the fact that the presence of the West Slavic element is observed on all linguistic levels (except phonology / orthography) in Ruthenian proves that we are dealing with consistent linguistic interference rather than a borrowing of individual lexemes and linguistic structures.

## From Language Mixing to Koineization

As a mixed language, Ruthenian is best described as a koine – a form of language resulting from a compromise between various mutually intelligible languages and lacking certain localizing features of the participating linguistic systems. The term koine comes from the Greek κοινη διάλεκτος, 'common dialect.' It originally referred to a fairly uniform variety of Greek, largely based on the Attic dialect, spoken and written from the fourth century B.C. until approximately the eighth century A.D. in Greece, Macedonia, and parts of Africa and the Middle East that had come under the influence of Greek or Hellenistic rulers. Before the fourth century B.C. there was no linguistic unity in Greece; each city state used its dialect as an official language. There were several literary languages, the use of which was determined by the literary genre rather than by the native dialect of the writer: epic poetry was written in a Homeric Ionic, lyric po-

[42] This term is used here with the meaning provided by Weinreich: "the practice of alternately using two languages" (Weinreich 1968, 1). It should not be confused with the term *diglossia* which refers to language functions.

etry in a Doricizing Greek, prose in a variety of dialects. The political and cultural dominance of Athens brought about Koine, a supranational dialect, based chiefly on the Attic dialect, which was no longer rooted in the speech of a particular region. This was a language of administration, literature, the Septuagint, and the New Testament.[43]

Since the original Koine represented the result of dialect contact, the term koine has been mostly applied to describe the contact of dialects. However, as research on language contact shows, it could be just as fittingly applied to refer to contact between mutually intelligible languages. A number of languages have been termed koine, for example, the "interdialects" of Macedonian, Belgrade-based Serbo-Croatian, Israeli Hebrew, and Canadian French.[44] Depending on the language in question, scholars have emphasized different features of the original Koine: (i) its function as a regional lingua franca, (ii) its being a standard language for a politically unified region, (iii) its being a form of language resulting from a compromise between various dialects. All these are true of Ruthenian. Furthermore, the driving force behind the genesis of Ruthenian was similar to that of Greek Koine: just as the political authority and intellectual prestige of Athens led to an increasing use of Attic as a lingua franca in Greece, the Ruthenian variety of Vilnius acquired a similar status in the Grand Duchy of Lithuania.

A koine is formed by means of koineization, which generally combines three processes: language mixing, language leveling, and simplification.[45] Koineization is a gradual process that requires a situation of bilingualism or multilingualism, in which speakers use more than one language interchangeably depending on their activity. However, the primary stimulus to koineization is the attainment of mutual understanding. This situation brings about linguistic interference, which results in the appearance of a large number of variants, i.e. in a language mixture. In a pre-koine stage various forms of the languages/dialects in contact are used concurrently and inconsistently. Sometimes koineization does not continue beyond this unstable stage. In the next stage focusing occurs by means of leveling – an accommodation of variants by the loss of marked and/or minority variants.[46] When leveling is complete, lexical, morphological, and phonological compromise forms from the languages or dialects in contact are fixed

[43] For more information on Greek Koine see, for example, Browning 1995, 19–52.

[44] For a more complete list see Siegel 1985, 359.

[45] For a detailed study of these phenomena in application to English dialects, see Trudgill 1986.

[46] Trudgill 1986, 126.

so that there is little variation. Leveling is usually accompanied by simplification – a selection of linguistically simpler forms.

## Mechanism of Koineization

A comprehensive study of the transfer and the mechanism of koineization in a language would have to address a number of issues. Besides establishing linguistic categories (levels of grammar, parts of speech, sub-classes) most susceptible to interference, transfer and koineization, its goal would be to determine what linguistic phenomena favor it and whether this process is sporadic or regular. The present study aims at outlining certain tendencies and regularities that may become a starting point for a more thorough future analysis.

It is evident from the examined Ruthenian translations that the lexicon is the area most responsive to linguistic transfer and koineization. Moreover, lexical transfer is occasionally responsible for the mixture of the West Slavic and East Slavic phonological, morphological and syntactical components of Ruthenian. (Consider the above discussed non-pleophonic forms, the fall of the initial *ji*–; the use of the verb **ймѣти** ('to have') to indicate predestined future, and the use of **тѻт** ('that') as a referential expression.)

It goes without saying that linguistic transfer is especially strong when there is contact between two genetically related languages. In the contact of Czech and Polish with Ruthenian, transfer is facilitated by the effect of similar components on all linguistic levels (phonological, morphological, syntactical, and lexical). Let us examine several types of adaptation that bring together West and East Slavic features in the language of a Ruthenian speaker.

Phonological adaptation (transphonemization) of Czech and Polish words into Ruthenian is carried out smoothly due to the similarity between phonemes and the existence of regular correspondences. For example, the Ruthenian *r* consistently replaces the Czech *ř* and the Polish *rz* (cf. **потребȣ** (S 212), Czech *potřeba* and Polish *potrzeba*); the Ruthenian *u* and *ja* substitute the Polish *ą* and *ę*, respectively (cf. **подѧковала** (S 20), Polish *dziękować*; **ѡ҆кръгле** (S 48–49), Polish *okrągły*).

Morphological adaptation (transderivation) is realized as a result of the similarity between derivational models and the existence of common morphemes. Common Slavic suffixes, prefixes and roots, although in unusual derivational combinations, make foreign Slavic words recognizable and, therefore, prone to adaptation and transfer. For example, the root **вѣд**– exists in both East and West Slavic. However, its valence in these groups of languages is different.

Such derivations as the Ruthenian з̑вѣдала (S 26) with prefix з–, and ѿповѣдила (S 40) with prefixes ѿ– and по– are not attested in Old East Slavic documents but are present in West Slavic (cf. Czech *zvěděla, odpověděla*, Polish *odpowiedzieć*). The adaptation of the Ruthenian ѕвѣздарька (S 2) from Czech *hvězdářka*, along with existing the Old East Slavic ѕвѣздочьтьца, is explained by the presence of constituents in East Slavic (ѕвѣзд–, –арь–, –к–, –а). The Ruthenian лавичька (T 51) 'bench' with West Slavic suffix –ичь– (Czech *lavice, lavička*) may be explained by its similarity to the proper East Slavic form лавьчька with suffix –ьчь–, later vocalized into лавочка. The existence of the suffix –ост– in the East Slavic derivational inventory allows for the infiltration of West Slavic words that consist of common Slavic roots with this suffix: горкостию (T 25) 'heat' (vs. Old East Slavic жаръ), великости (T 47) 'size' (vs. Old East Slavic величина), свѣтлость (T 66) 'light' (vs. Old East Slavic свѣтъ).

A similar phenomenon can be observed on a syntactical level, for example, the second position in a sentence of the reflexive particle сѧ and the usage of common Slavic prepositions with characteristically West Slavic government.

In a few cases phonetic similarity causes the emergence of phonetic but not semantic equivalents of West Slavic lexemes. For example, the Ruthenian краль (T 76), cf. Czech *král* 'king,' used to signify 'Lord' (the East Slavic equivalent for 'Lord' would be цесарь (written usually as цр҃ь); горкостию (T 25), Czech *horkost* 'heat' (горькыи in East Slavic means 'bitter,' and the East Slavic semantic equivalent would be жаръ); мѣ́ста (S 205), Czech *město* 'city' (the word место in East Slavic means 'place;' the East Slavic semantic equivalent would be городъ). Ruthenian [w] реча[X] (T 20) meaning 'about things' is phonetically translated from Czech *řeč* and Polish *rzecz*, 'thing'; the East Slavic equivalent in this case would be [w] вещє[X] as in (S 25).

Further examination of a larger number of Ruthenian texts of various genres will produce more definite conclusions about the regularity of patterns of the interaction of West and East Slavic features in Ruthenian, and the receptiveness of particular structures to this interaction and subsequent koineization. Tentatively, based on the three examined Ruthenian texts, it is possible to list the following grammatical forms and syntactical structures as an example of linguistic phenomena most regularly subject to transfer and koineization:

**MORPHOLOGY**

- Nominative plural ending *–ove/–eve*;
- Methods of comparison and intensification;
- Adverbs in *–e*;

- Passive participles without *l*–epentheticum;
- Periphrastic predestined future;

### SYNTAX

- Individual prepositions;
- Conjunctions in subordinate clauses;
- Position of reflexive particle сѧ;
- Demonstrative (deictic) pronoun as referential expressions;
- Conjunction *a* meaning 'and' in compound sentences;
- Ruthenian as a "have" language;

### LEXICON

- Fall of initial *ji*– in мѣти / ймѣти and з / из;
- Czech-type non-pleophonic forms;
- Particles ж(є) то and то.

The linguistic shift from East Slavic dialects to Ruthenian was characterized by language mixing, koineization and the convergence of East and West Slavic linguistic features. However, Ruthenian never reached the stage of a stabilized koine (although separate variants of Ruthenian, such as, for example, the chancery language, did attain superior uniformity and elaboration). As a literary language, Ruthenian was prevented from becoming a stabilized koine by extra-linguistic causes: the use of Ruthenian in administrative, political and official cultural spheres was no longer tolerated in the seventeenth-century Polish-Lithuanian Commonwealth, and finally came to an end when the Grand Duchy of Lithuania ceased to exist as a political entity.

## ANATOMY OF RUTHENIAN

The formation of Ruthenian vernacular may be graphically shown as follows:

IMPERFECT LEARNING > SUBSTRATUM INTERFERENCE > LANGUAGE MIXING > KOINEIZATION

The above scheme is of course an abstraction. The phases indicated describe different aspects of the same process, interweaving in time, and, therefore, may not be clearly isolated to form a coherent chronology. Rather, this scheme reflects their causal relationship.

The language of Ruthenian translations may therefore be treated as a special form of written koine, a product of linguistic shift and literacy contact. Linguistically, it is a compromise language between East and West Slavic, where East Slavic dialects (that later gave rise to modern standard Belarusian and Ukrainian) constitute a substratum and the West Slavic component constitutes a superstratum. Orthographically, Ruthenian is a supradialectal language as well.[47] However, linguistic analysis of Ruthenian translations demonstrates that not all linguistic levels are equally mixed. The orthography (partially reflecting phonology) and morphology, while displaying fluctuation between Belarusian and Ukrainian linguistic features, remain essentially East Slavic, whereas the syntax and lexicon are dominated by West Slavic forms.

[47] Graphically Ruthenian is represented by a combination of general East Slavic, specific Belarusian-Ukrainian, and Church Slavonic phonological features.

## Final Remarks

### Glagoljaši among Ruthenians

There are still many unanswered questions in the history of the Kleparz Slavonic Monastery of Holy Cross, home to the Glagolite monks who came to Poland from the Prague Emmaus Monastery. One of the central unresolved issues has been the question of the monastery's purpose and mission. Historians have hypothesized that the task of the Kleparz Slavonic Monastery, as it used the Roman Rite, was to conduct missionary work among the Orthodox Ruthenians. However, since almost no literary artifacts associated with it have been identified yet, most scholars question this hypothesis.

It would be rather hasty to assume a common origin for all of the Ruthenian translations from Czech and Croatian discussed in this monograph. Nevertheless, their sources suggest that the creation of at least some of these translations could be associated with the Kleparz Glagoljaši. Further, these Ruthenian translations may provide evidence of the proselytizing activity of the Catholic Glagoljaši among Orthodox Ruthenians in the fifteenth century. While the origins of the Ruthenian *Book of Taudal the Knight* (**кн҇ига ѿ таоу́дале рыцари**), the *Tale of Sivilla the Prophetess* (**сказаниѥ́ ѿ сивил҇ле п҇р ͦрчици**) and the *Book of Tovit* (**книга товиѳъ**) are more open to interpretation, strong evidence links the Ruthenian *Song of Songs,* the *Marian Mass* and Cyrillic Latin prayers with the venture of the Kleparz Glagoljaši.

These Ruthenian translations, despite many similarities, differ among themselves in language and translation technique, and therefore most likely were not made by a single individual. It appears that there could have been a wider circle of scribes engaged in translating Czech texts into Ruthenian at Kleparz. The fact that these texts are found in thematic clusters copied by the same hand suggests that they are of a common provenance. The inspiration and assistance for this translating activity could have emanated from the Emmaus Glagolite monks in Kleparz.

Quite likely there is no single answer regarding the mission of the monastery. The motives of the Polish Queen Jadwiga and King Władysław Jagiełło in inviting the Glagoljaši to Kleparz could be numerous. On the one hand, they could have wished to provide instruction in the Catholic Rite for formerly Orthodox Ruthenians and Lithuanians who came to the Polish Court from the Grand Duchy. On the other, Jagiełło could have been hoping one day to reconcile his newly acquired Catholic home kingdom with the vast Orthodox population in his native Lithuania, and thought the Glagoljaši could be of assistance in that cause.

## Adaptation of Catholic Texts in the Orthodox Ruthenian Milieu

The Ruthenian texts that have been translated from Catholic sources underwent apparent assimilation to the Orthodox context, in language as well as in content and interpretation. All Ruthenian translations show signs of "Orthodox" language; that is, they consistently translated Latin sounding names into familiar Orthodox names: *Taudal* became *Faudal*, *Job* and *Tobiaš* became *Iov* and *Tovit*, and several names in the *Song of Songs* also acquired an Orthodox dress. The content of some of the translations, too, underwent modification. In the Ruthenian *Book of Taudal the Knight* a few details relevant to Catholic readers were omitted and others even further condensed in the Church Slavonic *Edifying Story Told by Faudal*. Augustine's discourse *On the Three States* that follows the Church Slavonic *Edifying Story* lost its author, and was reduced to a short homily. Several historical details lost specificity in the Ruthenian *Tale of Sivilla the Prophetess* and its political message, applicable to European political life, lost its relevance in Ruthenia.

Adaptation and reinterpretation of Ruthenian translations sometimes led to the modification of their genre or function. The manuscript context shows that some Ruthenian translations changed their original setting when they migrated into Orthodox miscellanies. In Latin and Czech, both the *Visio Tundali* and the *Sibylla Tiburtina* are frequently found in historical compendia, annals or alongside other chronicles and historical treatises. Both of these eschatological works were evidently perceived as historical texts, whether commenting on current events or biblical history in general.

In the Ruthenian translation the *Book of Taudal the Knight* is followed by Augustine's discourse *On the Three States* that teaches how to avoid the sin of fornication and lead a chaste life. The close connection between these two texts is confirmed when the digest of Augustine's composition becomes almost embedded in the Church Slavonic translation, the *Edifying Story of Faudal the Warrior*. In the Ruthenian context, the *Visio Tundali* was viewed through the lens of Augustine's discourse and turned into a devotional text and an instructive story. Similarly, in losing its political and historical overtones the Ruthenian *Tale of Sivilla the Prophetess* became less of an historical treatise and more of an instructive text, accentuating the theological and devotional meaning of the prophecy. Finally, the Ruthenian *Song of Songs* was taken out of the Czech Bible, supplied with an instructive and interpretative commentary and set alongside the *Marian Mass*, reinforcing its relationship with Marian imagery and the theme of spiritual love.

## Fifteenth-Century Ruthenia as Borderland Civilization

The late sixteenth and early seventeenth centuries witnessed heightened opposition to, and criticism of, Catholicism and Latinity in the Orthodox milieu. Ruthenian polemical treatises severely censured the Catholic Rite as well as Catholic translations of the Holy Scripture. Fifteenth-century Ruthenian men of letters, by contrast, were not only uncritical of Catholic and, generally, Latin script texts but they apparently perceived no significant disagreement between Catholic and Orthodox textual traditions. They were well aware of both the potentialities and limits of foreign, non-Orthodox sources and of the linguistic choices that could be made in adopting them. Evidently, fifteenth-century Ruthenians found no contradiction between observing the Orthodox Rite and using Roman-Catholic texts as sources for translations: the translators of the Ruthenian *Song of Songs*, the *Tale of Sivilla*, the *Book of Taudal*, and the *Book of Tovit* were not troubled by the fact that their Czech sources were Catholic in origin. Their primary concern must have been the availability and comprehensibility of a source (indeed, quite a humanistic approach), whereas the use of Cyrillic orthography provided their translations with a passport for entry into Orthodoxy.

This confessional tolerance shows how indistinct the borders were between *Slavia Romana* and *Slavia Orthodoxa* (i.e. the cultural and political division of all the Slavs into those who followed the Roman-Catholic Church and those who adhered to the Greek Orthodox faith).[1] Although this terminological division is essential for understanding the cultural and confessional diversity of Slavic civilization, in many cases the interaction of these two spheres and their internal heterogeneity complicate easy categorization.

## *Ruthenica Bohemica*

The morphological, syntactical, and lexical analyses of these Ruthenian translations have demonstrated that their language is a mixture of East Slavic and West

[1] Picchio 1984.

Slavic (Czech) linguistic features, and that these translations follow their Czech sources very closely.

As numerous Czech and Polish equivalents have demonstrated, in the linguistic analysis of Ruthenian texts the quest to distinguish Bohemisms from Polonisms may not be very productive, unless the source text of a Ruthenian translation is established. The essential point in this regard is that Bohemized Polish language, interacting with Ruthenian, facilitated the reception of Czech texts.

## Literacy Contact

The multicultural and multilingual situation in the Grand Duchy of Lithuania and the Polish-Lithuanian Commonwealth provided the socio-historical circumstances for the emergence of a composite Ruthenian language and culture. One of the major factors in the formation of Ruthenian linguistic culture has been language contact between Polish (West Slavic) and East Slavic dialects. However, the linguistic processes that shaped Ruthenian as a language of writing were not only connected with language contact and language shift but were also governed by the nature of written discourse and literacy acquisition. To understand the mechanism of Ruthenian written language I have proposed to view it as a result of literacy contact. The term "literacy contact" is reminiscent of the term "language contact" but refers to a different function of language, that of writing. It occupies a niche between the linguistic concept of "language contact," which emphasizes the systemic linguistic relationship between participating languages and the semiotic term "text contact," which emphasizes the relationship and interaction between complete texts. The following formula describes the anatomy of Ruthenian:

**RUTHENIAN LITERACY = VERNACULAR + LITERACY,**

where

**VERNACULAR** = Belarusian + Ukrainian spoken dialects + spoken Polish

**LITERACY** = Church Slavonic + Polish literary languages

Since Ruthenian as a vernacular did not have its own literary tradition, it came to assume Church Slavonic and Polish literary models. The situation of literacy contact is not specific to the history of Ruthenian writing. Similar prerequisites for literacy contact may emerge in any literary language that develops on the basis of more than one language and their writing and literary conventions.

## A *Modus Operandi* of Ruthenian Men of Letters

The expression of intellectual curiosity and individuality, as well as considerations of linguistic accessibility, helped Ruthenian men of letters to reshape and animate their language. In summarizing what has been said about the language of Ruthenian translations, the following processes account for linguistic, orthographic and stylistic variation in Ruthenian written language and were essential in its formation:

1. Interference, mixing, and koineization occurred as a result of contact between Polish and Belarusian and Ukrainian dialects. The formation of Ruthenian vernacular may be graphically shown as follows:
   **imperfect learning > substratum interference > language mixing > koineization**
2. Interference and mixing were also caused by literacy contact and translation.
3. Striving for individual expression affected authors' stylistic considerations and prompted a variety of Ruthenian idiolects.
4. Ruthenian texts' generic heterogeneity derived from the operation of functional styles (in the Bakhtinian sense of "speech genres").

Using the approach of literacy contact along with theories of language mixing and koineization, I suggest that we view Ruthenian as a literary koine, a compromise language, in which East Slavic (Belarusian and Ukrainian) dialects constitute a substratum and the West Slavic component constitutes a superstratum.

It is my conviction that one should not be guided by a modern division of languages in characterizing and identifying Ruthenian texts. The concept of a national standardized literary language is the product of a modern linguistic mentality, and does not apply to pre-modern Ruthenian literary tradition.

Just as nationalist mentalities have manifested themselves in linguistics, a scholarly nationalism has been practiced in literary studies. These traditionally discuss texts translated from other languages as something marginal and not necessarily representative of a particular national tradition. However, as the linguistic analysis above has demonstrated, Ruthenian translations, albeit reliant on their sources, show sufficient individuality and assimilation to Ruthenian environment to be a part of both the Ruthenian linguistic and literary corpus.

# *Appendices*

# Appendix I. The Ruthenian *Song of Songs*[1]

## К҆нига є҃ⷭ сиꙗ неразꙋмномⷹ даєⷮ разꙋмеⷮ

Бл҃жен҃ъ чл҃вкъ тои. и҆же бꙋдеть чести книги сі́а. а҆ вси слова таꙗ҆ дх҃овно разꙋмѣвающи а҆ в любоⷡ бж҃ію з ниⷯ сѧ запалѧючи. А҆ ништо свѣтьскѡⷢ а҆ни на похоти тѣлесныѧ своеⷢ оума. ани мыслей ѻ҆борочаючи. Проклѧⷮ тоть которыи бы тыи кьниги чоⷧ. а҆ тые҆ бы слова на похоти женьскіи собѣ складалъ. а҆ ѻ҆борочалъ запалѧючиⷭ з҆ ниⷯ к҆ нимъ вь млѡⷭ. а҆ говорѧчи с ними тыми словы. приводѧчи иⷯ а҆ розмовлѧючи на блꙋⷣноую похоть. Бѣда а҆ горе чл҃вкоу томꙋ лꙋчши бы е҆мꙋ не родити. нижли тогоⷭ допꙋстити. Но сама прм҃дрѡⷭ бж҃іа которыиⷤ є҃ⷭ сн҃ъ бж҃іи складалъ є҃ⷭ самѣ тыи к҆ниги череⷭ оу҆ста мдрѡⷢ соломона. длѧ млⷭти своее҆. а҆быⷭ дш҃а с ниⷨ такъ оу҆миловала. бо є҃ⷭ є҃ⷢ невѣста а҆ ѡнъ е҆е беⷥсмр҃тныи нб҃ⷭныи жениⷯ милыи. саⷨ є҃ⷭ хⷭ҃ъ бг҃ъ :· А҆ третіи к҆ниги црѧ҃ премдрѡⷢ соломона. рекомыи пѣⷭ пѣснеⷨ. ѡ҆ млⷭти бж҃іи и҆ любьви:

Глаⷭ невѣсты дш҃а к҆любимомꙋ женихꙋ хⷭ҃оу ѿ велико палимыѧ любьве. въпіеть к немꙋ глѧ҃.

1:1 Цѣлꙋи мѧ цѣлованіемъ оу҆стъ своиⷯ. бо лѣпши оу҆стъ[2] пе҆рси твои над
виноⷨ

1:2 бл҃говон҆нѣиши ниⷤли а҆роматы мастіи налѣпьшиⷯ . ѡ҆леи и҆зліанныи и҆мѧ
твое҆. прото молоⷣци миловали сꙋть тебѣ.

1:3 тѧгни мѧ по собѣ. побѣгнеⷨ в доброво́нности ма́стѣи твоиⷯ. оу҆вел мѧ
є҃ⷭ црь до ви́нниць своиⷯ. радоватиⷭ бꙋдемъ а҆ веселити в тобѣ.
памѧтливыи боуⷣчи персеи твоиⷯ наⷣ вино. правии милоують тебѣ.
глаⷭ дш҃и къ събороу ст҃ыхъ. || (f. 39v)

1:4 Чорна е҆смь а҆ле красна дщ҆ѣри и҆ерⷧмⷭкіхъ. ꙗ҆ко станы кедⷬа. ꙗ҆коже то
кожа соломонова.

1:5 неⷣбаите мѧ знамѣнати же смѣда е҆смь. бо мѧ є҃ⷭ сл҃нце на беⷬвѣ
промѣнило. сн҃ове мт҃ри моее҆. боіѡ҆вали соуть. противъ менѣ поставили
мѧ сꙋть стороже ⷨ оу҆ ви҆нница ⷯ винници мое҆е не ѡ҆стерегала е҆смь.
глаⷭ ст҃ои црк҃ви. а҆ набж҃нои дш҃и. к҆ женихꙋ хⷭ҃ꙋ.

1:6 Оу҆каⷤ ми е҆гоⷤ милꙋеть дш҃а моѧ. гд҆ѣ пасѣшь. гд҆ѣ ѿпочива́ешь ѡ҆
полꙋдн҃е. а҆ть сѧ тꙋлѧть не поⷱноу. по стадеⷯ товарышоⷡ твоиⷯ.
глаⷭ хⷭ҃въ кь цѣрькви ст҃ои. а҆ к невѣсте милои дш҃и.

---

[1] Moscow Synod Collection Miscellany #558, ff. 39–45, the State Historical Museum (Moskovskaia Sinodal’naia Biblioteka, Gosudarstvennyi Istoricheskii Muzei);

[2] This is, most likely, a corruption of соуть.

# The Czech *Song of Songs*[3]

**Abbreviations**:

| | |
|---|---|
| Vf | Fojtův Starý Zákon (1484–1488) |
| Ax | Klementinská Bible neznámého původu (1440–1460) |
| Aw | Lobkovická Bible (1480) |
| An | Nymburská Bible (1462–1463) |
| At | Talmberská Bible (1460–1480) |

The numbers of the chapters and verses are absent in manuscripts. Ligatures in the Czech text are resolved in parentheses.

1:1 Polib mye polibenim vſt ſwych . neb lep˙ſie gſu prſy twe nad vino.

1:2 wonniey˙ſie nežli maſti naylep˙ſie . Oley wylity gmeno twe . proto mladicie
milowali ſu tie .
1:3 Tahni mye po ſobie . pobiehnem u woni maſtij twych . Vwedl mie g(es)t kral do
piwnic ſwych . Radowati ſie budem a weſeliti w tobie . pamietliui gſuc prſij
twych nad vino . Prawij milugij tie.
*Hlas synagogy .*
1:4 Czrna gſem ale kraſna . dcery geruzale(m)ſke . yako ſtankowe cedar . yakožto
kožie ˙ſalomunowa .
1:5 Nerodte mne znamenati . že ſmieda gſem . neb mye g(es)t ſlunce na baruie
p(ro)mienilo. Synowe matře me boiowali ſu proti mnye . poſtauili ſu mye
ſtražnu u winniciech . vinnicie me neoſřiehala ſem .
*Hlas cierkwe k kryſtoui .*
1:6 Vkaž mi gehož miluge du˙ſie ma . kde paſeś . kde odpociwaś o poledni . at ſie
tulati nepocznu po ſtadech towaři˙ſow twych .
*Hlas kriſtow k cierkwi .*

[3] The *Padeřovská Bible* (1432–1435), Österreichische Nationalbibliothek, Cod. 1175.

1:7 Не знаешь ли себѣ ѡ прекраснаꙗ межи жонами. выиди иди и послѣдꙋи
стад. а паси козлы твои. подле стаи пастыревых.
1:8 ѣздьцом моим оу возех фараѡновых. прировнала есмь тобѣ прїетелко моꙗ.
1:9 красны сꙋть ꙗгодки лица твоег. ꙗко горълицка шїа твоꙗ. *ꙗко златое*
*монисто.*
1:10 *сноурки золотыи оучинимо тобѣ перевиꙗныи сребром*
*глас црькви а дши ѡ хс̃ѣ.*
1:11 *Коли есть былъ црь оу ѣдлѣ*[4] нардꙋсъ мои. дал есть вонность свою.
1:12 снопок мирры милыи мои мьнѣ. межи персеи моих пребывати бꙋдеть.
1:13 грезнъ кипрски милыи мои мнѣ оу винницах екгадди.
глас хс̃въ къ црькви а къ дши.
1:14 Ѡи красна еси ты. прїетелко моꙗ милаꙗ. оочи твои голꙋбиныи.
глас црькви а дши къ хс̃ꙋ
1:15 Ѡи красны еси ты милыи мои витяжныи. постелꙗ наша краснаꙗ
свѣтлостїю
1:16 покрытье домовъ нашихъ кедрово. склепове наши кипарисовы.
глвa в. глас хс̃въ а къ црькви свои а дши боголюбимои.
2:1 Ꙗ квѣт полныи а лилиꙗ оудольнаꙗ.
2:2 ꙗко лилїа межи тернїемъ. так милаꙗ моꙗ || (f. 40) межи дщерями.
глас въ црькви къ хс̃ꙋ своемꙋ любимомꙋ женихꙋ.
2:3 Ꙗко же то ꙗблонь межи древїемъ лесным. такъ милыи мои межи станы.
под тѣнем его ж то есмь жедала сѣдела есми а овоцїе его сладко горлꙋ
моемоу.
2:4 оувелъ мꙗ есть црь до винничнаг покоꙗ. израдилъ есть въ мнѣ любов.
2:5 ѡтыкаите мꙗ квѣтїемъ. а ѡсыпаите мꙗ ꙗблоки. бо ѿ великое мл̃сти не
могꙋ.
2:6 левїца его под главою моею а правица ег обоимет мꙗ.
глас хс̃въ
2:7 Заклинаю вас дщери ерлмскїа. черес олени а серны полныи. абысте не
боудили ани прочютити казали милое моее. докꙋль сама въсхочеть.
глас црькви ꙗже есть всꙗкаꙗ дша любꙗщиꙗ ба. того дѣлꙗ зоветь сꙗ
невѣста милаꙗ хс̃ва.
2:8 Голос милого моег. а и тот то есть пришолъ скачючи по горах а
перескакиваючи погорки. и холмы.

---

[4] The text in italics is written in a different hand.

1:7 Nezna˙ſli ſebe o kraſna mezi ženami . wygdi a gdi po ſledu ſtad . a pas kozly twe. podle ſtawadl paſtyřowych .

1:8 Giezdczo(m) mym u woziech faraonowych přirownal ſe(m) tie přietelnicie ma .

1:9 Kraſne gſu yahodky licij twu yako hrdlicie. ˙ſige twa yako ſpinadla .

*Hlas přatel .*

1:10 Rzetiezky zlatte vczinime tobie provigiene ſtřiebrem .

*Hlas cierkwe o kriſtoui .*

1:11 Když g(es)t byl kral w gedle ſwem[5] . nardus moy dal g(es)t woni ſwu .

1:12 Snopek mirry mily moy mnie . mezi prſmi mymi přebywati bude .

1:13 Hrozen ciprſky mily moy mnie u vinniciech engady .

*Hlas kriſtow .*

1:14 Ay kraſna gſi ty přietelnice ma . oczi twogi holubicie .

*Hlas cierkwe .*

1:15 Ay kraſny gſi ty mily moy y wytecny . ložce na˙ſe ſtkwucie .

1:16 Lemiezowe domow na˙ſich cedroui . ſklepowe na˙ſi cipreſſouij .

II *Hlas kriſtow .*

2:1 Ya kwiet polſky[6] . a liliu(m) vdolnie .

2:2 Yako liliu(m) mezi trnim . tak přietelnicie ma mezi dcerami .

*Hlas cierkwe .*

2:3 Yakožto yablon mezi dřiewi(m) leſnim . tak mily moy mezi ſyny[7] . Pod ſtienem geho gehožto ſem žadala ſediela ſem . a owotce geho ſladke hrdlu memu .

2:4 Vwedl mie g(es)t kral do pokoge vinneho . zřiedil g(es)t we mnye laſku .

2:5 Otycieyte mye kwietim . oſipte mye yablky . nebot pro miloſt nedužim .

2:6 leuicie geho pod hlawu mu . a prauicie geho přituli mie .

*Hlas křiſtow .*

2:7 Zaklinam was dcery geruzalemſke ſkrzie ſrny y geleny polſke[8] . aby˙ſte nebudili . ani procititi kazali zmilele . donidžt ſama chce .

*Hlas cierkwe .*

2:8 Hlas mileho meho . Ay tento g(es)t při˙ſel ſkacie po horach . přeſkakuge pahorky .

---

[5] *w gedle* Aw.
[6] *polni* An, Aw, At.
[7] *stieny* Aw.
[8] *polni* An, Aw, At.

2:9 поⷣⷪбны єⷭ милыи мои серне а̀ ланѧти ѐленемꙋ. а̀ и ѡⷩ то стоиⷮ за стѣною
нш҃ею. смотрѧчи сквозе ѡ̀кна. а̀ преглѧдаючи череⷭ боронки.
2:10 а̀ милыи мои мовиⷧ ко мнѣ въстаⷩ поспешиⷭ прїетелко моа милаѧ.
голꙋбиⷱко моѧ краснаѧ а̀ поиди
2:11 бо оу̀же ѕима поминоула. превалъ лютости ѿшоⷧ и̇ ѿстꙋпиⷧ
2:12 к̏вѣтїе оу̀казалоⷭ оу̀ нашои земли. чаⷭ ѡ̇брезыванїа вин̏ниць. оу̀жо єⷭ
пришелъ голоⷭ горъличинъ. слышаⷩ єⷭ вь земли нашой.
2:13 ѳиниⷦ выдаⷧ єⷭ первые̇ ѡ̀вощи свои. вин̏ници квитꙋчи дали сꙋть вин̏ность
свою.
глаⷭ хⷭвъ къ црк҃ви ст҃ои дш҃и къ своѐи мл҃ои невѣсте.
Въстань милаѧ моѧ краснаѧ. а̀ поиди
2:14 в диреⷯ скалныⷯ а̀ в печеркаⷯ каменѧ. оу̀каⷤ ми тварь твою. а̀ть звиниⷮ
голоⷭ твои въ оу̀шїю мою. бо голоⷭ твои слаⷣкїи а тваⷬ твоѧ красна.
глаⷭ црк҃ви ст҃ои протиⷡ кацерем || (f. 40v) а̀ еретикомъ
2:15 Зымаите наⷨ лисенѧта малаѧ которыи ж то казѧⷮ вин̏ници бо винница
нш҃а квиⷮла єⷭ.
глаⷭ црк҃ви ст҃ое дш҃и къ своѐмꙋ женихꙋ хⷭоу.
2:16 Милыи мои мнѣ а̀ ѧ ѐмꙋ. ѐжь сѧ пасеⷮ межи лилїами
2:17 докоуⷧ сѧ дн҃ь не наклониⷮ а̀ не оу̀хилѧтьⷭ тѣневе. неврать сѧ[9] милыи
мои поⷣⷪбенъ бꙋди серне а̀любо ланѧтъкꙋ ѐленемꙋ на гораⷯ веѳиль.
глⷡа . г҃ . глаⷭ црк҃ви и̇ ст҃ыхъ дш҃ь выбраныⷯ с поганоⷡ в невѣсты къ
своѐмоу миломꙋ женихоу хⷭꙋ ѡ̇броученыⷯ ѐмꙋ вѣрою и̇ любовїю.
3:1 На ложи моѐмъ в̏ ночи глѧдала ѐсмь ѐгоⷤ милꙋеть дш҃а моѧ. искала
ѐсми ѐго а̀ не нашла.
3:2 в̏станꙋ а̀ ѡ̀боидꙋ мѣсто по рынцѣⷯ а̀ по оу̀лицаⷯ и̇скати боудꙋ єⷢ ѐгоⷤ
милꙋеть дш҃а моѧ̀. и̇скала ѐсми ѐго а̀ не нашла ѐсми.
3:3 знашли мѧ соуⷮ сторожеве к̥торыиⷤ то ѡ̀стерегали мѣста.
в церькваⷯ невѣсⷮныи дш҃и . по хⷭе сѧ пытають.
Ци видали ѐсте ѐго же милоу̀еть дш҃а моѧ.
3:4 маленько колиⷤ ѐсми проминꙋла ѐсми. нашла ѐсми ѐгоⷤ милꙋеть дш҃а
моѧ. держала ѐсми єⷢ а̀ниⷤ ѐго пꙋщоу. а̀лиⷤ ѐго въведꙋ до домꙋ мт҃ри
моѐѧ.
глаⷭ хⷭвъ ѡ̇ своеи невѣсте дш҃и.
3:5 Заклинаю ваⷭ дочки и̇ѐрⷭлмкїа чересъ серны а̀ ѐлени полные. а̀бысте не
боудили а̀ни прочютити казали милое моѐе. докꙋль бы сама ѡ̀лиⷤ
хотѣла.

[9] Instead of наврать сѧ.

2:9 Podobny g(es)t mily moy ſrnye . a k koluchoui geleniemu . Ay ont ſtogi za
ſtienu na˙ſi . hledie ſkrzie okna . prohledage ſkrzie mrzieżie .
2:10 A mily moy mluui mnie . Wſtan poſpieś přietelnicie ma . holubice ma .
kraſna ma . a pod .
2:11 Neb giż zima pominula . přewal od˙ſel y odſtupil .
2:12 Kwietie vkazala ſu ſie w zemi na˙ſie . czas obřezowanie vinnic g(es)t při˙ſel .
Hlas hrdlici ſly˙ſan g(es)t w zemi na˙ſie .
2:13 Fik wydal g(es)t prwnie owotce ſwe . Vinnicie ktwuce daly ſu woni ſwu .

*Hlas kriſtow .*
Wſtan přietelnicie ma . kraſna ma . a pod .
2:14 holubicie ma w dierach ſkalnych . w dupatech hrazie . Vkaż mi twař twu . at
wzni hlas twoy w v˙ſij mu . Neb hlas twoy ſladky . a twař twa kraſna .
*Hlas proti kacieřſtwim .*
2:15 Zlapayte li˙ſencie malicke nam . ktereżto kazie vinicie .
*Hlas cierkwe k żenichoui .* Neb vinnice na˙ſie zkwetla g(es)t .
*Hlas cierkwe .*
2:16 Mily moy mnye a ya gemu . genż ſie paſſe mezi lilium .
2:17 donidż ſie den nenakloni . a neuchylee ſie ſtienowe . Nawrat ſie podoben bud
mily moy ſrnie . nebo koluchoui geleniemu na horach betel .
III
*Hlas cierkwe wywolene z pohanow .*
3:1 Na lożci mem po nocech hledala ſe(m) . gehoż miluge du˙ſie ma . hledala ſem
geho a nenalezla ſem .
3:2 Wſtanu a obegdu mieſto po rynciech a po vliciech hledati budu gehoż miluge
du˙ſie ma . Hledala ſem geho a nenalezla ſem .
3:3 Nalezli ſu mie hlaſnij kteřiż oſtřiehagij mieſta .
*Cierkew o kriſtoui die .*
Zdali ſte vidieli gehoż miluge du˙ſie ma :
3:4 Maliczko když gie přegidech . nalezla ſem gehož miluge du˙ſie ma . Drżala ſem
geho . aniż puſtim aż uwedu gey do domu mateře me . a do pokogika
roditedlnicie me.
*Hlas kriſtow .*
3:5 Zaklinam was dcery geruzalemſke ſkrzie ſrny a geleny polſke[10] . aby˙ſte
nebudili.ani procititi kazali zmilele donidż by ſama chtiela .

[10] *polni* An, Aw, At.

Съборъ ст҃ыхъ пытаѥть ѡ д҃ши а ѡ ц҃ркви ст҃ои рекꙋчи.

3:6 Котораꙗ є҇ то таꙗ жь то оустꙋпаеть чере҇ поустыню ка҇ бы столпъ домныи. з добровонныⷯ рѣчеи ми҇рры а ливана а всꙗкого пороховоу миропольⷤнаго. апатекарева зложенаго з розноли҇ныⷯ зелеи :

Гла҇ ц҃рковныи а д҃ши ѿ х҃е ѡ своемъ миломъ женисѣ.

3:7 Ложе соломоново. ѯ҃ моцныⷯ || (f. 41) ѡбъстꙋпили из насилнеишиⷯ изрлⷭ҇киⷯ.

3:8 а вси деръжачи мечи а к боѥмъ велми оумѣлыи. а единаго кождого мечь на бедраⷯ є҇ про страхи но҇ныи.

ѿ х҃е д҃ша говорить повѣдаючи

3:9 пр҃тлъ вечерꙗдло оучинилъ собѣ ц҃рь соломонъ з древа ливанова

3:10 столпы є҇ сребрꙗны оучинилъ. ѿпочивало золотое стꙋпени златые. з особное мл҃ти и любовноѐ распростеръль є҇ про дщери иер҃лмьскїи.

гла҇ церькви ст҃ое ѿ х҃е.

3:11 Выидете дщери иер҃лмьскїа а ѡгладаите ц҃рꙗ соломона в корꙋнѣ котороюⷤ є҇ его короуновала м҃ти его въ д҃нъ веселїа срⷣца его.

Гл҇а д҃. гла҇ х҃въ къ своеи милои невѣсте ц҃ркви д҃ши. похвалꙗючї ю а говорꙗчи к҇ неи такъ.

4:1 Ѽ коль красна еси ты милаꙗ моꙗ коль красна еси. оочи твои голꙋбиныи. кромѣ того што сꙗ внꙋтрь таꙗть. волосы твои ꙗко стадо козъ которыиⷤ стꙋпили з горы галаадъ.

4:2 зꙋбы твои ꙗко стадо стрыженыⷯ ѻвець которыиⷤ сꙋть вышли з мытели. вси маючи по ⷣвою ꙗгнꙗто҇. а мллова не є҇ ни жадна межи ними.

4:3 ꙗко сноурокъ черленыи оуста твоꙗ. а вымова твоꙗ слаⷣка ꙗко же то оуломокъ раиска҇ ꙗблока. та҇ ꙗгоⷣки твое҇ лица кромѣ того штоⷤ сꙗ оунꙋтрь таить.

4:4 ꙗко вежа д҃вдва. шїа твоꙗ котораꙗⷤ то є҇ оудѣлана з дѣлы пꙋшечными. а)[11] А щитовъ висить из҇ нее и всꙗкїи гарнаⷲ моцьныхъ.

4:5 два҇ сесца твоꙗ ꙗко два҇ телꙗтъка дикои козы близнꙗтка. ꙗжь сꙗ то пасꙋ на кьриноⷯ лилїѡвыⷯ

4:6 докꙋль сꙗ д҃нь не наклонить. а не схилꙗть сꙗ тѣневе. поидꙋ на горꙋ ми҇рры а на погоро҇ кадила ливанова.

4:7 всꙗ красна еси || (f. 41v) милаꙗ моꙗ. а посквернь нѣтъ на тобѣ.

4:8 поⷣ ѿ ливана милаꙗ моꙗ невѣсто поⷣ ѿ ливана поⷣ а бꙋдешь корꙋнована почень҇ши ѿ головы а маючи наверхꙋ саниⷬ а гермонъ з отъпочива҇ ливовыⷯ.

---

[11] This abbreviation should signify "1000." The following capital "A" shows that the scribe probably did not understand the numerical meaning of the letter and interpreted it as a conjunction "a".

*Synagoga o cierkui .*

3:6 Ktera g(es)t tato ge˙ſto wſtupuge přeſpu˙ſt yakožto ſlup dymny . z wonnych
viecij mirry a kadidla . a w˙ſelikeho prachu apatekařowa ſloženeho z rozlicnych
viecij :

*Hlas cierkwe .*

3:7 Ay poſtelku ˙ſalomunowu . ˙ſeſtdeſat ſilnych obkliczugij . z nayſilniey˙ſich
izrahelſkych .

3:8 w˙ſickni držiece mecie . a k bogiem převmielij a gednoho každeho mecz na
bedrach geho pro bani nocznie.

*O kriſtoui die .*

3:9 Weczeradlo vcinil ſobie kral ˙ſalomun z dřieuie libanſke(ho) .

3:10 Slupy geho vczinil g(es)t ſtřiebrne . odpociwadlo zlatte . wſtupowanie
zlattohlawne z obecne laſky proſtřel g(es)t pro dcery geruzale(m) ſke .

*Hlas cierkwe o kriſtoui .*

3:11 Wygdiete dcery ſyonſke. a ohledayte krale ˙ſalomuna w korunye. kteruž g(es)t
gey korunowala matie ge(ho). w den otdanie geho. a w den weſele ſrdcie ge(ho).

IV

*Hlas kriſtow .*

4:1 Kterak kraſna gſi přetelnice ma . kterak kraſna gſi . oci twogi holubicie . kromie
toho czož ſie wnitrz tagi . Wlaſy twogi yako ſtada koz . kterež ſu wſtupily s hory
galaad .

4:2 Zubowee twogi yako ſtada ſtřiženich owec. ktere ſu wſtupily z vmywadla .
W˙ſiecky magice po dwem gehnec. a yalowa nenie mezi nimi.

4:3 Yako ˙ſnorka czrwena rtowe twogi. a wymluwnoſt twa ſladka . Yako vlomek
zrnateho yablka . tak yahodky licij twu . kromie toho czož ſie wnitrz tagi .

4:4 Yako viežie dauidowa ˙ſige twa. kteražto g(es)t vdielana s alkeři. Tiſic ˙ſtitow
viſi z nie . w˙ſelike odienie ſilnych.

4:5 Dwa prſy twa yako dwie telatcie diwoke kozi blizenci. ge˙ſto ſie paſſu na
liliu(m) .

4:6 dokudž ſie den nenakloni . a neſchyle ſtienowe . Pogdu na horu mirry . a
na pahorek kadidla .

4:7 W˙ſiecka kraſna gſi přetelnice ma . a po˙ſkwrny nenie na tobie .

4:8 Pod z libana choti ma. pod z libana. pod˙ budeś korunowana. z hlawy amana. z
wrchu ſanir a hermon. z odpocziwadl lwowych. z hor pardowych.

4:9 Оу́ранила є̓си срдце мое̓ сестро моѧ милаѧ невѣсто. оу́ранила є̓си срдце
моє ѡ̓дным възглѧденїємъ оо̓чїю твоих. а̓ оу̓дномъ влосꙋ шїи твоеи.
4:10 коль красны сꙋть перъси твои над вино. а̓ вонѧ мирра мастїи твоих. надо
вси доброво́нныи рѣчи.
4:11 стѣнник каплють оу̓ста твоѧ. милаѧ невѣсто. медъ и млеко под ѧзыком
твоим. а̓ вонѧ ѡ̓дѣѧнїѧ твоег ꙗ̓ко вонѧ кадила ливанова.
4:12 ѡ̓городокъ замкненыи . а̓ источникъ запечатаныи.
4:13 выпꙋканїа твоа̓ раи зернѧтых ꙗ̓блѡк со ѡ̓вощомъ ꙗ̓блоновым. Кѵ́прове с
нардом.
4:14 нардъ съ сахаромъ. ѳистꙋла а̓ циномонъ съ всѧкимъ древомъ ливановым
мирра. а̓ а̓лое съ всими первыми мастьми.
4:15 колодѧз затверженыи про глꙋбинꙋ вод живых. которыи жь текоу̓ть
быстринѧми прꙋдкостїю ѿ ливана.
глас ѿ црькви невѣсты хсвы милои дши.
4:16 Въстанъ вѣтре ѿ полночи. а̓ встань вѣтре полꙋденныи провеите
ѡ̓городокъ мои. мироположных а̓патѣкъ доброво́нныхъ рѣчеи е̓е̓.
глва е. дша ѡ̓пѧть къ хсꙋ говорить.
5:1 Прїиди милыи мои до заграды своє̓и. а̓ ежь ѡ̓вощи ꙗ̓блонеи своих.
хсъ къ дши говорить.
Подь до ѡ̓горо́да моє̓го сестро моѧ милаѧ невѣсто. пожалъ є̓сми миррꙋ
мою з доброво́нными рѣчми мои̓ми. е̓лъ є̓сми стѣнникъ медꙋ моег.
пилъ є̓сми вино мое с молокомъ моимъ.
голосъ хсвъ посполито къ всимъ вѣрным дшамъ.
Єжьте прїєтели мои а̓ оу̓пиваи || (f. 42) тесѧ намилеишїи мои.
5:2 ꙗ̓ сплю а̓ срдце мое чюет.
О̓пѧть дша къ хсꙋ говорить.
Голос милого моег толкꙋчего до менѣ. ѿтвори ми сестро моѧ милаѧ
голꙋбичко моѧ непоскверненаѧ. бо голова моѧ полна ес росы. а̓ челюсти
мои кропей ночных.
5:3 Сволокла є̓сми с себѣ сꙋкню мою. какъ сѧ в нее ѡ̓болокꙋ. оу̓мыла є̓сми
ноги мои какъ их и̓змараю̓.
Тоу ѡ̓пѧть дша с великою жалостїю къ хсꙋ говорить выповедꙋючи свои
пригоды :
5:4 Милыи мои стѧгнꙋлъ ес рꙋкꙋ свою скквозе[12] дирю а̓ брюхо мое
задрыжало ес з дотъкненїа ег.
5:5 встала є̓смь а̓бых ѿтворила миломꙋ моє̓моу. рꙋце мои ка́пали сꙋть

[12] The first к has been changed into a с producing сıсквозе.

4:9 Ranila ſi ſrdce me ſeſtro ma choti . ranila ſi ſrdce me w gednom oczi twych. a w gednom wlaſu ˙ſige twe.

4:10 Kterak kraſne gſu prſy twe . ſeſtro ma choti . Kra˙ſ ſie gſu prſi twe nad vino . a wonie maſti twych nade w˙ſiecky wonne vieci .

4:11 Plaſt kapagici rtowe twogi choti . ſtred a mleko pod yazikym twym . a wonie rucha tweho yako wonie kadidla .

4:12 Zahrada zawřena ſeſtra ma choti. zahrada zawřena. ſtudnicie zaznamenana.

4:13 Wypukanie twa rag zrnatych yablek . s owotcem yablkowym . Cyprowe s nardem .

4:14 nardus a ˙ſafran . fiſtula . a ſkořice ſe w˙ſim dřiewim libanſkym . Mirra a aloes ſe w˙ſiemi prwnimi maſtmi .

4:15 Studnicie zahradnie . pro hlubnie wod żiwych . ktereż teku[13] z libana .
*Kriſtus cierkwi dary ducha dobre dawa* nebo *Hlas cierkwe . duch dary dawa .*

4:16 Wſtan vietře od puolnoci a přid vietře poledni . produn zahradku mu . a poteku wonne vieci gegie .
*kapitola V Cierkew o kriſtoui die .*

5:1 Przid mily moy do zahrady ſwe . a giez owotce yabloni ſwych .
*Kriſtus die .*
Pod do zahrady me ſeſtro ma choti . pożal ſem mirru mu s wonnymi viecmi mymi . Giedl ſem plaſt s ſtrdi mu . pil ſem vino me s mlekem mym.

*Kriſtus k apo˙ſtolom die .*
Giezte přietele pite a zapite ſie naymiley˙ſij

5:2 Ya ſpim a ſrdce me bdi .
*Hlas cierkwe .*
Hlas mileho meho tlukucieho . Otewři mi ſeſtro ma . přietelkynye ma . holubice ma . nepoſkwrnyena ma . neb hlawa ma plna g(es)t roſy . a lilikowe mogi kropij nocnich .

5:3 Swlekla ſem s ſebe ſukni mu. kterak ſie w ni obleku : Vmyla ſem nohy me. kterak gie zprznim :

*Hlas cierkwe o kriſtoui .*

5:4 Mily moy puſtil g(es)t ruku ſwu ſkrzie dieru . a břicho me zatřaſlo ſie k dotceni geho .

5:5 Wſtala ſem abych otewřiela milemu memu . Rucie mogi kapale ſu mirru . a

---

[13] *teku prudkoſti* An, Aw, At, Ax, Vf.

мирр8 прейск8шеноу .
5:6 заклепъ двереи моих ѿворила есми миломоу моемѹ. але ѡнъ са оуже
был оухилилъ ѿшолъ дша моа расплыла са ес. коли мовилъ къ мнѣ
милыи мои гладала есми а не нашла есми ег. кликала есми а не ѡзвалъ
ми са.
5:7 Знашли ма с8ть сторожеве которыиж то с8ть ѡбхоживали мѣсто. били
ма соуть и ранили. и взали ми плащь мои сторожеве міра.
5:8 Заклинаю вас дщери иерслмскіа знаидете ли ми моего милого. абысте
ем8 оузъавили. же ѿ великое млсти по немъ не мог8.
Глас збор8 стаго къ невѣсте хсве црквии стѣи милои дши.
5:9 Таковыи ес милыи твои любимыи ѡ накрашшаа жь жонъ каковыи ес
любимыи твои. же еси нас такъ заклала.
Дша ѿповедаеть стом8 збор8 ѡ своем миломъ женисѣ хсе. выповѣд8ючи
его красоу и сличность въ подобеньствах размоитых рѣчеи.
5:10 Милыи мои бѣлыи а червеныи выборныи ис тисачеи.
5:11 голова || (f. 42v) его золота налѣпшее. чело ег іако листіе палмовое.
черны іако гавронъ
5:12 оочи ег іако гол8бины над подтоки[14] водными которыиж с8ть молокомъ
ѡбъмыты. а сѣдать подле полных быстрин.
5:13 іагодки лица ег іако заградки добровонных рѣчеи посажены ѿ апатекаревъ .
оуста его лиліа капаюча мирр8 перв8ю.
5:14 р8цѣ его оуглажены златы полны ацинтковъ. брюхо ег слоново
передѣлено шафирми.
5:15 голени его столпове марморяны. которыиж то соут оуставлены на
покладах златых. тварность ег свѣтлость ливанова. выборныи іако кедръ.
5:16 горло ег пресладко. а вес възъжаданы. таковыи ти есть мои милыи. а
тотт то ес любимыи мои дщери иер8солимьскіа.
Глас збор8 стаго к невѣсте хсве а к милои дши. Глва ѕ.
6:1 Камъ ес ѿшол милыи твои ѡ накрашшаа з жонъ. кам са ес оухилилъ
милыи твои. а б8демъ ег гладати с тобою.
Дша ѿповѣдаеть напротивъ збор8 стом8 ѡ своемъ миломъ женисѣ хсе.
6:2 милыи мои ст8пилъ ес до заграды своеи. на мѣстцѣ бл҃говонных рѣчеи .
абы са паслъ оу заградах а ліліе збирал.
6:3 іа милом8 моем8 а милыи мои мнѣ. ежъс пасѣть межи крыны ліліами.
Тоут ѡпа хсъ говорит къ своеи милои невѣстѣ црквии дши похвалаючі ю
зъ ее добрых дѣлъ. а приподоблаючі ю многимъ размоитымъ рѣчемъ.

[14] Originally, this was most likely потоки (cf. Czech *potoky*).

prſtowe mogi plny mirry přezku˙ſene .

5:6 Zaworu dweřij mych otewřiela ſem milemu me(mu). ale on ſie bie˙ſe vchylil a
za˙ſel . Du˙ſie ma rozpuſtila ſie g(es)t yakż g(es)t mluuil[15] . hledala g(es)t[16] a
nenalezla geho . Wolala ſem a neodpouiediel g(es)t mnie.

5:7 Nalezli ſu mie ſtrażnij kteřiż obchaziegij mieſto . bili ſu mie y ranili ſu mie .
wzieli ſu mi plaſt moy ſtrażnij zdij .

5:8 Zaklinam was dcery geruzalemſke . nalezneteli mileho meho aby˙ſte
zwieſtowali gemu . żet pro miloſt nedużim .

*Hlas ſynagogy .*

5:9 Kteraky g(es)t mily twoy z mileho . o naykra˙ſ ſie z żen : Kteraky g(es)t mily
twoy z mileho . żes nas tak zaklela :

*Hlas cierkwe o kriſtoui .*

5:10 Mily moy biely a czrweny . wyborny z tiſicow .

5:11 Hlawa geho zlatto naylep˙ſie . k˙ſticie geho yako liſtie palmowe . czrne yako
hawran.

5:12 Oczi geho yako holubice nad potoky wodnymi . ktereż gſu mlekem omyte . a
ſedie podle plnych byſtřin .

5:13 Yahodky licij ge(ho) yako zahradky wonnych vieci . poſazene od apatekařow .
Rtowe geho lilia kapagic mirru prwni .

5:14 Rucie geho vhlazenie zlatte . plne yacinctow . Břicho geho ſlonowe . rozdielne
zafiry .

5:15 Hnatowe geho ſlupowe mramorouij . kteřiżto gſu vſtaweni na podkladiech
zlattych . Twarnoſt geho yako libanowa . wyborny yako cedrowe .

5:16 Hrdlo geho přechutne . a weſken żaduci . Takowyt g(es)t mily moy . a te(n)tot
g(es)t přietel moy dcery geruzalemſke .

VI *Hlas ſynagogy k cierkwi .*

6:1 Kam g(es)t od˙ſel mily twoy . o naykra˙ſ ſie z żen : Ka(m) ſie g(es)t vchylil mily
twoy. a budem geho hledati s tebu :

*Hlas cierkwe .*

6:2 Mily moy sſtupil g(es)t do zahrady ſwe . na mieſti˙ſtie wonnych vieci . aby ſie
paſl w zahradach a lilia ſbieral .

6:3 Ya milemu memu . a mily moy mnie . genż ſie paſſe mezi lilium .

*Hlas kriſtow k cierkwi .*

---

[15] *mily mluvil* Aw, At, Ax, Vf.

[16] *sem* An, Aw, At, Ax.

6:4 Красна ѥси милаѧ моѧ. слаⷣка и витѧжна. ꙗко иерⷭ҇лмъ. грозна ꙗко
спица к бою зрѧженаѧ.
6:5 Ѿврати очи твои Ѿ менѣ бо тыи соуть ми оучинили абыⷯ оулѣтеⷧ҇.
волосы твои ꙗко стадо козъ. котороеⷤ то сѧ оуказало з галаадъ.
6:6 зѹбове твои ꙗко стадо овець. || (f. 43) которыиⷤ сѹть вышли из мытели
оумывальноє вси по двою ꙗгнѧтокъ имѹще. а ѧловоє нѣтъ межи ими.
6:7 ꙗко кожа раискаⷢ ꙗблока. такъ ꙗгоⷣки лица твоеⷢ кромѣ таиныⷯ рѣчеи
твоиⷯ.
6:8 ѯ҃ есть црⷭ҇веⷩ а п҃ моужниⷯ жонъ а молодицамъ нѣтъ числа.
6:9 одна еⷭ҇ голѹбоⷱка моѧ доконалаѧ моѧ єдина еⷭ҇.[17] мтⷭ҇ри свои выбрана
родителници своєи видѣли соуть дщ҃ери иерⷭ҇лмьскїа єє а преблⷢ҇гословенѹю
соуть ю взывали. црⷭ҇вны а мѹжнїи жоны хвалили соуⷮ ю.
6:10 котораѧ еⷭ҇ то таѧ ꙗжь сѧ береть ꙗко зарѧ поѹстоваючи красна ꙗко
мⷭ҇ць выбоⷬна ꙗко слⷩ҇це. грознаѧ ꙗко спица к бою зрѧженаа.
Дш҃а говорить Ѿ великои радости къ зборѹ стоⷨⷹ
6:11 Стоупила есмь до заграды орѣховоє. абыⷯ огледала ꙗблока оудольнаѧ.
а осмотрела кьвитоут ли винници. а расплoжают ли сѧ ꙗбьлока раискаѧ
6:12 невѣдала єсми дш҃а моѧ засмѹтила мѧ про возы аминодавовы.
Хⷭ҇ къ дш҃и говорить а къ црⷭ҇кви в бѣдаⷯ а в напастѣⷯ и в покѹсохъ
бѹдоучеи. Ѿ свѣта Ѿ тѣла Ѿ дїавола приводѧчї ю опѧть к собѣ а
рекѹчи.
6:13 навротьⷭ҇ навроть сѧ сѹмантѧньни навроть сѧ навроть сѧ. ать на тебе
смотрю.
Дш҃а Ѿповѣдаеть емѹ велми жаловне. б҃ъ бо такъ хотѣⷧ кого оⷩ
милѹеть того и казнить тоуⷮ на томъ свѣте ꙗко злато оу огⷩ҇ни такъ
ю искѹшаеть здѣ многими скорбьми и бѣдами размаитыми. и печальми.
а протоⷤ она Ѿповѣдѹеть а рекѹчи такъ. Глⷡа з҃ .
7:1 то[18] иноⷢ видишь на соумантѧныни. одно застѹпы боюⷭ҇ючиⷯ[19] .
Тоуⷮ Хⷭ҇ опѧⷮ Ѿповѣдалъ єи тѣшѧчї ю. а милыми словы || (f. 43v)
похвалѧючї ю за то штоⷤ его раⷣⷶ миле вси бѣды тыє и напасти и
покѹсы на неє перепѹщоный з доброю волею то все еⷭ҇ претерпѣла. а
мовѧчи к неи таⷦ.

---

[17] On the margin, there is an encircled comment: прчⷭ҇теи двц҃и марии разоумнѣи, 'interpret as the Most Holy Virgin Mary.'

[18] This word should be read as Что. There is a space left before то for an initial but never filled.

[19] The meaning of the superscript с is unclear. Most likely, it was added during later copying.

6:4 Krafna gſi přitelnice ma . chutna a wytecna yako geruzalem . hrozna yako ſpic
ſtanowy zpoſobena .

6:5 Otwrat oczi twogi ote mne . neb ty gſu mi abych vletiel vcinili . Wlaſowe twogi
yako ſtada kozie kteražto ſu ſie vkazaly z galaad .

6:6 Zubowe twogi yako ſtado owcie . kterež ſu wze˙ſly z vmywadla . W˙ſiecky po
dwem gehnet magice . a yalowe nenie mezi nimi .

6:7 Yako kora zrnateho yablka . tak yahodky licij twych . kromie taynych vieci
twych .

6:8 Śe˙ſtdeſat g(es)t kralowen . a oſmdeſat ženim . a mladiciem nenie cziſla .

6:9 Gedna g(es)t holubice ma dokonala ma . gedna g(es)t mateři ſwe . wywolena
roditedlnici ſwe . Vidieli ſu gi dcery ſyonſke . a přeblahoſlawenu ſu ohlaſowaly .
kralowny a ženimy chwalili ſu gi .

6:10 Ktera g(es)t tato kteražto ſie beře yako zařie powſtawagic . kraſna yako mieſiec .
wyborna yako ſlunce . hrozna yako ſpic ſtanowy zpoſobena .
*Hlas cierkwe k ſynagoge .*

6:11 Stupila ſem do zahrady ořechowe . abych ohledala yablka vdolnie . a opatřila
ktwu li vinnicie . a wzplodila li ſu yablka zrnata .
*Hlas ſynagogy k cierkwi .*

6:12 Neuiediela . du˙ſie ma zarmutila mie g(es)t pro wozy aminadabowy .

*Hlas vtie˙ſeny cierkwe k ſynagogie .*

6:13 Nawrat ſie nawrat ſie ſunamitſka . nawrat ſie nawrat ſie at na tie patřime .

VII *Hlas ſynagogy o cierkwi .*

7:1 Czo vzrziś na ſunamitſke gednie zaſtupy rytieřugicich?
*Hlas kryſtow o cierkwi .*

Коль красны соуть ходы и ст8паніа твоа. оу вов8ви дщеро кнжти.
свазкове бедръ твоих гако же то запонки которыиж то коуть[20] скованы
р8ками золотарьскими.
7:2 И поупок твои гако рєпичка оуглаженаа николи не треб8ючи напоєвъ.
брюхо твое гако стогъ пшеничныи ѡбложеныи лиліами.
7:3 два сосца персєи твоих гако двоє телатокъ близнатокъ дикое козы.
7:4 шіа твоа гако вежа слонова оочи твои гако рыбники оу зевоне которыиж
то соут оу броны дчерь множества. носъ твои гако вежа ливанова гаж то
зрить против8 дамашк8.
7:5 голова твоа гако кормилъ. а волосы головы твоєи гакъ багоръ златт
тканыи цревъ причиненыи к жолобомъ
7:6 Коль красна єси витажна намилеишаа оу роскошах.
7:7 а постава твоа приподобана єс палмє. а сесца персеи твоих грезнови
винном8.
7:8 реклъ єсми оуст8плю на палмоу. а похвачю ѡвощіє єє и боуд8ть перси єє
гако гронове винничніи, а вона оустъ твоих гако раиских габлокъ.
7:9 горло твое гако вино наилепшее.
свєста хсва дша поуп[21] ѡ своем милом женисє хсє. такъ говорить.
годно милом8 к8 пити а оустомъ и з8бом єго къ пережюванію.
7:10 га милом8 моєм8 а ко мнє ѡборочаніє єго.
Тоут д8ша ѡпать познавши млс а любовь своег милог жениха хса к собє
тыми словы говорить к нем8.
7:11 Поиди милыи мой а выидимо на поле. пребыва в селех.
7:12 рано вьстанмо до винниць. а ѡсмотремо сквитла лі єс винница.
расплодилис ли соуть квє || (f. 44) тьа ѡвощіи, заквеtли ли с8ть оуже
раискаа габлока. тоут дам тобє перси мой.
7:13 мандракгоры дали с8ть воню свою. оу бронахъ наших вса габлока новаа
и ветхаа милыи мои сховала єсмь тобє.
Глва и. И ѡстаточнаа тых то милых книжокъ. тоутъ то дша милаа
невєста хсва. распаливший великою любовію а горачею мтью къ своєм8
милом8 жених8 хсоу. желаючи оуже с ним быти на вєки в небє. а
хотачи єго видєти лицем вь лице. а протожь чересъ набжное
размышленіє а оумноє бговидєніє. к немоу тыми словы, говорить.
просачи а молачис єм8.
8:1 Кто ми та дасть братца милого моег сс8чего перси мтки моєа. абых та

[20] Instead of соуть.

[21] свєста and поуп instead of невєста and тоут.

Kterak gſu kraſnij krokowe twogi w obuwi dcero knieżiete . Swazowe[22] bedr twych . yakożto zapony ge˙ſto gſu skowany ruku remeſlnikowu .

7:2 Pupek twoy yako řepice vhlazena . nikdy nepotřebugic napoiow . Břicho twe
yako ſtoh p˙ſenicny obloženy liliumem .
7:3 Dwa prſi twa yako dwie telatcie blizenci diwoke kozy .
7:4 Śige twa yako vieżie ſlonowa . Oczi twogi yako rybnici w ezebon . kteřižto gſu
w branie dcery mnozſtwie . Nos twoy yako vieżie libanſka . ge˙ſto patrzi proti
dama˙ſku .
7:5 Hlawa twa yako karmelus . a wlaſi hlawy twe yako zlattohlaw . kralow
přicinyeny k żlabom .
7:6 Kterak gſy kraſna a wytecna naymiley˙ſie w rozko˙ſech .
7:7 Poſtawa twa připodobniena g(es)t palmie . a prſi twe hroznom .
*Żenich o křiżi die .*
7:8 Rzekl ſem wſtupim na palmu polapim owotce gegie . *Żenich o choti* . Y budu
prſi twe yako hroznowe vinnicnij. a wonie vſt twych yako zrnatych yablek .
7:9 Hrdlo twe yako vino naylep˙ſie .
*Cierkew o kriſtoui die .*
Hodne milemu memu ku pitij. a rtom y zubom geho k přežiwani .
*Chot o żenichoui .*
7:10 Ya milemu me(mu) . a ke mnie obracenie geho .
*Cierkew o kriſtoui .*
7:11 Pod mily moy wygdieme na pole . přebywayme we wſech .
7:12 rano wſtanme do vinnicie . opatrzme zkwetla li g(es)t vinnicie . zplodili li ſu
kwietowe owotce . zakwetla li ſu zrnata yablka . tu dam tobie prſi me .

7:13 Mandragory daly ſu woni w branach na˙ſich . W˙ſiecka yablka nowa y wetcha
mily moy ſchowala ſem tobie .

VIII

*Hlas patriarch o kriſtoui .*

8:1 Kto mi tie da bratra meho sſucieho prſy matky me. abych tie nalezla wnie. a

[22] *Swazkowe* An, At.

знашла на дворѣ а поцеловала тя. а оуже мною тогды ни жадинъ не погорди^т.

8:2 а оухвачю тя и поведꙋ до домꙋ мт҃ри моеи. а да покойка ро^ди тельници моеи. тамъ мя бꙋдешь оучити. а я да^м тобѣ напои з вина ссchallаданаго. а смакъ раиски^х ꙗблокъ мои^х.

8:3 левица е^г по^д главою моею а правица е^г ѡбоиметь мя.

Голо^с х^свъ къ зборꙋ ст҃ыхъ ѡ своеи милои невѣсте дш҃и.

8:4 Заклинаю ва^с дщери иер^слмьскїа. абы есте не бꙋдили ани прочютити казали милое моеи. докꙋль бы ѡли^ж сама хотѣла.

Голо^с збороу ст҃аго ѡ невѣсте х^све. дивячи ся ѡ неи а пытаючи^с тыми словы рекоучи.

8:5 Ѡ которая е^с тая ж то оуст8паеть с п8стыни роскошми ся размогаючи. възлегши на милого свое^г.

голо^с женихо^в к невѣсте.

Подъ деревомъ ꙗблоновы^м оубꙋди^л есми тебѣ. тоутъ порꙋшена е^с мт҃ка твоя. тоу^т растлѣна есть ро^дите || (f. 44v) льница твоя.

К дш҃и х^съ говорить выповѣдꙋючи еи какъ е^с моцна млⷭ҇ его с нею, какъ пожиточьна е^с еи къ сп҃сенїю ега.

8:6 поло^ж мя ꙗко печа^т на ср^дци свое^м а ꙗко знамя на ремени твое^м. бо е^с силна ꙗко смрть милⷭ҇. а твердо ꙗко пекло желанїе. лампы ея ꙗко лампъı пламенныя а ѡгненыи.

8:7 воды многи не могли сꙋть оугасити любви. ани рѣки затопити ее. коли да^с члвкъ все што имѣеть за любь[23]. и бꙋдеть ꙗко^ж бы ничто^ж погꙋби^в.

Цркв ст҃ая говорить къ дш҃амъ которыи теперь ново починають миловати х^са в вѣрѣ еще боудꙋчи ^несъвершени. ани доскональни. а рекꙋчи.

8:8 сестра нш҃а маленька а персеи не има^т што оучинимъ сестре нш҃еи. въ дн҃ь коли ж то маеть быти намовлена. алюбо смовлена.

Са^м х^съ ѿповѣдаеть за нее а рекꙋчи.

8:9 ест ли мꙋръ влаимо^ж. на неи поушки серебряныи. пак ли сꙋть двери ѡгородѣм же и^х порканы кедровыми.

Дш҃а невѣста х^сва которо^ж ся ба размиловала говорить

8:10 ꙗ есми мꙋро. а перси мои ꙗко веж^да. зане^ж есмь оучинена пере^д нимъ. ꙗко покои наиденыи.

Ст҃їи ѡ црквии х^све. ѡ его милои невѣсте говорять тыми словы рекꙋчи.

8:11 виннница была е^с покоиномꙋ котора^ж то маеть люди да^л е^с ю

[23] Instead of любовь.

polibila tie . a giż mnu ni żadny nepohrzie :

8:2 Chytim tie a powedu tie do domu mateŕe me . a do pokogika roditelnicie me . tu
mie budeś vciti . a dam tobie napoy z vina ſkadaneho . a meſt zrnatych yablek
mych .
8:3 Leuicie ge(ho) pod hlawu mu . a prauicie geho obegme mie .
*Hlas kriſtow .*
8:4 Zaklinam was dcery geruzalemſke . aby˙ſte nebudily ani procititi kazali zmilele
donidż by ona ſama chtiela .

*Hlas ſynagogy k cierkwi .*
8:5 Ktera g(es)t tato ge˙ſto wſtupuge z pu˙ſtie . rozko˙ſmi ſie rozmahagic . zpoleh˙ſi
na milem ſwem :
*Hlas żenichow k neuieſtie .*
Pod dŕiewem iabloniewym vbudil ſem tie . tu poru˙ſena g(es)t matka twa . tu
po˙ſkwrniena g(es)t roditedlnicie twa.

*Cierkew k kriſtoui .*
8:6 Polož mie yako znamenie na ſrdce twe . yako znamenie na rameni twem . neb
g(es)t ſilna yako ſmrt miloſt . twrde yako peklo milowanie . Lampy geho yako
la(m)py ohniwe a plamenne .
8:7 Wody mnohe nemohly ſu vhaſiti laſky . ani ŕieky zatopie gi . Da li clouiek
we˙ſken ſtatek domu ſweho za milowanie . yako nic nepohrzie gim .

*Kriſtus k ſynagoge o cierkwi .*
8:8 Seſtra na˙ſie malicka . a prſij nema . Czo vcinime ſeſtŕie na˙ſie . w den kdyžto
namluwana ma byti .
*Kriſtus ſobie odpouieda .*
8:9 Geſtli zed wzdielayme na nie alkeŕie ſtŕiebrne . pakli gſu dweŕie ohradme gie
prkny cedrowymi .
*Odpouieda cierkew .*
8:10 Ya gſem zed . a prſi me yako vieżie . poniewadż ſem vciniena pŕed nim yako
pokog nalez˙ſi .
*Synagoga k cierkwi die .*
8:11 Vinnice byla g(es)t pokoynemu w tee kterażto ma lidi. dal g(es)t gi ſtrażnym.

сторожемъ. м8жь приноситъ за ѡ҆воци є҆ѣ ҂а҃ сребреникоⷡ.

Хⷭ҇ъ говоритъ ѡ҆ своє҆и невѣстѣ ст҃ои цр҃кви.

8:12 винн҇ица моѧ преⷣⷪ мною єⷭ҇ ҂а҃ твоиⷯ мѷ҇рныⷯ а҆ с҃ тыⷯ ѡ҆стерегаюⷮ которыи ѡ҆вощоⷡ є҆ѣ.

Голоⷭ҇ хⷭ҇въ къ блж҃нои а҆ къ ст҃ои дш҃и котораѧ є҆м8 набж҃не беⷥ престани сл8житъ въ дн҃и и҆ в҇ ночи молѧчиⷭ҇ є҆м8 въ ѱл҃мѣхъ и҆ в пѣⷭ҇хъ и҆ в҇ пѣнї а ⷯ дх҃овныⷯ а҆ въ всемъ волю єⷢ҇ чинѧчи. а҆ наⷣ все толк҇о є҆го самоⷢ҇ вѣрьне мил8ючи. а҆ ни ѡ҆ што ѡ҆ и҆ное на томъ свѣте дь || (f. 45) баючи.

8:13 Котораѧ живешь оу҆ виноградѣⷯ милого. посл8хаю голоса твоєⷢ҇ даи ми єⷢ҇ слышати.

Дш҃а ѿповѣда є҆тъ къ своє҆м8 миломоу милом оу жених8 хⷭ҇8 просѧчи єⷢ҇ а҆бы є҆ѣ оу҆же с того свѣта взѧⷧ҇ к҇ собѣ в҇ горн҇ее҆ црⷭ҇тво нбⷭ҇ное. гд҇ѣ єⷭ҇ соло ⷣкость всѧкї а вони бл҃гооу҆ханїа бжⷭ҇твнаго. и҆ великаѧ радѡⷭ҇. нбⷭ҇ное веселїе неи҆зрѣчен҇ное . и҆ вѣчн҇аго живота оу҆тѣшенїе. и҆ млⷭ҇ти бж҃їа и҆ любьви єⷢ҇ слаⷣкое насыщенїе а҆ конечн҇ее с милымъ бг҃омъ своиⷨ милыⷨ женихоⷨ вѣчноє҆ с ниⷨ милованїе. и҆ оу҆тѣшенїе.

8:14 Поиди милы҇ мои а҆ приробнаи сѧ дикои козе. а҆ ланѧтк8 є҆ленеⷨ⁸ на гораⷯ бл҃говонн҇ыⷯ рѣчеи.

Muż přina˙ſie za owotce gegie tiſic ſtřiebrnych .

*Kriſtus die .*

8:12 Vinnicie ma přede mnu g(es)t . Tiſic twych pokoynych . a dwieſtie tiech kteřiż
oſtřiehagij owotcie gegieho .

*Hlas kriſtow .*

8:13 Kteraż bydliś w zahradach přietelé poſluchagij hlaſu tweho . każ mi ſly˙ſieti gey.

*Hlas cierkwe k kriſtoui .*

8:14 Vtecz mily moy . a přirownay ſie k diwoke kozie . a k koluchoui gelenyemu na
horach wonnych viecij .

## Appendix II. The Ruthenian *Book of Taudal the Knight*[1]

(f. 144) **Починаетсѧ книга ѿ таоудале рыцари**
лѣта ѿ нарожениїа сн҃а бж҃иаго тисѧчаго триⷣцатого девѧтого было дрѫгое лѣто цр҃ѧ таврата цесарѧ римъского вале҇ⷱного ишто есть валькоу про ер҃лимъ мѣлъ, а четвертаго лѣта, ꙗко же есть еѵгенїюсъ папежемъ былъ воленъ, в томъ лѣте тако еѵгениюсъ папеⷤ възратил сѧ есть былъ до рима з влаⷯ ишто словоу гамїа[2] а тогоⷤ лѣта стыи малахиа въ манастыри, иже то слове глозоналъ, изшелъ с того свѣта.

С того мѣста былъ есть единъ моуⷤ родомъ, емоуⷤ имѧ было таоудалъ, родоу словоутного але дѣлъ велми недобрыхъ, по тѣлоу витѧⷤный а велми смѣлый, а ѡ спасенїи своеа дш҃а мало ибо ничого не смотрѧше. то емоу прелишь бѧше противно, а штобъ хто ѐмоу хотѣлъ мало ѡ спасенїи дш҃и повѣдати . до цр҃кви такеⷤ не ходѧше а нищихъ ненавидѧше преⷣ собою, але играцемъ и пистцоⷨ а гоуⷣцомъ выдалъ есть что мѣлъ . але мѣлъ много таваришовъ а приꙗтелевъ добытыхъ . и любимого имѣлъ ѐсть товариша единого в ритеръствѣ, тотъ емоу былъ должеⷩ три кони . Тогда таоудалоусъ ждалъ емоу до оурочного рокоу и напоминалъ емоу и по тоⷨ роце приехалъ к немоу . а ѡнъ его любовъно || (f. 144v) привиталъ и былъ оу него три дни а три нощи . никаⷨ емоу не далъ ити тоутъ пилъ с ниⷨ а мовилъ с ниⷨ ѡ различныⷯ речаⷯ .

(f. 146v) **глава. ·г҃·** Егдаⷤ поидоша посполоу. Ѿидоста немѣюще жаⷣное свѣтлости ниⷤли ѿ аг҃гла. и прїидоша до долоу прелишь грозного а велми темного, а тотъ бѧше велми глꙋбокїи а полнъ горѧщого оуглїа а на тоⷨ долоу покрывало желѣзное толъстотою на десѧть локотъ а то своею горкостию примогаше. тоу бѧше ѿ того покривала такїи смраⷣ, ишто бѧше дѫша търпѣла всѣхъ моукъ, премогалъ тотъ смраⷣ. а в тотъ долъ грозный что поⷣ покривалоⷨ идѧхоу много доуши грѣшныⷯ а на тоⷨ железноⷨ покривале горѧщеⷨ парѧхоу ихъ, ꙗко бы ѡскварокъ въ панви. с того со всего еще бѧше наигорше, иже

[1] The following three fragments from the Ruthenian *Book of Taudal the Knight* are taken from the Swidziński Miscellany and are reproduced here according to the edition by Alexander Brückner (Brückner 1881, 199–212) with several corrections and modified word divisions.

[2] Should be read as галлїа.

# The Church Slavonic *Edifying Story Told by Faudal the Warrior* [3]

(f. 259) ПоложенѦ быⷭ҇ сиѝ повѣсть во .в҃і. гл҃хъ.

Повеⷭⷮ полезна сиа҆ сказаⷩ҇ є҆ фаоу҆далоⷨ . воиноⷨ . приклюⷱ҇шаⷽ҇сѧ є҆моу҆ . каⷦ҇ быⷭ҇ мр҃твъ . три д҃ни . и҆ паки ѡ҆живе . и҆ тамо видѣ мноⷢ҇личнаꙗ҆ м҃чниꙗ҆ а҆дова . и҆ грѣшныⷯ жилища . и҆ велики҅ скорби . и҆ ноужⷣа . и҆ насиліа҆ . томлений бесъ въскыⷯ търпеⷧ҇ . а҆г҃гль бо б҃жи҅ видиⷧ҇ єⷢ҇ и҆ тамо є҆моуⷤ҇ и҆ сказаваше по рѧдоу҆ . коє҆го ради греха каⷦ҇ єⷭ҇ кто моучиⷨ . и҆ каꙗ҆ м҃чніа҆ лютаꙗ҆ . ждоуⷮ҇ грѣшныⷯ нехотѧщиⷯ сѧ каꙗти . и҆ є҆ще тамо видѣ . каковыⷯ бл҃гъ споⷣбленії д҃ша правеⷣныхъ :- глⷡ҇а . а҃ . блⷭ҇ви ѡ҆҃че проⷱ҇ : +

Поведавы наⷨ сиа҆ и҆меноуе҆мы҅ фаоудаⷧ҇ . рожение҆ и҆ воспитаніє҆ єⷢ҇ . въ граⷣⷡ ри҅ⷨстиⷨ бл҃гороуⷣноу и҆ богаⷮ҇у радителю с҃нъ нрав же сверепъ и҆ жестокъ . телесеⷨ крѣпоⷦ҇ . и҆ во воеⷯ же храбръ напрасно . смр҃ти же и҆ доу҆шевноⷢ҇ попеⷱ҇ніꙗ҆ никогда же помѧноуⷡ҇ и҆ всѧⷦ҇ гл҃ѧй е҆мꙋ полезнаꙗ҆ противень тоу҆ ꙗ҆влѧшеⷭ҇ . во црк҃въ же на || (f. 260) м҃лтвꙋ не входѧ . и҆ нищиⷯ и҆з лиха ненавидѧ. и҆ всѧ е҆лика и҆мѧше в҅ гоусли . и҆ тиⷨ паны прочаꙗ҆ . таковаꙗ҆ брацаю҆щиⷨ раздоваше . и҆ многыхы дроугоⷨвъ[4] пꙋстоⷲ҇ныⷯ сиⷨ притѧжа· но ѡ҆баче е҆динъ ѿ воиⷩ҇ люблѧше · и҆скрено е҆моу же и҆ долъженъ бѣ три конѧ . и҆ жд҅авъ е҆мꙋ до времене речеⷩ҇ного и҆ прийде взѧти долгъ сво҅ . єⷢ҇ же любовъне прие҆мъ и҆ доволъными · трапезы ї пьꙗ҆ньствы оу҆чредивъ .

(f. 264) а҃[5]

И҆доущима же нама вкꙋпе и҆ свѣтъ погибе токъмо а҆г҃гловъ свѣтѧщесѧ и҆ при҅дохомъ ко пропасти темнѣ и҆ страшне . не и҆мы҅ конца глоубинѣ полъна же ю҆гли горѧщиⷯ . и҆ на н҅е покрывало железно . толъ.сто лакти десѧть пре ѡ҆девааꙗ҆ лютостию҆ . ѿ него же и҆схожаше смрадъ и҆ преже видимыхъ . д҃ши моеи҆ горъчае҆ши . и҆ в тоу҆ю҆ пропасть . покровеноу҆ю҆ множество ниⷥсходѧхъ д҃шь грѣшныⷯ . и҆ на томъ прикрывале зномъ[6] прѧгоуть иⷯ ꙗ҆ко сало в котлѣ скварѧщее҆сѧ . всѣхъ же горъшей ꙗко сквозѣ ѡ҆ное҆ прикривало . д҃шь техъ цѣдѧть ꙗ҆ко воскь сквозѣ мѣхъ и҆

[3] The whole text of the *Edifying Story of Faudal the Warrior* is found in a late fifteenth or early sixteenth-century miscellany from the National Library in Warsaw, Biblioteka Ordynacji Zamojskich #92 on ff. 259–288 (briefly described in Shchapov 1976a and 1976b).

[4] The superscript м is probably a corruption.

[5] Written on the margin.

[6] This is, most likely, a mistake during copying from the word желѣзномъ.

скрозе то || (f. 147) покрывало цѣдıахоу тїи грѣшныа доуши, и ıако воскъ скрозе плат цедѧть. апѧть тамъ сѧ ѡбновлѧхѹ во ѡгни к моукам. Тогда аг҃лъ к дѫши рече та моука есть вражебниковъ приготована ѿцовъ а брати а иным тымъ, которыи же даремно поволнѣ враждоують дѣлом. и рече агг҃лъ по той тѧ моуце поведоу до большихъ. а ты какъ же былъ еси враждѣлникъ, ѡбаче того не боудешь тръпѣти. Потом прїидоша к горѣ велми великои а прелишь къ грозной. а тоу бѧше поут велми оузкый съ единое страны тое горы и с тое горы плапоташе ѡгонь смолы а з серы а велми смрадныи а прелишь темныи а з дрѫгое страны снѣгъ с ледомъ а ветръ велми силно великыи. на тои же то горѣ было есть полно катовъ бѣсовъ съ пламенными гребла, съ оудицами желѣзными, ѡ трехъ розехъ вельми ѡстрыми, нимиж то доуши давѧхоу, которыи хотѣли черес тоу горѫ проити. и вътръгахоу ихъ в тыи моукы а по хвили оувращахѫ ихъ въ ѡгонь и ѡпѧтъ засѧ въ моукы. и повѣда агг҃лъ тоут есть моука льстивыхъ а гнѣвливых невѣрныхъ. Потом доуша таоудалова про великыи страхъ а грозоу оупадаше за агглом идоущи. прїидоша до глоубокого долоу нечистого а велми темного, егож великости не могла дш҃а дозрети а едно слышала звоукъ реки пловоущѹю серою а рыдание доушь в тои реце, || (f. 147v) иже моучахоу сѧ в ней. Ѿтоудѫ выхожахоу дивове и ıако з мръхи и вельми смрадныи смрад, иже премоглъ былъ вси моукы, что есть доуша была перво видѣла ихъ. Тоу пакъ бѧше една лавичька велми длъга съ единое горы на дроугоую и ıако мостокъ черес долъ преглоубокїи оу даль на милю а единъ в ширинoу перъстень мостокъ ити. не было льзе жадъномоу преити нижли божемоу зволенъцоу с тогож то мостъка таоудалова доуша видѣла много доушь падающих, нижли единъ законникъ презвитеръ тотъ его прошолъ безъ шкоды, иже былъ поустынникъ, неслъ есть палмоу сирѣчь знамѧ в рѹце а ѡблъченъ былъ в ризы законскы. а тот есть мнихъ наперееи прешолъ. Агглъ оутѣшаа дѹшю повѣдилъ есть не бои сѧ, боудешь збавена тое то мѹкы, але иный моусишь терпѣти. а ида напред и нѧвъ его и превелъ черес тот мостокъ безъ оуразоу. И повѣдилъ есть гл҃ѧ тот то долъ гордых есть моужеи пышныхъ всѣхъ немилостивыхъ.

**глава аı҃·** Мало егда же бѣıаста отошла, оузрѣли дом || (f. 158) дивно оукрашенъ, ѿ злата, ѿ срѣбра а ѿ драгаго каменїа а не бѧше двереи ани ѡконець в томъ домоу, ѡбаче вси которыи хотѣли, шли ѿ того домѹ. а в том домоу такаа бѧше всѣтлость, же не гл҃ю иже бы едно сл҃нце свѣтило, но ıако неколико сл҃нцов было. тот домъ былъ паки во ѿгни ѡбъновлѧхоу сѧ на моуки . тогда а҃ггль рече ми се ѥсть моука оуготованъна тоуне гнѣвающимъсѧ . на ѿц҃а и на братию и на всехъ чл҃вкь и рече ми сею моукою поведоу тѧ к болъшимъ ты же аще си врагъ бывъ но сихъ . не имаши . терпѣти :·

гл҃ⷡа в҃ [7] По семъ прийдоⷯ къ горе привелицей и зѣло страшней . и со ѥдиныѧ страны горы пȣⷮ велми оузокъ . и из горы тое клоко || (f. 265) таше ѿгнь смолы сѣры темъный веⷧми и смрадъный . ѿ дроугое же страны . снѣгъ с лѣдомъ и вѣтрь жестокъ . гора же сиѧ исполнена . бысть бѣсовъскими . мȣчители со тризоубъци . ѿгнеными . и с ȣдами железными . три роги имоуща вельми . ѡстрыⷯ ими же дш҃ь бодахȣ . хотѧщиⷯ прейти гороу ѡноу и въ моуки реющи . и паки вмале вь ѿгнь влагахоу иⷯ и по сиⷯ моуки и каза ми . а҃гглъ се ѥсть моужей моука лⷭтивыⷯ и враждȣющиⷯ . и невѣрныхъ по семъ дш҃а моѧ ѿ великаго . ради страха . и прениꙗ последоуѧ а҃гглȣ претыкашесѧ :·

гл҃ⷡа . · г· Прийдохомъ же в ровъ глⷹоубокий . нечистоты и тмы исплъненъ [8] . ѥго же величества доуша моѧ . не возможе до конца видити . токмо слышаⷯ реченое стремъленїе . текоущее . сѣрою и вопль доушевный миноующесѧ тамо . и ѿ толе исхожаѧ многовидънаꙗ томлениѧ моукамъ . и ꙗко троупъный смрадъ превосходѧ . прежⷣе нихъ моукъ видимыхъ дш҃и моей . и тоу бѧше лава долготою . велика ѿ горы к то [9] дроузей горе ꙗко мостъ . чересъ ровъ преглоубокий . долготою ꙗко пѧтьма поприщий . и широка ѿ прьстей ѥдиномъ ѥꙗ же прийти никако же мощно . токмо истиⷩно работавшиⷯ бг҃оу . и ѿ мостȣ сего видеⷯ много падающиⷯ дш҃ь . ѥдинъ же презъвитеръ . || (f. 266) во мнишеской ѡдежи въши [10] в поустыни и носѧ нѣкое . знаменїе божие в рȣцѣ своеи . сей прейде мость ѡнъ долъгий . не запѧтъ ничиⷨ же сиѧ сказа а҃ггль оутешаѧ мѧ не боисѧ рече сеѧ мȣки свободь . боудеши иныⷯ же претерпети . имайши . и шествȣѧ приведе мѧ безъ врьда и гл҃а ми сий ровъ ѥсть . чл҃вкъ грьдыⷯ и немлⷭтивыⷯ :·

(f. 284) гл҃ⷡа ·аі· Мало же намь ѿшедъшиⷨ и се домь диⷡно оукрашень златомъ сребромь и многоцѣⷩными камений врать же не имый ни

[7] Written on the margin.

[8] The letter ъ is modified from an о.

[9] Should be тои.

[10] This is probably a corruption of ѡдежи живъши.

прешироки̇и а ѡкрѫглы а всѧ оутворена ѿ хр8сталѧ и ѿ злата а ѿ драгаго каменїа а повлаць та всѧ ѿ злата и ѿ драгаго каменїа бѧше. Такъ смотрѧ таоудалюс оузрѣ единъ златыи прстлъ, предрагими поставци повлеченъ, а приправлена ѿ всѧкого найдражшаг каменїа. А на том прстлѣ крал кромѣрътга сѣдел надрагой ѡдежи что есть на том то свѣте наидражши. Єгдаж стоꙗше дивѧшес. поиде множествїе ихъ до того дом8 з дары своими пред кралѧ а кажды емоу приношаше свои дары велми веселе и с радостию. Таоудалюс егдаж такъ долго стоѧше пред своим кралем, и ꙗкож есть был его краль на свѣте, съедег много поповъ а дїаконовъ ѡблъчены в ризы и въ всю сщенническ8ю ѡдежю, и ꙗко хотѧще литргїю сл8жити. а тоу тот дом ѡздобѧхоу и и оукрашахѫ, а наставлѧх8 к том8 златыхъ чашеи а к8ѳликовъ а кал8ховъ. и довнимал, иже бы иное вѧще хвалы въ нбсномъ црствїи не было, здало быс досыт тое радости, что есть т8 было а тоут вси слоужахоу пред кралем приходѧще || (f. 158v) припадали емоу глюще блжнъ еси и добро тобѣ боудеть, ибо бѫдешь добре оуживати въ силѣ [in the margin въ крѣпости] р8къ своих.

ѿконець ѿбаче живоущий в немь исхождаꙗхоу и восхождааху никимь же возбраняемий . в домоу томь свѣтоу быти не ꙗко ѿ единого слнца . но ꙗко многыя слнца просвѣщааху лоуча своя круглостию и широтою превекь[11] бѣ вся же оутворениа хроусталнa и злата и камения драгаго . полаты же в неⷨ . златый всякого мноⷢцѣннаго каменїа оустроены . и се видехъ престолъ злать пестрыми оуброусы поокрове но и всячскими различай многоцѣнными оукрашень на неⷨ же сѣдяше црь знаемы ми во ѿдежди многоцѣнной иже во мирѣ семь надражшая и стогаⷯ дивяся и се иде множество в доⷨ ѿный з дары кь црю и вся приношениа емоу исполнь раⷣⷪсти и веселиа . и стоящя ми преⷣ ниⷨ на долзе . ꙗкоⷤ црь мнѣ быⷭ и в животѣ сый . абие прийде множество презвитеⷬ съ диаконы. ѿбольчени въ свщнические ѿдежⷣа . ꙗкоⷤ хотяще совершати бжⷭтвеноую литргию . и всячскими красотами оутваря || (f. 285) хоу доⷨ ѿный преⷣпоставляюще чяши златыя коубъки и потири. мнѣти ми ꙗко сиⷯ болше и нѣⷭ хвалы в небесноⷨ црⷭтви несказанная бо радость тоу бяше ꙗко всѣⷨ слоужити црви и приходяще кланяхоуся емоу глюще блжень еси добро тобѣ боудеть оудержиши бо блгая крѣпости роукь своиⷯ

---

[11] Should be превеликь.

# Appendix III. The Latin *Visio Tundali*[1]

*De raptu animae Tundali, & eius viſione*
Cap. LXXXCIII

Anno domini 1149. qui fuit annus secundus expeditionis Hieroſolymorum, Co(n)radi Regis Romanorum, & annus quartus Eugenii Papæ, in quo anno ipſe Papa de partibus Galliarum Romam reuerſus eſt, in quo etia(m) anno ſanctus Malachias in Clareualle defunctus eſt, viſa eſt hæc viſio.

Duae ſunt Metropoles in Hibernia, Ardiacha ſeptentrionalium Hibernenſium, Auſtralium Caſelenſis, de qua ortus fuit vir quidam, Tundalus nomine, nobilis genere, crudelis actione, forma corporis egregius, fortitudine robuſtus, de ſalute animæ suæ nihil ſolicitus; grauiter ferebat ſi quis ei vel breuiter de ſalute animæ loqueretur. Eccleſiam negligebat, pauperes Chriſti nec videre volebat, ſcurris & ioculatoribus pro vana gloria diſtribuebat, quicquid habebat. Hic cum multos haberet amicos & ſodales, inter eos habebat vnum, qui co(m)militonis debito, trium equorum debitor erat. Hic cum ſtatutum terminum præſtolaret, tranſacto termino, illu(m) conuenit, qui cum bene receptus ab eo pere(n)dinaret tribus noctibus coepit tractare de cæteris rebus. [...]

*De valle horribili, & ponte anguſto.* Cap. XC.
Cvmque longius ſimul pergerent, nullumque præter ſplendorem Angeli lumen haberent, venerunt ad vallem terribilem & tenebroſam valde, & opertam mortis caligine. Erat autem profunda, & carbonibus ardentibus plena, operculum ferreum habens ſpiſſitudinis 6. cubitorum, quod ardore nimio ipſos carbones ſuperabat ardentes. Cuius fætor omnes, quas hucuſque paſſa fuerat anima tribulationes, ſuperabat. Super illam laminam deſcendebat multitudo miſerarum animaru(m), & illic cremabantur, donec ad modum cremii in ſartagine liqueſcerent, & quod erat grauius per prædictam laminam colabantur, ſicut colari ſolet cera per pa(n)num, & iterum in carbonibus ignis ardentibus renouabantur ad tormentum. Hæc erat pæna patricidarum, fratricidarum, homicidarum vel facto vel conſenſu. Sed poſt hanc pænam, inquit Angelus, ducentur ad maiores. Tu autem quamuis homicida ſis, modo tamen iſtam non patieris. Poſt hæc venerunt ad montem miræ magnitudinis & horroris, magnæ & vaſtæ ſolitudinis qui transeuntibus anguſtum valde præbebat iter. Ex vna parte illius montis erat ignis putridus ſulphureus & tenebroſus, ex altera parte nix glacialis & ventus horribilis. Erat mons ille tortor-

[1] Vincent de Beauvais [1624] 1964, 1127–1133.

ibus plenus, qui furcas habeba(n)t ferreas ignitas, & tridentes acutiſſimos, quibus iugulabant animas tranſire nolentes, & ad poenas trahebant, & per vices de niue & grandine mittebant eas in ignem, & econuerſo. Hæc eſt, inquit Angelus, poena inſidiatorum & perſidorum. Poſt hæc anima illa præ timore pedete(n)tim angelum ſequens, venit ad vallem profundam, & putridam nimis & tenebroſam, cuius profunditate(m) ipſa quidem anima videre non poterat, ſonitum tamen ſulphurei fluminis, & vlulatum patientium in eo audiebat. Fumus vero de ſulphure & cadaueribus inde ſurgebat foetidus, qui ſuperabat omnes poenas quas prius viderat: ibi erat tabula lo(n)giſſima de vno monte in aliu(m) montem porrecta, in modum pontis ſuper vallem extenſa, quæ mille paſſus habebat in longitudine, in latitudine pedem vnum. Quem pontem nemo niſi electus tranſire poterat. De hoc po(n)te vidit hæc illa anima multos cadere, & vnum ſolum presbyterum illæſum pertranſire, qui erat peregrinus portans palmam, & indutus ſclauinia, & primus ante omnes intrepidus pertranſibat: Angelus autem timentem conſolans animam dixit: Ne timeas, ab hac ſiquidem poena liberaberis, ſed aliam patieris. Et præcedens tenuit eam, & vltra pontem duxit illæſam dicens: Hæc eſt, inquit, vallis horribilis in poena ſuperborum.

Cvm autem modicum procederent, viderunt domum mirabiliter ornatam, cuius paries & omnis ſtructura ex auto & argento erant,& ex omnium lapidum precioſorum generibus, ſed fenistræ ibi non erant nec oſtium, & tamen omnes qui intrare volebant intrabant. Erat autem intus tam ſplendida, acſi non dico vnus Sol, ſed quaſi ibi multi ſplenderent Soles. Eratque nimis ampla & rotunda, & nullis columnis fulta, & totum etiam eius veſtibulum auro & lapidibus precioſis erat ſtratum. Circum ſpiciens autem Tundalus, vidit vnum ſedile aureum, cum gemmis & ſerico & omnibus ornamentis ornatum, & Regem Cormarcum in ipſo throno ſedere, veſtitum mirabilibus veſtimentis, & precioſiſſimis ſupra omne precium terrenum. Etcum ſtaret admirans, venerunt plurimi in domum illam cum muneribus ad Regem, & offerebant ſinguli cum gaudio munera ſua. Et dum ſtaret Tundalus diutius, ante Dominum ſuum Regem Cormarcum, erat enim Dominus ſuus in ſæculo, veneruntque multi ſacerdotes, & leuitæ ſolenniter induti, ſicut ad Miſſam cantandam cum ſericis caſulis, & alijs ornamentis valde precioſis, & ornabatur vndique domus illa regia mirabili atque præcioſiſſimo ornamento. Ponebant enim cyphos & calices aureos & argenteos & pixides eburneas ſuper paxillos & tabulas, & ſic domus illa ornabatur, vt ſi maior gloria in regno Dei non eſſet, iſta poſſe ſufficere videretur. Omnes ergo illi qui miniſtrabant ante Regem venientes, & genua flectentes dicebant: *Labores manuum tuarum quia manducabis*.

## Appendix IV.
## The Church Slavonic *On the Three Lawful States* [1]

(f. 288) Гл҃еть писание̑ ѿ треⷯ в҇законениꙗⷯ хрⷭ҇тиѧноⷨ преданыⷯ ю҆ноша и҆ли дв҃а и҆ вдова . и҆ли ѿ брака женоу҆ моу҆же и҆мый и҆ всѧкъ слышавый . и҆ несохранѧꙗ҆ заповѣдей сиⷯ нѣⷭ҇ подобень гⷭ҇оу н҇шомоу҆ і҆с҃ хⷭ҇оу . ѡ҆ сеⷨ бо пишеть є҆зекиѧ҆ прр҃ⷪкъ гл҃ѧ в дн҃ь соу҆да ни є҆динъ же сп҃сень боу҆деть раз҇вѣ треⷯ моу҆жей сирѣⷱ[2] лота и҆ѡ҆ва данийла но ѡ҆ сиⷯ да раꙁꙋмѣє҆мь а҆ще бы є҆динемь сиⷨ спⷭ҇тисѧ . а҆нꙵ никто же не боу҆дито но ѡ҆баⷱ тий три є҆прона знамеꙋю҆ть три взаконѣниѧ҆ ѿ и҆ѡ҆ва женѧщий ѿ лота вдовьствоу҆ю҆щий ѿ данийла . дв҇ⷭтвеници и҆ сими вз҇а || (f. 289) конений хрⷭ҇тиꙗ҆не спⷭ҇ени боудоу҆ть во дн҃ь соу҆д҇ный а҆ є҆же єⷭ҇ кто кромѣ сего закона погиб҇неть ꙗ҆ко же гл҃еть ст҃ый павеⷧ҇ бл҇оуд҇никоⷨ и҆ прелюбодѣеⷨ бог осоу҆дить ѡ҆нѣмь соу҆доⷨ сꙋдить погибели веч҇ней гл҃еть бо ст҃ый гераси ⷨ ꙗ҆ко бл҇оуда ради гⷭ҇ь реⷱ҇. каю҆сѧ ꙗ҆ко сотвориⷯ чл҃вка никоє҆го же бо грѣха сице гⷭ҇ь не мстиⷧ҇ єⷭ҇ . ꙗ҆въно ꙗ҆ко ꙗ҆ко блоу҆дъ содомоу҆ и҆ гомороу҆ и҆ныⷯ грады во а҆дъ преврати и҆ бл҇оу҆да ради веⷭ҇ мирь потопи бл҇оуда ради все колѣно вениꙗ҆миново погоубилъ бл҇оуда ради . много тысѧщь жидовъ напрⷭ҇ною҆ смр҃тию҆ поразити . бл҇оуда ради . ꙗ҆ко же и҆н҇де пишеть . гⷭ҇ь б҃ь до҇лго воп҇лотитиⷭ҇ не хотѣль . и҆ прпⷣбны҇ гераси мъ гл҃ть . ꙗ҆ко родиⷭ҇ во полоуноци . є҆гⷣа вси блоуⷣници напрасною҆ смр҃тию҆ погибоша . сего дѣлѧ всѧⷦ҇ хрⷭ҇тиѧ҆нинь . да пребываєть в҇ закони . в неⷨ же восхощеть . ѡ҆ставив҇ши вси свой похоти . ли закон҇но женившиⷭ҇ . и҆ли во вдовъстви съхранѧꙗ҆ цѣломⷣрие̑ . и҆ли в҇законений каю҆щиⷯсѧ . и҆ли во оу҆стави . дв҃ъственикъ . бг҃оу н҃шемоу҆ сл҃ва съ ѡ҆ц҃мь и҆ ст҃ыⷨ : ~ :

---

[1] Transcribed from a late fifteenth or early sixteenth-century miscellany from the National Library in Warsaw, Biblioteka Ordynacji Zamojskich #92, ff. 288–289.

[2] In the manuscript, it is written спрѣⷱ.

# Appendix V. The Ruthenian *Tale of Sivilla the Prophetess*[1]

Ѕказаніе ѡ сивиллє прⷪ҇рчици f. 171v

Того чаⷭ҇ꙋ за моꙋдраго црѧ саломона. бѣѧше прⷪ҇рчица ѕвѣздарька именеⷨ сивилла, а та бѣѧше велми моꙋдрâ. иже въ звѣзⷣахъ мно-гый вещи в бꙋдѧщиⷯ речаⷯ провидѣла. преⷤ многыⷯ тысѧщь лѣⷮ. что сѧ в землѧⷯ стати маѐть, та ѐй моꙋⷣрость еⷭ҇ ѿ бга дана. и зна-ѐма бѣѧше. и бѧше красна. à богата. але ѐдинꙋ ногꙋ къ поⷣⷪбенъствꙋ гоꙋсинꙋ ногꙋ мѣла, и за тꙋ сѧ велми смоꙋщашеⷭ҇. а протоⷤ на ней стоꙗла и ходила. теⷤ и ꙗкоⷤ то и иный люⷣⷶ стоꙗть. àбо ходѧⷮ. Сивилла оуслыша-вши ѡ моуⷣрости саломоновѣ, и ѿ красе его двора. въсхотѣла своима ѡчима видѣти ѐго. и иде к немоꙋ. â ѐгдаⷤ то црь оувѣдалъ. противъ неѐ пойде. понеⷤ слышаⷧ ѿ ней повѣ-дающи. много. и приꙗлъ ю с великою честїю и раⷣⷪстию. гла радꙋйсѧ возлюбленнаà гости. â ѡна емоꙋ подѧковала велми миле. и рече к не црь. сивилла и почто еси сеⷨ працовала. и ѿвѣ-ща сивилла. црю тоѐ и ꙗ хощꙋ повѣдати àбы изволилъ вѣдати. мнѣ ѐсть ѡ твоѐй моуⷣро- f. 172 сти. и ѿ красотѣ твоѐго двора повѣдано и такъ и ѿныⷯ вещеⷯ много и рада быⷯ то за пра-вдꙋ звѣдала. Тогда црь рече. не хощꙋ без того быти. моусишь первеѐ со мною ѐсти. â ѐгда же идѧше с ниⷨ сивилла къ дворꙋ. иже с ниⷨ ѐсти имѣла. и пригоⷣⷶло сѧ и ꙗко сѧ стати могло преⷭ҇ àдамово древо ити. à ѐгдаⷤ тоѐ древо добре ѡсмотрела, и не хотѣла ѐсть черезъ ѐго ити à в тоⷮ чаⷭ҇ сталъ сѧ ѐсть дивъ ѿ бга. иже сиви-лле гꙋсиѧ нога ѐсть была оуздравена. и ꙗкоⷤ

[1] The text of the *Tale* is reproduced from Karskii's edition (Karskii 1898, 2–10) with corrections and additions made with the help of the Czech source texts (Zíbrt 1910 and Menčík 1879). Line numbers – despite a couple of errors – are also reproduced from Karskii's edition.

то члвчиа нога, и возрадовала ся есть томоу сивилла велми. а црь то баше молча все видѣвъ. ани чтож не реклъ. ажь было и по обѣде на цареве дворе. И рече црь къ сивилле. сивилло повѣж. что еси то оумѣнила. иже еси со мною черес тое древо не шла. а она ем8. Ѿповѣдила. вѣдай црю. иже ся маеть дитя ис тебе[2] на тот то свѣт народити. зъ двы. а маеть оумрти на том древе. а многомоу члвчеств8 помоци з ноуже которыж боудеть в него вѣрити. и такъ двѣ мтри его. Црь рече. сивилло повѣдай ми Ѿк8дя еси тоу моудрость взяла хотел бых того радъ вѣдати. она емоу Ѿповѣдала. Повѣдаю тобѣ иже [f. 172v] видим звѣздя на нбе а крстъ а окр8г. а в том окр8гле двиц8. а едино дитя. и иный оучителный. вещи. которыиж соут мнѣ нне Ѿ бга зъявлены. Тогда црь саломон. больше въпрошааше ея гля вѣси ли когда дитя тое народитися маеть. а какъ емоу имя дано боудет. И Ѿвѣща сивилла Ѿ том га црю во истинн8 вемъ. безъ всякое измѣны. боудет члкъ. и истинны бгъ. а боудет іс хс назван. И тот боудет оучити на земли люди. како бы могли живи быти на небесех. И боудет онъ оучити оуставеня нова. и приказанья многа. и вси люди боудоут верети в него. и последовати боудоут оученію его. Потом его имя и его бжествие воистинн8 познано боудет. по всей земли розглашено. и боудет бгъ чтоущій и моляційся всем народомъ. и Ѿ него хрстианъство боудеть розмножено. И жидовъство боудет потлачено. иже потом жадного царя. ани князя никогда вяще не боудят мѣти. То оуслышавъ цръ видѣла ся ем8 та реч р8гава и неистинна. и не хотел ся на то обратити. ани томоу верити. бы жидовъство мѣло скажено быти.

[2] This is a mistranslation of the Czech *jistě*, 'without doubt, certainly': "Věz, to králi, že se má dietě naroditi jistě na tento svět z panny, a to má na tom dřevě potom umřieti." (Zíbrt 1910, 77.)

и҆ ч҇то є҆м8 ѿ х҃е гл҃аше. ничем8 том8 не вѣроваше. Сивил҇ла рече ты мнѣ цр҃ю не вериⷲ. вѣрь иже а҆зъ є҆см҇и то на звѣздаⷯ оу҆смотре f. 173 а҆ то сѧ҆ вс҇е мае́ⷮ стати. И҆ оу҆сл҇ышавъ то цр҃ь оу҆мол҇че того чаⷭ҇у. И҆ нача є҆ѧ҆ дале въпр҇ошати гл҃ѧ. сивил҇ло. ч҇то ми є҆си повѣдала ѿ х҃е а҆ християнеⷯ. а҆чьколвекъ том8 не мог8 вѣрити ѿбаче ѿ тоⷨ раⷣ сл҇ышати. и҆ є҆гдаⷤ пакъ хрⷭ҇тиа҆не боу҆доуⷮ. какъ боу҆деⷮ в тыи҆ часы на зем҇ли. сивил҇ла рече. то ѧ҆ цр҃ю повѣдаю҆ тобѣ. а҆жь и҆ не веришь м҇нѣ. жидовъ б҃ѫдеⷮ вел҇ми мало. и҆ б8джⷮ жидове хрⷭ҇тиа҆ноⷨ поⷣдани быти, а҆ є҆гдаⷤ сѧ҆ боу҆деⷮ хрⷭ҇тиа҆нъст҇во м҇ножити. тог҇да ваши люⷣи жиⷣовъскїи҆ боу҆доуⷮ гин8ти. а҆ которыи҆ боу҆доуⷮ хрⷭ҇тиа҆нъск8 вѣр8 др҇ъжати добре. боу҆доуⷮ бл҃жни. и҆ ѧ҆коⷤ и҆ ѧ҆ ѿ тоⷨ имаⷨ верити. И рече цр҃ь. вопр҇ошаю҆ тѧ҆ того спр҇авн҇е.[3] какъ долг҇о свѣⷮ маеть ст҇оѧ҆ти. и҆ ѿна ѿвѣща целе и҆ ѧ҆ того не мог8 вѣдати. и҆ є҆гда соуⷣн҇ыи҆ д҃нь маеⷮ прїйти. ѿ тоⷨ вем҇ъ поведати ч҇то хощеⷮ за прав҇д8 прїйти. є҆гда боу҆деⷮ по четырьнадесѧтиⷯ стеⷯ летеⷯ. по хⷭ҇вѣ нарожен҇їи. в тыи҆ часы наст҇анеⷮ є҆дина звѣз҇да на н҃бѣ. а҆ хв҇ост҇ъ и҆моу҆щи ѧ҆ко набобъ. а та боу҆деⷮ зн҇аменати. иже м҇нозѣ дивове настаноуⷮ межи хрⷭ҇тиа҆нъ. моры. глади. потопы. зем҇ли тресенїє҆ поганыⷯ нахоженїє҆. прелест҇и. фал҇шенїє҆. ближнихъ ѿбол҇ганиє҆. недостаⷮкы м҇ногыⷯ. на водаⷯ на землѧⷯ. и все то f. 173v ѿ тыⷯ видимо боудеⷮ кои҆ живи боу҆доуⷮ. И҆ потоⷨ и҆ пакы вѣⷨ что сѧ҆ маеть ст҇ати. по первоⷨ и҆ по сеⷣми десѧти летеⷯ. хрⷭ҇тиа҆нъст҇во боу҆деⷮ пол҇но кнѧⷤст҇во. а҆ кнѧ҆зи сѧ҆ боу҆джⷮ. не рѧⷣне ховати. а҆ гаⷩбы не боу҆доуⷮ сѧ҆ хотети боронити. а҆ погорше҇є҆. и҆ пр҇отоⷤ люⷣи не боу҆доуⷮ ихъ въ ч҇ти мети. а҆ниⷤ боу҆доуⷮ и҆хъ сл҇8хати хотети. И҆ пакы цр҃ь рече. зн҇аменаи на звѣ-

[3] The word спр҇авн҇е is a mistranslation of the Czech *zprav mě*, 'tell me, explain to me': "Král vece: Tieži tebe, zprav mě toho, kterak dlúho svět má státi." (Zíbrt 1910, 79.)

зⷣахъ. а҆ ѹ҆зъꙗ́ви ми. како в ты часы боудеⷮ и҆ ѿна рече. господарьство боудеть несправеⷧливо. таковый и҆хъ боудоуⷮ вои. и҆ богаре и҆ слоугы по иⷯ прикладеⷯ. А тїи кой бы мели земли боронити. боудоуⷮ при собѣ мордери. а҆ злодей ховати. господиⷩ боудеⷮ злодей. а҆ злодеѧ господина застѹпати и҆ ѿцищоваⷮꙵ и҆ ѻкрⷭтъ ихъ боудеⷮ много злыⷯ людей на земли. но е҆гда бы господїе҆ хранили правдѫ былъ бы на земли покой и҆ всѧка добродѣтеⷧ и҆ престали бы злости. но востанеⷮ браⷮ на брата. а҆ сн҃ы противъ ѿцоу. а҆ такъ каⷤдый боудеⷮ хотети быти е҆динъ на дрѹгого. а҆ моць наⷣ ниⷨ и҆мѣти. А҆ сⷮ того сѧ повозⷣвигноуⷮ рати в землѧⷯ. зде и҆ и҆нде и҆ прїйдеть е҆динъ и забие҆ть дрѹгого. и҆ такъ погоубиⷮ е҆динъ дрѹгого и҆ свой живоⷮ. И҆ востаноуть два цр҃и. е҆диⷩ лоудвикъ. а҆ дрѫгыи фридрикъ. тїи f. 174 за ѿдно боудѫⷮ воевати. вѧще ниⷤли за седмь летъ ѿ риⷨское҆ црⷭтво ѿбаче томоу мѹси сѧ здразити[4] а҆ царьствїе҆ риⷨское҆ силне боудеⷮ боронити. И҆ рече црь саломонъ. дай ми разѹмъ тыⷯ двѹ. сивилла рече. и҆ е҆динъ боудеⷮ назваⷩ црь а҆лбретаⷮ. а҆ дроугїй а҆долфоуⷭ. третїй боудеть слоути лоудвиⷦ. а҆ четвертый боудеⷮ фридиⷯ. А то ꙗ҆ повѣдаю. и҆же тоⷮ е҆гда цесаⷬ боудеⷮ. тоⷮ прїязни ѿ кнѕѧ и҆ и҆ дѫховныⷯ и҆мѣти не бѹдеⷮ. и҆ пакы црь лоуⷣвикъ црⷭтвовати боудеⷮ . а҆ по е҆го смрти не боудеть вѧще цр҃ей ниⷤ е҆динъ цесарь на земли . а҆ тотъ мае҆ть црь карѹ слыти. и҆ ꙗ҆кокоⷧве тїи цареве. и҆ цесарь црⷭтвовати боудѫⷮ. ѿбаче риⷨское҆ црⷭтвїе҆ велми ѿпоустееть. и҆ скажено боудеⷮ. и҆ ѿбницщае҆ть. такъⷤ редъкїй оу҆споминати е҆го боудеть. И҆ рече црь саломоⷩ. како сѧ црю карлови вести маюⷮ. сивилла рече. боудѫть въ времена е҆го. замоутокъ а҆ псота велика. хрⷭтїане боудѫⷮ своего бга моучити. присѧгаⷨ

[4] This is a mistranslation of the Czech *zdařiti*, 'to happen': "Avšak tomu se musí zdařiti." (Zíbrt 1910, 80.)

боуджт. через тѣло его и кровъ его. а моучити б8доут словы своими. рек8ще присягам бг8. присягам милом8 бгж в годин8 многократ. и ꙗкобы его сами своими р8ками били. И для того [на не] рана ѿ бга послана боудет ѿ неб[а на землю. ве]тръ. голодградобитїе, непоча[сие земли тресенїе][5] потопы а воды. иже то боудоут великїи шкоды f. 174v чинити. и на ѿвоцы сходжати боудет. много недостатъковъ людии на свѣте търпети боудоут морди л8пежи ѿгни зрады фальши. злости много вады. чтож николи ѿ людей слоухано и не исповѣдано было межи людми. боемъ збито боудет а оу велик8ю н8ж8 и въ хоудоб8 много их оупадет. много съжьжено а побиено боудет много мечем а звлаштие господарьство[6] погыбнет а воинъство. И во велик8ю ганьб8 и н8жоу господа оуроженый падуть. И боудет имъ ꙗко червове земстїи си реч селяне за долгїи час господствовати боудоуть. а в тое время превеликих дивовъ много станеть и мало або ничтоже полепшенїе в людех боудеть. Чим старшїи а тым горшїи. а чим богатшїи а тымъ ск8пейшїи. а боудоут знаходити нахоженїа нова. и понеже найдоут какъ бы доплънени были грѣхове. нечистыми грѣхи. розличными ѿбычаи. а гордости и пыхы неизреченны а злым ѿбходом добывающи богатства. або скаръбовъ. какъ бы богати были безъ млсти божее. А людии боудоут носити ѿдеж8 предивн8. господоу бг8 невгодн8. на панях або паннах. боудет розличных [ных фалдов]ъ крой. А такъ воидоут. людїе съ [бгомъ въ] вой великїи а боудоут мало дба[ти на ... ][7] вченїе. к сим къ старшим не б8д8т

[5] Here and further in this edition the text in square brackets is missing from Karskii's transcription. It is reconstructed according to the Czech *Proroctví Sibyllino*: "A proto bude na ně rána od boha poslána od nebe sěm na zemi, vietr, krúpy, hromobitie, nepočasie, země třesenie, potopy a vody, ješto veliké škody budú činiti." (Menčík 1879, 25.)

[6] Karskii transcribed this fragment as а звлашти егосподарьство and suggested interpreting it as а звлашти его господарьство. However, the Czech source reads: "A zvláště panstvo," suggesting that this phrase should be read in Ruthenian as а звлаштие господарьство.

[7] This fragment is reconstructed according to the Czech: "Ale potom viece budú nésti oděv předivný a Pánu Bohu jich nevzácný, na paniech anebo na pannách bude rozličných

f. 175

и҆мети послȣшаніа а҆ни. караніа и҆ базни.[8] но каждый боуⷣеⷮ хотети свою̑ волю̑ и҆мѣти. како ходиⷮ господинъ такъ хощеⷮ и҆ селѧнинъ ходити носиⷮ ли господинъ ѿдежȣ болѧрьскȣ. и҆ селѧнинъ хощеⷮ и҆мети таковоуⷤ, носиⷮ ли господинъ клобоукъ болѧрьскіи. и҆ селѧнинъ хощеⷮ мети таковый же. такоⷤ настаноуⷮ и҆ ѡбȣви дивны. Бѫдоуⷮ знаменіа на торжищи и҆ на оулицаⷯ. и тако впишетъ сѧ много замысловъ. иже бы моглъ мȣдрый то вѣдаⷮ и҆ выйти ис смысловъ.[9] Правда в тый часы загинеⷮ. невѣрность а҆ фальшьность та сѧ множити боудеⷮ. боудѫⷮ соуⷣи не справеⷣливи. вырченіе наⷣ нищими несправеⷣливое и҆ кривое и лживое выдаⷣуть. боудѫⷮ сȣдити моужи и жены воⷣле приазни. си рѣчь мъзды раⷣи. а не поⷣле правды. и҆ того ради великаа многа рана бжіа прійдеⷮ на люⷣи. и҆ прото ижеⷭ жаⷣнаа правда скоро не станеть. и҆ не можетьⷭ стати сиротаⷨ або нищиⷨ. И҆ рече црь къ сивилле. и҆ еще сповѣдай наⷨ что ещо напреⷣ маеть быти. И҆ ѿвѣща ѡна. потоⷨ на звѣздаⷯ есми видѣла. что сѧ їереѡⷡ раⷣи маеть сѧ стати. їерей велми ѡмдлеюⷮ духовній и҆ свѣⷮскій. таⷦ иже боудеⷮ сварь межи їерей папежи. и҆ [їерархи и҆ епспы и҆ прочими ерей ................ тели свѣта того и҆ сребра... [каждый з ниⷯ имѣт-][10]

falduov kroj. A tak vejdú lidé se Pánem Bohem u veliký boj a málo budú tbáti na kněžské kázánie a k svým svrchním nebudú mieti poslušenstvie ani bázni." (Zíbrt 1910, 82.)

[8] Karskii transcribed this word as **казни**, 'punishment,' but most likely it should be read as **базни**, 'fear'. See the Czech source in previous footnote.

[9] This fragment contains several mistranslations and reinterpretations of the Czech source: "A taky každý bude chtieti svú vuoli mieti. Jak chodí pán neb panoše, takéž chce sedlák choditi jako jinoše. A jestliže pán ponese klobúk špičatý, sedlák bude chtieti mieti takový, budelit' na pánu kukla bez cípa, musít' být na sedláku taková. Také nastanú třevíce s dlúhými špicemi a budú známy po rynku i po ulicech. A tak bude v pýše mnoho zámysluov, že by múdrý to vida mohl z smysla vystúpiti." (Zíbrt 1910, 82.) See analysis in "Text Adaptation" in Chapter Four.

[10] In the Czech source this fragment reads as follows: "Na hvězdách sem dále vidala, co skrze popy lotry má se státi, že popi a kněžie velmi zemdlejí tak duchovní i světští, tak že bude svar mezi popy, papeži, biskupy i obecnými kněžími. Mají li neb mieti budú kde co ještě, každý z nich bude chtieti mieti věčie, ve cti žádati a duostojenstvie věčieho dojíti a budú velmi lháti a o zbožie velmi státi budú." (Menčík 1879, 26.)

f. 175v и боудеть вѧ҃ще хотети. и жедати боⷧшего достоиⷩства. а боудоуⷮ велм҇и лгати. а оу скарб҇ы велм҇и стати. мест҇а и веси и зем҇ли. раⷣи бы вѣдали бы все было въ иⷯ вѣне. Й егда же все то ст҇анеть. слово бж҃іе которыⷨ оучити боудꙋⷮ люⷣи. въ ихъ срⷣци не ѿстанеть. ибо то чт҇о ѿни казати боудж҃ⷮ. того сами въ делеⷯ чинити не бꙋдоуⷮ. и дл҃ѧ ихъ пыхи и горд҇ости позⷣвиженїе ихъ боудеть велико и погорш҇енїе. понеже боⷧше бꙋдоуⷮ жедати мимо потребꙋ мети. и ѿ людей боудоуⷮ оукарѧ҃еми. Й абїе цр҃ь рече. како то боудеть. иже гь҃ бг҃ъ допоуст҇ити из҇волить. правомоу и лоукавомоу. въ единоⷨ месте. и ѿна рече то пр҇ото абы искоусиⷧ своиⷯ оу вере. а ктоⷤ боудеⷮ ст҇алый оу вере тоⷮ боудеⷮ сп҇асенъ. а ктоⷤ не ст҇алый а нестривалый тоⷮ погыбнеть.

На потоⷨ гь҃ бг҃ъ дасть вѣч҇ное прироженье свѣтꙋ пѧⷮ. а четырьдесѧⷮ дн҃ии. которыⷨ бы чл҃къ наоучил҇ сѧ его дѣлоⷨ боудꙋчи недоверенъ. а по неⷨ постꙋпиⷧ. абы в тоⷨ прироже҃ни каꙗлъ сѧ а меⷧ съкрꙋшенїе срⷣца. абы затрачо҃нъ чл҃къ не быⷧ но радее избавленъ. Потоⷨ гь҃ бг҃ъ сил҇ный егда бѣси възнес҇ꙋть ан҇тихриста к небоу [подъ обл҇]аки съкрꙋшиⷮ его ѿгнеⷨ доловъ а дх҃омъ [ажь до] испоⷣнѧго ада а таⷨ ѿстанеⷮ [съ люцинероⷨ до][11] вѣка. Кой пакъ сл҇оуги антихрист҇овы слепїи въ его вере ѿстаноуть. f. 176 боудоуⷮ сѧ веселиⷮ ажь сѧ имъ зл҇е стане. а таⷦже [сѧ] с ниⷨ дїаволꙋ достанꙋ.[12] Потоⷨ гь҃ і҃с х҃с прїйдеⷮ бг҃ъ живый а вѣч҇ный. а боудеⷮ соудити живыхъ и мр҇твыⷯ. а преⷣ тыⷨ неⷤли сѧ то ст҇ане. много сѧ дивъ станеⷮ. въ пѧⷮнадесѧти дн҃ехъ. а в каⷤдый дн҃ь. звлаштный дивъ сѧ станеть

[11] This fragment is reconstructed according to the Czech: "Potom pán buoh svú mocí, když dáblové vznesú Antikrista k nebi pod oblaky, srazí jej dolóv ohněm a sírú a povětřím až do kořenu pekla. A tam musí zuostati s Luciperem věky věkoma bez konce." (Menčík 1879, 28.)

[12] Karskii notes that the meaning of this phrase is unclear to him. However, it becomes clear when we compare it to the Czech source: "...budú se veseliti a potom se jim zle stane, tak že se s ním čertu dostanú." (Zíbrt 1910, 85.)

а̓ в̓ первый дн҃ь стане ⷮ дивъ. море выше всѣхъ гⷪръ стане ⷮ. а̓ крапла̑ е̓го не оу̑канеть. дрꙋгы̑ дн҃ь дивъ сѧ станеть море ѿ пѧ ⷮ доловъ спадне ⷮ. а сровнае̑т сѧ зъ землею ровно. На третїй дн҃ь дивъ сѧ̑ стане ⷮ. рыбы а̓ морьскїй потворы жалостию великою воспою ⷮ а̓ заревоу̑ть. На четвертый дн҃ь дивъ сѧ̑ станеть. текоу̑щїй воды горети боу̑дж ⷮ. На пѧтый дн҃ь листвїе̑ кровавы ⷨ пото ⷨ потити сѧ̑ бꙋде ⷮ. На шесты̑ дн҃ь. паде ⷮ всѧкое̑ древо. Се ⷣмый дн҃ь горы и̓ скалы поу̑кати сѧ боу̑дж ⷮ. Въ ѿсмый дн҃ь землѧ̑ трести сѧ̑ боу̑де ⷮ. Въ девѧтый дн҃ь. сровнаю ⷮ сѧ̑ горы и оу̑доли. Въ десѧтый дн҃ь кто колве бꙋдеть гдⷣе сѧ̑ съкры ⷧ. во ⷩ выйде ⷮ ѿ великое̑ грозы.[13] Въ первый на десѧ ⷮ дн҃ь мртвїй востаноу ⷮ. Въ вторый на десѧтый дн҃ь. звѣзды боу̑доу̑ть падати с неба. Въ третїй на десѧтый дн҃ь. землѧ̑ и̓ все коренїе̑[14] згори ⷮ ѿгне ⷨ. На четверты̑ на десѧты̑й дн҃ь землѧ̑ всѧ̑ [згори ⷮ и вѧще н]ичто ⷤ не боу̑де ⷮ к томꙋ. и̑ злато и сребро. и вси f. 176v житейскый вещи погыноу ⷮ.[15] и̓ все конець во ⷥ ме ⷮ. и̓ е̓дини праве ⷣнїй не погиноу ⷮ. тїй съ господе ⷨ бг҃о ⷨ в рад ⷣ ⷪсти боу̑дж ⷮ. Въ пѧтый на десѧтый дн҃ъ сꙋдити прїиде ⷮ съ нбси г҃ь бг҃ъ живы ⷯ и̓ мртвы ⷯ И̓ воздасть комꙋждо по дѣломъ е̓го а̑минь·:[16]

[13] *hruozy* (‘horror’) in Czech.

[14] *stvořenie* (‘creature’) in Czech.

[15] “čtrnáctý den střiebro i zlato i všecko sbožie užitečné v zemi i všecky věci, což bylo shuoří a zahyne, a již nic nebude.” (Menčík 1879, 29.)

[16] The last fragment in the Ruthenian translation differs from the Czech in that it includes a mention of the Second Coming and Last Judgment. Both Czech versions show the following reading: “patnáctý den budú nebe i země obnovena a přestane veškeren běh hvězdy i planety i slunce i měsíc. Slunce stane na východ a měsiec na západ; tu tak stanú až na věky. A tu již konec všecko vezme a zahyne; všickni rozděleni budú, zlí do věčné žalosti a dobří do věčné radosti. Amen.” (Menčík 1879, 29.)

# BIBLIOGRAPHY


Alekseev, A. A. 1980. *"Pesn' pesnei" v drevnei slaviano-russkoi pismennosti.* Chast' 1–2. Institut russkogo iazyka AN SSSR. Predvaritel'nye publikatsii, 134. Moskva.

--------. 1983. "'Pesn' Pesnei' v cheshskoi biblii i vostochnoslavianskie perevody XV–XVI v." *Slavia* 52:283–289.

--------. 1999. *Tekstologiia slavianskoi biblii.* St. Peterburg.

--------. 2002. *Pesn' pesnei v drevnei slaviano-russkoi pis'mennosti.* St. Peterburg: Dmitrii Bulanin.

Altbauer, Moshé. 1992. *The Five Biblical Scrolls in a Sixteenth-Century Jewish Translation into Belorussian (Vilnius Codex 262).* Jerusalem: Dorot Press.

Anderš, Josef. 1976. "Do pytannia pro ches'ko-ukraïns'ki movni zv'iazky naidavnishnoï doby." *Slovo i trud.* Kyïv. 59–66.

--------. 1998. "K česko-ukrajinským jazykovým kontaktům." *Slavia* 67 (1/2):19–23.

Astell, Ann W. 1990. *The Song of Songs in the Middle Ages.* Ithaca and London: Cornell University Press.

Auty, Robert. 1980. "Czech." *The Slavic Literary Languages: Formation and Development.* Alexander Schenker, Edward Stankiwicz, and Micaela S. Iovine, eds. Yale Russian and East European publications, no. 1. New Haven: Yale Concilium on International and Area Studies.

Bakhtin, Mikhail. 1986. "The Problem of Speech Genres." *Speech Genres and Other Late Essays.* Caryl Emerson and Michael Holquist, eds. Austin: University of Texas Press. 60–102.

Banenis, E. D. 1978. "Pisari diplomaticheskoi sluzhby v kantseliarii Velikogo kniazhestva Litovskogo v nachale XVI veka." *Materialy mezhrespublikanskoi nauchnoi konferentsii po istochnikovedeniiu i istoriografii narodov pribaltiiskikh respublik Soiuza SSR. Istochnikovedenie.* Vilnius.

Bartoš, František. 1926. *Soupis rukopisů Národního musea v Praze.* Svazek I. Praha.

Barycz, H. 1948. "Dziejowe związki Polski z Uniwersytetem Karola w Pradze." *Przegląd Zachodni* 3.

Bednov, V. A. 2002. *Pravoslavnaia tserkov' v Pol'she i Litve (no Volumina Legum).* Minsk: Luchi Sofii.

Beliakov, A. A. and E. V. Beliakova. 1992. "O peresmotre eskhatologicheskoi kontseptsii na Rusi v kontse XV veka." *Arkhiv russkoi istorii* 1. 7–31.

Beyer, Rolf. 1987. *Die Königin von Saba. Emgel und Dämon. Der Mythos einer Frau.* Bergisch Gladbach: Gustav Lübbe Verlag.

Borkovskii, V. I. and P. S. Kuznetsov. 1963. *Istoricheskaia grammatika russkogo iazyka.* Moskva: Akademiia Nauk SSSR.

Browning, Robert. 1995. *Medieval and Modern Greek.* Cambridge: Cambridge University Press.

Brückner, Alexander. 1881 "Die Visio Tundali in böhmischer und russischer Übersetzung." *Archiv für Slavische Philologie* 13:199–212.

Brynychová, Věra. 1927. "České Proroctví Sibyllino v ruském překladě." *Český Lid* 27:49–60.

Bulyka, A. M. 1988. *Mova belaruskai pis'mennastsi XIV–XVIII st.* Minsk: Navuka i tekhnika.

Bulyka, A. M. et al. 1979. *Histarychnaia marfalohiia belaruskai movy*. Minsk.

Bulyka, A. M., A. I. Zhuraŭski and U. M. Sviazhynski. 1990. *Mova vydanniau Frantsyska Skaryny*. Minsk: Navuka i tekhnika.

Buslaev, F. I. 1884. *Svod izobrazhenii iz litsevykh apokalipsisov po russkim rukopisiam s XVI-go veka po XIX-yi*. Moskva: Sinodal'naia tip.

Čekmonas, Valeriy. 2001. "On some Circum-Baltic features of the Pskov-Novgorod (North-Western Central Russian) dialect." *Circum-Baltic Languages. Volume I: Past and Present*. Östen Dahl and Maria Koptjevskaja-Tamm, eds. Studies in Language Companion Series 54. Amsterdam/Philadelphia: John Benjamins Publishing Company.

Chadraba, Rudolf. 1975. "APOSTOLUS ORIENTALIS. Poselství Jana z Marignoly." *Z tradic slovanské kultury v Čechách. Sázava a Emauzy v dějinách české kultury*. Praha: Univerzita Karlova. 127–133.

Cinke, Vladimír. 1975. "Slovanské prvky v kronice Marignolové." *Z tradic slovanské kultury v Čechách. Sázava a Emauzy v dějinách české kultury*. Praha: Univerzita Karlova. 135–136.

Coetsem, Frans, van. 1988. *Loan Phonology and the Two Transfer Types in Language Contact*. Publications in Language Sciences 27. Dordrecht, Holland/Providence, RI: Foris.

--------. 2000. *A General and Unified Theory of the Transmission Process in Language Contact*. Monographien zur Sprachwissenschaft 19. Heidelberg: Winter.

Cooper, Henry R., Jr. 2003. *Slavic Scriptures: the Formation of the Church Slavonic Version of the Holy Bible*. Madison: Fairleigh Dickinson University Press.

Cope, Gilbert. 1959. *Symbolism in the Bible and the Church*. London: The Camelot Press.

Corin, Andrew. 1993. "Variation and Norm in Croatian Church Slavonic." *Slovo* 41–43:155–196.

Crasinius, Joannes. 1574. *Polonia*.

Cuřín, František. 1985. *Vývoj spisovné češtiny*. Praha: Státní pedagogické nakladatelství.

Czyżewski, Feliks. 1986. *Atlas gwar polskich i ukraińskich okolic Włodawy*. Lublin.

--------. 1998. "Polsko-ukraińskie interferencje językowe na Podlasiu. Problemy metodologiczne." *Slovo i kul'tura*. Moskva: Indrik.

Daley, Brian E. 1986. "The "Closed Garden" and the "Sealed Fountain": Song of Songs 4:12 in the Late Medieval Iconography of Mary." *Medieval Gardens*. Elisabeth B. MacDougall, ed. Washington, D.C.: Dumbarton Oaks Research Library and Collection.

Danylenko, Andrii. 2006. "'Prostaia mova', 'Kitab', and Polissian Standard." *Die Welt der Slaven* 51:80–115.

Długosz, Joannes. 1864. *Liber beneficiorum diocesis cracoviensis*. Vol. 3. Alexander Przeździecki, ed. Kraków.

Dmitrieva, R. P. 1972. "Chet'i sborniki XV veka kak zhanr." *Istoriia zhanrov v russkoi literature X-XVII vekov. Trudy Otdela Drevnerusskoi Literatury* 27:150–180.

Dobrianskii, F. 1882. *Opisanie rukopisei vilenskoi publichnoi biblioteki, tserkovnoslavianskikh i russkikh.* Vilnius: Tipografiia Syrkina.

Downing, Pamela, Susan D. Lima and Michael Noonan, eds. 1992. *The Linguistics of Literacy.* Amsterdam/Philadelphia: John Benjamins Publishing Company.

Drzazgowski, Mariusz. 1991. "Zapożyczenia ruskie w języku pisarzy kresowych i środkowopolskich XVII–XIX wieku." *Studia z filologii polskiej i słowiańskiej* 28:51–64.

Dudík, B. 1867. *Archive im Königreiche Galizien und Lodomerien.* Archiv für Österreichischer Geschichtsquellen. Wien.

Durnovo, Nikolai. 1969. *Vvedenie v istoriiu russkogo iazyka.* Moskva: Nauka.

Emler, Josef, ed. 1882. *Fontes rerum Bohemicarum = Prameny dějin českých.* Vol. 3. Praha: Nákl. N. F. Palackého.

--------. 1893. *Fontes rerum Bohemicarum = Prameny dějin českých.* Vol. 5. Praha: Nákl. N. F. Palackého.

Enea Silvio Piccolomini. [1458] 1967. "*De Europa.*" *Opera omnia.* Minerva G.M.B.N. Frankfurt am Main: Unveränderter Nachdruck. 387–471.

--------. [1458] 1998. *Historia Bohemica = Historie česká.* Clavis monumentorum litterarum (Regnum Bohemiae), 1. Dana Martínková, Alena Hadravová, Jiří Matl, and František Šmahel, eds. Praha: Koniasch Latin Press.

Fałowski, Adam. 1984. *Kształtowanie się̨ kategorii superlatywu przymiotników w tekstach staroruskich i starorosyjskich XI–XVII w.* Monografie slawistyczne, 48. Wrocław: Zakład Narodowy im. Ossolińskich.

--------. 2001. "Rola jezuitów wileńskich w rozwoju szkolnictwa, języka i piśmiennictwa zachodnioruskiego w XVI w." *Krakowsko-wileńskie studia slawistyczne,* v. 3, Wanda Stępniak-Minczewa and Aleksander Naumow, eds. Kraków: Instytut Filologii Słowiańskiej Uniwersitetu Jagiellońskiego.

--------. 2003. *Język ruskiego przekładu Katechizmu Jezuickiego z 1585 roku.* Studia Ruthenica Cracoviensia. Kraków: Universitas.

Fine, John V. A. 2000. "The Slavic Saint Jerome: An Entertainment." *Cultures and Nations of Central and Eastern Europe. Essays in Honor of Roman Szporluk.* Zvi Gitelman, Lubomyr Hajda, John-Raul Himka and Roman Solchanyk, eds. Cambridge, Mass.: Harvard University Press. 101–112.

Florovskii, Antonii. 1935. *Chekhi i vostochnye slaviane. Ocherki po istoruu cheshsko-russkikh otnoshenii (X–XVIII vv.).* Vol. 1. Praha: Orbis.

--------. 1939. "Vliv staré české literatury v oblasti ruské." *Co daly naše země Evropě a lidstvu.* Praha: Evropský literární klub.

--------. [1946] 1988. *Cheshskaia bibliia v istorii russkoi kul'tury i pis'mennosti.* Reprint. München.

--------. 1947. *Chekhi i vostochnye slaviane. Ocherki po istoruu cheshsko-russkikh otnoshenii (X–XVIII vv.).* Vol. 2. Praha: Orbis.

Frick, David. A. 1994. "Foolish Rus'": On Polish Civilization, Ruthenian Self-Hatred, and Kasijan Sakovyč." *Harvard Ukrainian Studies* 18 (3/4):210–48.

--------. 1995. *Meletij Smotryc'kyj*. Harvard Series in Ukrainian Studies. Cambridge, Mass.: Harvard Ukrainian Research Institute

Gebauer, Jan. 1970. *Slovník Staročeský*. Praha: Academia.

Giles, Howard. 1977. "Social Psychology and Applied Linguistics: Towards an Integrated Approach." *ITL Review of Applied Linguistics* 35:27–42.

Giles, H. and P. Smith. 1979. "Accommodation Theory: Optimal Levels of Convergence." *Language and Social Psychology*. H. Giles and R. N. St. Clair, eds. Oxford: Basil Blackwell. 45–65.

Giles, Howard, Nikolas Coupland and Justine Coupland. 1991. "Accomodation Theory: Communication, Context, and Consequence." *Contexts of Accomodation. Developments in Applied Linguistics*. Howard Giles, Nikolas Coupland and Justine Coupland, eds. Cambridge: Cambridge University Press.

Golovatskii I. 1865. "Neskol'ko slov o biblii Skoriny i o rukopisnoi russkoi biblii iz XVI stoletiia, obretaiushcheisia v bibliotetse monastyria Sv. Onufriia vo L'vove." *Naukovyi Sbornik* I. L'viv.

Gorbachevskii, N. I. [1874] 1992. *Slovar' drevnego aktovogo iazyka Severo-Zapadnogo kraia i Tsarstva pol'skogo. (Wörterbuch der alten Urkundensprache des Grossfürstentums Litauen und des Königreichs Polen.)* Reprint. O. Horbatsch, ed. Specimina philologiae Slavicae 95. München: Verlag Otto Sagner.

Górnicki, Łukasz. 1954. *Dworzanin Polski*. Roman Pollak, ed. Biblioteka Narodowa, 109. Wrocław: Zakład im. Ossolińskich.

Gorskii, A. V. and K. I. Nevostruev 1862. *Opisanie slavianskikh rukopisei moskovskoi Sinodal'noi biblioteki*. otdel 2. ch. 3. Moskva.

Gröschel, Bernhard. 1972. *Die Sprache Ivan Vyšenśkyjs. Untersuchungen und Materialien zur historischen Grammatik des Ukrainischen*. Slavistische Forschungen, 13. Köln: Böhlau-Verlag.

Gudziak, Borys. A. 2001. *Crisis and Reform. The Kyivan Metropolitanate, the Patriarchate of Constantinople, and the Genesis of the Union of Brest*. Cambridge, Mass.: Harvard Ukrainian Research Institute.

Hamm, Josip. 1971. "Glagoljica u predrenesansno doba." *Studia Paleoslovenica*. Praha.

Havránek, Bohuslav. 1939. "Expanse spisovné češtiny od 14. do 16. století." *Co daly naše země Evropě a lidstvu*. Praha: Evropský literární klub.

--------. 1975. "Vztahy kláštera *Na Slovanech* k jazyku a literatuře charvátskohlaholské." *Z tradic slovanské kultury v Čechách. Sázava a Emauzy v dějinách české kultury*. Praha: Univerzita Karlova. 145–148.

Helinand de Froidmont. 1855. *Chronicon*. Jacques-Paul Migne, ed. *Patrologiae Cursus Completus: Omnium Sanctum Patrum, Doctorum Scriptorumque Ecclesiasticorum. Series Latina* 212:1038–1055. Paris: Garnier Fratres.

Helmling, Leandr, and Adalbert Horcicka. 1904. *Die Urkunden des königlichen Stiftes Emaus in Prag. Band I., Das vollständige Registrum Slavorum*. Prag: Verein für Geschichte der Deutschen in Böhmen.

Hercigonja, Eduard. 1975. *Povijest hrvatske književnosti*. Vol 2. *Srednjovjekovna književnost*. Zagreb: Liber Mladost.

Holdenried, Anke. 2006. *The Sibyl and Her Scribes: Manuscripts and Interpretation of the Latin Sibylla Tiburtina c. 1050–1500*. Aldershot, England & Burlington, VT: Ashgate.

Horvath, Julia and Wexler, Paul. eds. 1997. *Relexification in Creole and Non-Creole Languages*. Wiesbaden: Otto Harrassowitz.

Hruca, A. P. 1976. "Prynazoŭniki podle, podlug", v"podlug", vedle, vedlug u starabelaruskai move XIV-XVIII stst." *Belaruskaia linhvistyka* 10:64–70.

Hrushevs'kyi, Mikhailo. 1955. *Istoriia Ukraïny-Rusy*. Vol. 5. New York: Knyhospilka.

--------. 1995. *Istoriia ukraïns'koï literatury*. Tom 5. Kyïv: Lybid'.

Humets'ka, L. L. 1958. *Narys slovotvorchoï systemy ukraïnskoï aktovoï movy XIV–XV st.* Kyïv: Vyd-vo Akademiï nauk RSR.

--------. 1967. "Chy vplyvala staroches'ka mova na movu ukraïns'kykh hramot XIV–XV st.?" *Movoznavstvo* 4:92–95.

Humets'ka, L. L. et al., eds. 1977. *Slovnyk staroukraïns'koï movy XIV–XV st.* 2 vols. Kyïv: Naukova dumka.

Huňáček, Václav. 1975. "Klášter na Slovanech a počátky východoslovanských studií u nás." *Z tradic slovanské kultury v Čechách. Sázava a Emauzy v dějinách české kultury*. Praha: Univerzita Karlova. 175–186.

Iakovliv, Andrii. 1929. *Vplyvy staroches'koho prava na pravo ukraïns'ke litovskoï doby XV–XVI v*. Praha.

Isačenko, Alexander. 1974. "On 'Have' and 'Be' Languages (A Typological Sketch)." *Slavic Forum: Essays in Linguistics and Literature*. Michael S. Flier, ed. The Hague: Mouton. 43–77.

Isaevich, Iaroslav. 1966. *Bratstva ta ïkh rol' v rozvytku ukraïns'koï kul'tury XVI-XVIII stolittia*. Kyïv: Naukova dumka.

--------. 1990. "Istoriia izdaniia Ostrozhskoi biblii." *Ostrozhskaia bibliia. Sbornik statei*. Moskva: Institut russkogo iazyka AN SSSR. 3–17.

Iukho, I. A. 1978. *Pravovoe polozheniie naseleniia Belorussii v XVI v*. Minsk: Izdatel'stvo BGU.

Ivanov, Vyacheslav V. 2005. "Iazyki, iazykovye sem'i i iazykovye soiuzy vnutri Velikogo kniazhestva Litovskogo." *Speculum Slaviae Orientalis: Muscovy, Ruthenia, and Lithuania in the Late Middle Ages*. Vyacheslav Vs. Ivanov and Julia Verkholantsev, eds. UCLA Slavic Studies, n.s., IV. Moscow: Novoe Izdatel'stvo.

Ivir, Vladimir and Damir Kalogjera, eds. 1991. *Languages in Contact and Contrast. Essays in Contact Linguistics*. Trends in Linguistics. Studies and Monographs 54. Berlin and New York: Mouton de Gruyter.

Jahandarie, Khosrow. 1999. *Spoken and Written Discourse: A Multi-Disciplinary Perspective*. Stamford, Connecticut: Ablex Publishing Corporation.

Jakobson, Roman. 1953. "Polska literatura średniowieczna i Czesi." *Kultura* (Paris) 68 (6): 27–42.

--------. 1985. “The Beginning of National Self-Determination in Europe.” *Selected Writings. Volume VI, Part 1. Early Slavic Paths and Crossroads*. Berlin, New York, Amsterdam: Mouton Publishers. 115–128.

Jakubec, Jan. 1911. *Dějiny literatury české. Od nejstarších dob do probuzení politického*. Praha: Jan Laichter.

Janów, Jan, ed. 1947. *Jan Sandecki <Malecki>. Ewangeliarz z początku XVI w. i dwa późniejsze druki polskie tegoż autora. Biblioteka pisarzów polskich* 87. Kraków: Polska akademia umiętności.

Jansen, Olaf. 1939. “Český vliv na středověkou literaturu polskou.” *Co daly naše země Evropě a lidstvu*. Praha: Evropský literární klub.

Jireček, Josef. 1875. “Nové objevy z literatury staročeské.” *Časopis Českého Museum* 49.

Jurić, Šime, ed. 1993. *Katalog rukopisa Nacionalne i sveučilišne biblioteke u Zagrebu*. Vol. 2. Zagreb: Nacionalna i sveučilišna biblioteka.

Karpluk, Maria. 1985. “Cechy regionalne oraz rutenizmy morfologiczne i skladniowe w języku M. Stryjkowskiego (pol. 16 w.).” *Studia z filologii polskiej i slowiańskiej*. Warszawa 23:23–47.

--------. 1997. “Cerkiew i car w polszczyźnie Joannicjusza Galatowskiego (w. XVII).” *Słowanie Wschodni. Między językiem a kulturą. Księga jubileuszowa dedykowana Profesorowi Wiesławowi Witkowskiemu w siedemdziesiątą rocznicę urodyin*. Anna Bolek et al., eds. Kraków: Bohdan Grell. 127–135.

Karskii, Evfimii. 1894. “O iazyke tak nazyvaemykh Litovskikh letopisei.” Varshavskie universitetskie izvestiia (2/3):1–64.

--------. [1897] 1964. “Zapadnorusskii sbornik XV veka.” *Izvestiia Otdeleniia Russkogo Iazyka i Slovesnosti Imp. AN* II (3/4):964–1036. Reprint. Graz, Austria: Akademische Druck – U. Verlagsanstalt.

--------. 1898. “Zapadnorusskoe skazanie o Siville prorochitse po rukopisi XVI veka.” *Varshavskie uviversitetskie izvestiia* (2):1–31.

--------. 1921. *Belorusy. Vol. 3. Ocherki slovesnosti belorusskogo plemeni. Staraia zapadnorusskaia pis’mennost’*. Petrograd.

--------. 1955. *Belorusy. Iazyk belorusskogo naroda*. Moskva.

--------. 1962. “Chto takoe drevnee zapadnorusskoe narechie?” *Trudy po belorusskomu i drugim slavianskim iazykam*. Moskva.

Kędelska, Elżbieta. 1993. “Bohemizmy i rutenizmy w słowniku Mikołaja Volckmara z 1596 r.” *Studia z filologii polskiej i słowiańskiej* 31:131–146.

Keenan, Edward. 2007. “Why You Can’t Get Russian Cultural History Right Unless You Get “Ruthenian” History Right First.” Lecture presented at the Harvard Ukrainian Summer Institute.

Kiaupa, Zigmantas, Juratė Kiaupienė and Albinas Kuncevičius. 2000. *The history of Lithuania before 1795*. Vilnius: Lithuanian Institute of History.

Kłoczowski, Jerzy. 2000. *A History of Christianity*. Cambridge: Cambridge University Press.

Kostomarov, N. M. 1861. “Starinnyi iuzhnorusskii perevod Pesni Pesnei s posleslovijami o liubvi.” *Osnova* 11–12.

Kras, Paweł. 1998. *Husyci w piętnastowiecznej Polsce*. Lublin: Towarzystwo Naukowe KUL.

Krukowski, Józef. 1886. *O słowiańskim kościele św. Krzyża i klasztorze benedyktynów założonym przez Jadwigę i Jagiełłę na Kleparzu w Krakowie 1390 roku*. Kraków.

Kuraszkiewicz, Władysław. 1934. *Gramoty halicko-wołyńskie XIV–XV wieku: studjum językowe*. Kraków: Druk. Uniwersytetu Jagiellońskiego.

Kyas, Vladimír. 1955. "K rekonstrukci české předlohy staropolské bible." *Česko-polský sborník vědeckých prací*. II. Praha. 39–67.

--------. 1997. Česká bible v dějinách národního písemnictví. Praha: Vyšehrad.

Kyas, Vladimír and Jaroslava Pečírková. 1993. *Biblia Slavica I/1: Die Dresdener oder Leskowetz-Bibel*. Paderborn: Ferdinand Schöningh.

Labyntsev, Iurii. 1990. *Pachatae Skarynam. Belaruskaia drukavanaia litaratura epokhi Renesansu*. Minsk: Mastatskaia litaratura.

--------. 1992. *Mezhdunarodnaia slavianovedcheskaia programma "Istoriia knizhnoi kul'tury Podliash'ia."* Minsk.

Labyntsev, Iurii and Larisa Shchavinskaia. 1996. *Pravoslavnaia akademiia Khodkevichei i ee izdaniia*. Minsk.

Łesiów, Michał. 2000. "The Polish and Ukrainian Languages: A Mutually Beneficial Relationship." *Cultures and Nations of Central and Eastern Europe. Essays in Honor of Roman Szporluk*. Zvi Gitelman, Lubomyr Hajda, John-Raul Himka and Roman Solchanyk, eds. Cambridge, Mass.: Harvard University Press. 393–406.

Likhachev, N. P. 1899. *Paleograficheskoe znachenie bumazhnykh vodianykh znakov*. Obshchestvo liubiteleii drevneii pis'mennosti. St. Peterburg: V.S. Balamev i K.

Lur'e, IA. S. 1995. "Poslaniia Gennadiia Novgorodskogo i vopros o "kontse mira" v XV veke." *Harvard Ukrainian Studies* 19:563–577. [= Kamen' Kraeõgъlьnъ - Rhetoric of the Medieval Slavic World: Essays presented to Edward L. Keenan on his Sixtieth Birthday by his Colleagues and Students].

Łużny, Ryszard. 1966. *Pisarze kręgu Akademii Kijowsko-Mohylańskiej a literatura polska. Z dziejów związków kulturalnych polso-wschodniosłowiańskich w XVII–XVIII w*. Kraków.

Macůrek, Josef. 1960a. "K dějinám česko-ukrajinských a česko-rumunských vztahů 2. pol. 14. a 1. pol. 15. století." *Slovanské historické studie* 3. Praha.

--------. 1960b. "K otázce vztahů listiny české, ukrajinské a moldavské v druhé polovině 15. století." *Sborník praci filozofické fakulty brněnské univerzity* 9 (7).

--------. 1968. "Po stopach spisovné češtiny v jihozápadní Ukrajině koncem 14. a v 1. polovině 15. století." *Franku Wollmanovi k sedmdesátinám*. Praha.

Marcus, Brother. 1989. *The Vision of Tnugdal*. Translated by Jean-Michel Picard. Introduction by Yolande de Pontfarcy. Dublin: Four Courts Press.

Mareš, František Václav. 1971. "Hlaholice na Moravě a v Cechách." *Slovo* 21:133–199.

--------. 1975. "Emauzské prameny českého diakritického pravopisu." *Z tradic slovanské kultury v Čechách. Sázava a Emauzy v dějinách české kultury*. Praha: Univerzita Karlova. 169–172.

--------. 1976. "Moskevská Mariánská Mše." *Slovo* 25–26:296–359.

--------. 2000. *Cyrilometodějská tradice a slavistika.* Praha: Torst.

Martel, Antoine. 1938. *La langue polonaise dans les pays ruthènes. Ukraine et Russie Blanche 1569–1667.* Lille.

Martinet, André. 1952. "Diffusion of Language and Structural Lingiustics." *Romance Philology* 6:5–13.

Mathiesen, Robert. 1984. "The Church Slavonic Language Question: An Overview (IX-XX Centuries)." *Aspects of the Slavic Language Question.* Vol. I. Riccardo Picchio and Harvey Goldblatt, eds. Yale Russian and East European Publication 4-a. New Haven: Yale Concilium on International and Area Studies.

Matter, E. Ann. 1990. *The Voice of My Beloved: the Song of Songs in Western Medieval Christianity.* Middle Ages series. Philadelphia: University of Pennsylvania Press.

Mayenowa, Maria Renata. 1984. "Aspects of the Language Question in Poland from the Middle of the Fifteenth Century to the Third Decade of the Nineteenth Century." *Aspects of the Slavic Language Question.* Vol. 1. Riccardo Picchio and Harvey Goldblatt, eds. Yale Russian and East European Publication 4–a. New Haven: Yale Concilium on International and Area Studies.

McGinn, Bernard. 1979. *Visions of the End. Apocalyptic Traditions in the Middle Ages.* New York: Columbia University Press.

McMillin, Arnold. 1980. "Belorussian." *The Slavic Literary Languages: Formation and Development.* A. M. Schenker and E. Stankiewicz, eds. New Haven. 105–117.

Medynskii, E. N. 1954. *Bratskie shkoly Ukrainy i Belorussii v XVI–XVII vv. i ikh rol' v vossoedinenii Ukrainy s Rossiei.* Moskva: Akademiia pedagogicheskikh nauk.

Menčík, Ferdinand. 1879. *Zápisky kněze Václava Rosy.* Vídeň: J. Pašek v Jičíně.

Miakishev, Vladimir. 2000. "'Movy' Velikogo kniazhestva Litovskogo v edinstve svoikh protivopolozhnostei." *Studia Russica* 18:165–172.

--------. 2001. "Litovskii Statut na puti ot "ruskoi" redaktsii k pol'skomu perevodu (o rukopisnom ekzempliare iz fondov Berlinskoi korolevskoi biblioteki)." *Krakowsko-Wileńskie Studia Slawistyczne* 3. Wanda Stępniak-Minczewa and Aleksander Naumov, eds. Kraków: Instytut Filologii Słowiańskiej UJ. 173–192.

Michálek, Emanuel. 1975. "Poslání Emauzského kláštera a české památky s ním souvisící." *Z tradic slovanské kultury v Čechách. Sázava a Emauzy v dějinách české kultury.* Praha: Univerzita Karlova. 149–152.

--------. 1989. *Česká slovní zásoba v Klaretových slovnících.* Praha: Academia.

Mieses, Matthias. 1919. *Die Gesetze der Schriftgeschichte. Konfession und Schrift im Leben der Völker. Ein Versuch.* Vienna: W. Braumüller

Milčetić, Ivan. 1911. *Hrvatska glagoljska bibliografija.* Vol. 1. Opisi rukopisa. *Starine* 33. Zagreb: Judoslavenska Akademija Znanosti i Umjetnosti.

Mil'kov V. V. 1999. *Drevnerusskie apokrify.* Seria: Pamiatniki drevnerusskoi mysli. Issledovaniia i teksty. St. Peterburg: Russkii Khristianskii gumanitarnyi institut.

Mironowicz, Antoni. 2001. *Kościół prawosławny w dziejach dawnej Rzeczypospolitej.* Białystok: Wydawnictwo Uniwersytetu w Białymstoku.

--------. 2003a. *Kościół prawosławny w państwie Piastów i Jagiellonów.* Białystok: Wydawnictwo Uniwersytetu w Białymstoku.

--------. 2003b. *Bractwa cerkiewne w Rzeczypospolitej*. Białystok.

Morozova, N. A. and Temchin, S. Iu. 1997. "Ob izuchenii tserkovnoslavianskoi pis'mennosti Velikogo kniazhestva Litovskogo." *Krakowsko-Wileńskie Studia Slawistyczne* 2:7–39.

Morzy, Józef. 1959. "Geneza i rozwój cechów wileńskich do końca XVII w." *Zeszyty naukowe Uniwersytetu im. Mickiewicza, Seria Historia*. 3–93.

Moser, Michael. 2002. "Chto takoe 'prostaia mova'"? *Studia Slavica Hung*. 47:221–260.

Moszyńska, Donuta. 1998. "O polszczyźnie Sylwestra Kossowa." *Tematy. Księga jubileuszowa w 70. rocznicę urodzin profesora Leszka Moszyńskiego*. Slawistyka 9. Gdańsk: Wydawnictwo Uniwersytetu Gdańskiego.

Moszyński, Leszek. 1971. "Liturgija słowiańska i głagolskie zabytki w Polsce." *Slovo* 21:255–273. Zagreb.

--------. 1998. "Cerkiewnosłowiańska tzw. Moskiewska Msza Maryjna jako odzwierciedlenie litewsko-białorusko-polskich kontaktów kulturowych w XV wieku." *Czterechsetlecie unii brzeskiej. Zagadnienia języka religijnego*. Zenon Leszczyński, ed. Lublin: TN KUL. 21–35.

Naumow, Aleksander and Andrzej Kaszlej. 2004. *Rękopisy cerkiewniosłowiańskie w Polsce. Katalog*. Kraków: Scriptum.

Němec, Igor. 1975. "K podilu Emauzského kláštera na rozvoji staré češtiny." *Z tradic slovanské kultury v Čechách. Sázava a Emauzy v dějinách české kultury*. Praha: Univerzita Karlova. 165–168.

Neske, Ingeborg. 1985. *Die spätmittelalterliche deutsche Sibyllenweissagung. Untersuchung und Edition*. Göppinger Arbeiten zur Germanistik, ed. Ulrich Müller, Franz Hundsnurscher, and Cornelius Sommer. Göppingen: Kümmerle Verlag.

Obolensky, Dimitri. 1994. "Sts. Cyril and Methodius, Apostles of the Slavs." *Byzantium and the Slavs*. New York: St. Vladimir's Seminary Press. 205–217.

Ochmański, Jerzy. 1986. "The National Idea in Lithuania from the 16th to the First Half of the 19th Century: The Problem of Cultural-Linguistic Differentiation." *Harvard Ukrainian Studies* 10(3/4):301–315.

Ohienko, Ivan. 1930. *Ukraïns'ka literaturna mova XVI–ho st. i Krekhivskyi Apostol 1560 r.* Warszawa.

Olson, David. 1994. *The World on Paper: The Conceptual and Cognitive Implications of Writing and Reading*. Cambridge: Cambridge University Press.

Ong, Wlater J. [1982] 1988. *Orality and Literacy: The Technologizing of the Word*. Reprint. London and New York: Routledge.

Orloš, Teresa Zofia. 1993. *Tysiąc lat czesko-polskich związków językowych. Tisíc let česko-polských jazykových vztahů*. Kraków: Universitas.

Ostojić, Ivan. 1960. "Benediktinci glagoljaši." *Slovo* 9/10:14–42.

Pacnerová, Ludmila. 1975. "Česká hlaholská literatura v klášteře *Na Slovanech*." *Z tradic slovanské kultury v Čechách. Sázava a Emauzy v dějinách české kultury*. Praha: Univerzita Karlova. 155–162.

--------. 2000. *Česká Bible Hlaholská. Bible Vyšebrodská*. Praha: Euroslavica.

--------. 2001. "Česká bible Hlaholská (Bible Vyšebrodská)." *Slavia* 70(1):1–10.

--------. 2002. *Staročeský Hlaholský Comestor*. Praha: Euroslavica.

Palacký, František. 1831. "Jazyk český na dvoře litevském v XV století." *Časopis Českého Museum* 3.

Palmer, Nigel F. 1982. *"Visio Tnugdali." The German and Dutch Translations and their Circulation in the Later Middle Ages*. München: Artemis.

Paulová, M. 1950. "L'edée cyrillo-methodienne dans la politique de Charles IV et la foundation du monastère slave de Prague." *Byzantinoslavica* 11.

Pečírková, Jaroslava. 1998. "Czech Translations of the Bible." *The Interpretation of the Bible*. Jože Krašovec, ed. Journal for the Study of the Old Testament. Supplement Series 289. Sheffield: Sheffield Academic Press. 1169–1189.

Perets, V. N. 1903. *Povest' o trekh koroliakh-volkhvakh v zapadno-russkom spiske XV veka*. Pamiatniki drevnei pis'mennosti i iskusstva 150. St. Peterburg.

Perwolf, Josef. 1886. "Chervonorusskii perevod Vislitskogo Statuta." *Trudy VI Arkheologicheskogo s'ezda v Odesse (1884 g.)* 1. Odessa.

--------. 1874. *Slavianskaia vzaimnost' s drevneishikh vremen do XVIII veka*. St. Peterburg.

--------. 1893. *Slaviane, ikh vzaimnye otnosheniia i sviazi*. 3(1). Warszawa: K. Kowalewski.

Pesensen, Michael. 2007. "The Sibylline Tradition in Medieval and Early Modern Orthodox Slavic Culture." *Old Testament Apocrypha in the Slavonic Tradition*. Lorenzo di Tommaso and Christfried Boettrich, eds. Texts and Studies in Ancient Judaism. Tuebingen: Mohr Siebeck.

Petr, Jan and Šabouk, Sáva, eds. 1975. *Z tradic slovanské kultury v Čechách. Sázava a Emauzy v dějinách české kultury*. Praha: Univerzita Karlova.

Piccard, Gerhard. 1961. *Die Wasserzeichenkartei Piccard im Hauptstaatsarchiv Stuttgart: Findbuch*. Stuttgart: Kohlhammer.

Picchio, Riccardo 1984. "Guidelines for a Comparative Study of the Language Question among the Slavs." *Aspects of the Slavic Language Question*. Vol. 1. Yale Russian and East European Publications 4–a. Riccardo Picchio and Harvey Goldblatt, eds. New Haven. 1–42.

Piechnik, Ludwik. 1983. *Dzieje Akademii Wileńskiej. Rozkwit Akademii Wileńskiej w latach 1600-1655*. Vol. 2. Rome: Institutum Historicum Societatis Jesu.

--------. 1984. *Dzieje Akademii Wileńskiej. Początki Akademii Wileńskiej, 1570–1599*. Vol. 1. Rome: Institutum Historicum Societatis Jesu.

Pietkiewicz, Krzysztof. 1995. *Wielkie Księstwo Litewskie pod rządami Aleksandra Jagiellończyka*. Poznań: Wydawnictwo naukowe UAM.

Pliushch, Pavlo P. 1971. *Istoriia ukraïns'koï literaturnoï movy*. Kyïv.

Pollak, Roman, ed. 1966. *Antologia pamiętników polskich XVI wieku*. Wrocław–Warszawa–Kraków: Zakład narodowy im. Ossolińskich.

Pritsak, Omeljan. 1984. "A Historical Perspective on the Ukrainian Language Question." *Aspects of the Slavic Language Question*. Vol. 2. Riccardo Picchio and Harvey Goldblatt, eds. Yale Russian and East European Publication 4–b. New Haven: Yale Concilium on International and Area Studies.

Ptashitskii, S. L. 1887. "Opisanie knig i aktov Litovskoi Metriki." *Zhurnal Ministerstva Narodnogo Prosveshcheniia* 11:127.

Pugh, Stefan M. 1985. "The Ruthenian Language of Meletii Smotryc'kyj: Phonology." *Harvard Ukrainian Studies* IX(1/2):53–60.

--------. 1996. *Testament to Ruthenian. A Linguistic Analysis of the Smotryc'kyj Variant*. Harvard Series in Ukrainian Studies. Cambridge: Harvard University Press.

Pułaski, Franciszek. 1915. *Opis 815 rękopisów Biblioteki Ordynacyi Krasińskich*. Warszawa: Nakładem funduszu Świdzińskich. 76–78.

Rauch, H. D. 1973. "Das Bild des Antichrist im Mittelalter." *Beitraede zur Geschichte der Philosophie und Theologie des Mittelalters*, NF, 9.

Reczek, Józef. 1968. *Bohemizmy leksykalne w języku polskim do końca XV wieku*. Wrocław: Ossolineum.

Reczek, Stefan. 1968. *Podręczny słownik dawnej polszczyzny*. Wrocław–Warszawa–Kraków: Ossolineum.

Řeháček, Luboš. 1975. "Emauzský klášter a Polsko (K založení a významu filiálních klášterů Emauz v dolnoslezské Olešnici a v Klepařích u Krakova)." *Z tradic slovanské kultury v Čechách. Sázava a Emauzy v dějinách české kultury*. Praha: Univerzita Karlova. 203–222.

Richhardt, Rosemarie. 1957. *Polnische Lehnwörter im Ukrainischen*. Weisbaden: Otto Harrassowitz.

Różycka-Bryzek, Anna. 1983. *Bizantyńsko-ruskie malowidła w kaplicy Zamku Lubelskiego*. Warszawa: Państwowe Wydawnictwo Naukowe.

--------. 2000. *Freski bizantyńsko-ruskie fundacji Jagiełły w kaplicy Zamku Lubelskiego*. Lublin: Muzeum Lubelskie.

Rusanovskii, V. M. 1998. "Stanovlenie novogo ukrainskogo literaturnogo iazyka." *Slavianskie literaturnye iazyki epokhi natsional'nogo vozrozhdeniia*. G. K. Venediktov, ed. Moskva.

Rybandt, Stanisław. 1970. "O pobycie benedyktynów słowiańskich w Oleśnicy." *Sobótka* 25(4):665–680.

Sakař, Vladimír. 1975. "Klášter *Na Slovanech* v období husitského revolučního hnutí a jeho doznívání." *Z tradic slovanské kultury v Čechách*. Praha: Univerzita Karlova.

Schenker, Alexander. 1978. "The Role of Czech in the Formation of the Polish Literary Language." *American Contributions to the Eighth International Congress of Slavists* I. Henrik Birnbaum, ed. Columbus, Ohio. 574–596.

--------. 1983. "Glavnye puti leksicheskikh zaimstvovanii v slavianskikh iazykakh (na materialakh cheshskogo, pol'skogo i vostochnoslavianskikh iazykov X–XVI vv.)." *American Contributions to the Ninth International Congress of Slavists I. Linguistics*. Michael S. Flier, ed. Slavica. 255–267.

Schuchardt, Hugo. [1884] 1971. *Slawo-deutsches und Slawo-italienisches*. Reprint. Slavische Propyläen. Texte in Neu- und Nachdrucken 66. München: Wilhelm Fink Verlag.

Ševčenko, Ihor. 1991. "Byzantium and the Slavs." *Byzantium and the Slavs in Letters and Culture*. Cambridge, M.A.: HURI. 3–15.

--------. 1996. "Religious Polemical Literature in the Ukrainian and Belarus' Lands in the Sixteenth and Seventeenth Centuries." *Ukraine between East and West*. Edmonton & Toronto: CIUS Press. 147–163.

Shchapov, Ia. N. 1976a. *Vostochnoslavianskie i iuzhnoslavianskie rukopisnye knigi v sobraniiakh Pol'skoi Narodnoi Respubliki*. Moskva: Akademiia Nauk SSSR. 40–42.

--------. 1976b. "Biblioteka polotskogo sofiiskogo sobora i biblioteka akademii zamoiskoi." *Kul'turnye sviazi narodov Vostochnoi Evropy v XVI v. Problemy vzaimootnoshenii Pol'shi, Rossii, Ukrainy, Belorussii i Litvy v epokhu Vozrozhdeniia*. B. A. Rybakov, ed. Moskva: Nauka. 262–282.

Shcherba, L. B. 1974. "O poniatii smesheniia iazykov." *Iazykovaia sistema i rechevaia deiatel'nost'*. Leningrad: Nauka. 60–74.

Shevelov, George [Šerech-Shevelov, Yury]. 1952. "The Problem of Ukrainian-Polish Linguistic Relations from the Tenth to the Fourteenth Century." *Word* 8(4):329–349.

--------. [Šerech, Yury]. 1953. *Problems in the Formation of Belorussian*. Supplement to Word 9 (December).

--------. 1979. *A Historical Phonology of the Ukrainian Language*. Heidelberg: Winter.

--------. 1980. "Ukrainian." *The Slavic Literary Languages: Formation and Development*. Alexander M. Schenker and Edward Stankiewicz, eds. New Haven. 143–160.

Sidorov, A. A. et al., eds. 1979. *Belorusskii prosvetitel' Frantsisk Skorina i nachalo knigopechataniia v Belorussii i Litve*. Fedorovskie chteniia 1977. Moskva: Nauka.

Siegel, Jeff. 1985. "Koines and Koineization." *Language in Society* 14:357–378.

--------. 1993. Review article of Peter Trudgill's *Dialects in Contact*. "Dialect Contact and Koineization." *Koines and Koineization. International Journal of the Sociology of Language* 99:105–121.

Sielicki, Franciszek. 1997. *Polsko-ruskie stosunki kulturalne do końca XV wieku*. Wrocław: Wydawnictwo Uniwersytetu Wrocławskiego.

Sigalov, Pavel. 1995. "Istoriia slavianskikh narechii na –o/–ě." *Paleoslavica* 3:5–40.

Smržík, Stephen. 1959. *The Glagolitic or Roman-Slavonic Liturgy*. Series Cyrillomethodiana II. Cleveland, OH – Rome: Slovak Institute.

Smułkowa, Elżbieta. 1988. "Zagadnienia polsko-białorusko-litewskiej interferencji językowej na ziemiach północno-wschodniej Polski." *Z polskich studiów slawistycznych* II. Warszawa.

Sobolevskii, A. I. 1888. "Review of Doktor Frantsisk Skorina, ego perevody, pechatnye izdaniia i iazyk. Issledovanie P.V. Vladimirova." *Zhurnal Ministerstva Narodnogo Prosveshcheniia*. St. Petersburg.

--------. 1907. *Lektsii po istorii russkogo iazyka*. Moskva.

--------. 1910. *Materialy i issledovaniia v oblasti slavianskoi filologii i arkheologii*. St. Petersburg.

Sokołowski, August, and Anatol Lewicki. 1876. *Codex epistolaris saeculi decimi quinti*. Kraków: Nakładem Akademii umiejętności. Vol. 2.

Sokolski, Jacek. 1990. *Staropolskie zaświaty*. Wrocław: Wydawnictwo uniwersytetu Wrocławskiego.

Stang, Christian. 1935. *Die westrussische Kanzleisprache des Großfürstentums Litauen*. Oslo.

--------. 1939. *Die Altrussische Urkundensprache der Stadt Polotzk*. Oslo.

Štefanić, Vjekoslav. 1960 *Glagoljski rukopisi otoka Krka*. Djela Jugoslavenske Akademije Znanosti i Umjetnosti. Vol. 51. Zagreb.

Stejskal, Karel. 1968. "Nástěnné malby kláštera *Na Slovanech* v Praze z hlediska etnografického a kulturně historického." *Český lid* 55:125–150.

--------. 1974. *Klašter Na Slovanech*. Praha.

--------. "Emauzy a český helenoslavismus." *Z tradic slovanské kultury v Čechách. Sázava a Emauzy v dějinách české kultury*. Praha: Univerzita Karlova. 113–124.

Stone, Daniel. 2001. *The Polish-Lithuanian State, 1386–1795*. A History of East Central Europe, Vol. 4. Seattle: University of Washington Press.

Strumins'kyj, Bohdan. 1984. "The Language Question in the Ukrainian Lands before the Nineteenth Century." *Aspects of the Slavic Language Question*. Vol. 2. Riccardo Picchio and Harvey Goldblatt, eds. Yale Russian and East European Publication 4–b. New Haven: Yale Concilium on International and Area Studies.

Sviazhynski, U. M. 1990. *"Histarychnyia zapiski" F. Eŭlashoŭskaha*. Minsk: Navuka i tekhnika.

Tannen, Deborah, ed. 1982. *Spoken and Written Language: Exploring Orality and Literacy*. Norwood, NJ: Ablex.

Taube, Moshe. 1993. "On the Slavic *Life of Moses* and its Hebrew sources." *Jews and Slavs* 1: 84–119. Wolf Moskovich et al., eds. Jerusalem and St. Petersburg.

--------. 1995a. "The Kievan Jew Zacharia and the Astronomical Works of the Judaizers." *Jews and Slavs* 3: 168–198. Wolf Moskovich et al., eds. Jerusalem.

--------. 1995b. "The 'Poem on the Soul' in the *Laodicean Epistle* and the Literature of the Judaizers." *Harvard Ukrainian Studies* 19:563–577. [= Kamen' Kraeõgъlьnъ – Rhetoric of the Medieval Slavic World: Essays presented to Edward L. Keenan on his Sixtieth Birthday by his Colleagues and Students].

--------. 1997. "Posleslovie k Logicheskim terminam Maimonida i eres' zhidovstvuiushchikh." *IN MEMORIAM: Pamiati IA. S. Lur'e*. N. M. Botvinnik and E. I. Vaneeva, eds. St. Peterburg: Feniks. 239–246.

--------. 2004. "The Vilnius 262 Psalter: A Jewish Translation?" *Jews and Slavs* 14:27–38. Wolf Moskovich et al., eds. Jerusalem.

--------. 2005a. "The Fifteenth-Century Ruthenian Translations from Hebrew and the Heresy of the Judaizers: Is There a Connection?" *Speculum Slaviae Orientalis: Muscovy, Ruthenia and Lithuania in the Later Middle Ages*. Vyacheslav V. Ivanov and Julia Verkholantsev, eds. UCLA Slavic Studies IV, n.s., Novoe Izdatel'stvo.

--------. 2005b. "*The Book of Job* in Vilnius 262." *Jews and Slavs* 15. Wolf Moskovich et al., eds. Jerusalem – Sofia. 281–296

--------. (forthcoming). *The Logika of the Judaizers: A 15th Century Ruthenian Translation from Hebrew*. Jerusalem: Israel Academy of Sciences and Humanities.

Thomason, Sarah Grey. 2001. *Language Contact: An Introduction*. Washington, D.C.: Georgetown University Press.

Thomason, Sarah Grey and Thomas Kaufman. 1988. *Language Contact, Creolization and Genetic Linguistics*. Berkeley & Los Angeles: University of California Press.

Thomson, Francis. J. 1998. "The Slavonic Translation of the Old Testament." *The Interpretation of the Bible*. Edited by Jože Krašovec. Journal for the Study of the Old Testament. Supplement Series 289. Sheffield: Sheffield Academic Press.

--------. 1999. *The Reception of Byzantine Culture in Medieval Russia*. Aldershot – Brookfield – Singapore – Sydney: Ashgate.

Topolska, Maria Barbara. 1984. *Czytelnik i książka w Wielkim Księstwie Litewskim w dobie Renessansu i Baroku*. Wrocław: Ossolineum.

--------. 2004. "Mecenasi i drukarze ruscy na pograniczu kulturowym w XVI–XVIII w." Prawosławne oficyny wydavnicze w Rzeczypospolitej. Antonii Mironowicz, Urszula Pawluczuk, and Piotr Chomik, eds. Białystok: Instytut Historii Uniwersytetu. 33–51.

Trajdos, Tadeusz, M. 1988. "Fundacja klasztoru benedyktynów słowiańskich na Kleparzu w Krakowie." *Rocznik Krakowski* 54:73–89.

Trubetzkoy, N. S. 1987. *Izbrannye trudy po filologii*. Moskva: Progress.

Trudgill, Peter. 1986. *Dialects in Contact*, Oxford and New York: Blackwell.

Turilov, A. A. 1986. *Predvaritel'nyi spisok slaviano-russkikh rukopisnykh knig XV veka, khraniashchikhsia v SSSR*. Moskva: Akademiia nauk SSSR.

----------. 1998. "Perevody s latinskogo i zapadnoslavianskikh iazykov, vypolnennye ukrainsko-belorusskimi knizhnikami v XV – nachale XVI vv." *Kul'turnye sviazi Rossii i Pol'shi XI–XX vv. Związki kulturalne między Polską a Rosją XI–XX w.* Moskva: URSS. 58-68

Turska, Halina. 1995. *O powstaniu polskich obszarów językowych na Wileńszczyźnie*. Vilnius: Mintis.

Tymchenko, E., ed. 1930. *Istorychnyi slovnyk ukraïns'koho iazyka*. Kharkiv – Kyïv.

Urbańczyk, Stanisław. 1946. *Z dawnych stosunków językowych polsko-czeskich. Cz. I. Biblia królowej Zofii a staro-czeskie przekłady Pisma Świętego*. Rozprawy Wyd. Filol. 67. Kraków: Nakł. Polskiej Akademii Umiejętności.

Urbańczyk, Stanisław and Vladimír Kyas. 1965. *Biblia królowej Zofii (Szaroszpatacka) wraz ze staroczeskim przekładem Biblii*. Wrocław: Zadład Narodowy im. Ossolińskich.

Uspenskii, B. A. 2002. *Istoriia russkogo literaturnogo iazyka (XI–XVII vv.)*. 3rd ed. Moskva: Aspekt Press.

Verkholantsev, Julia. 2003. "A Fifteenth-Century Ruthenian Translation of the *Song of Songs* from Czech." *Slavia* 72:195–226.

Vincent de Beauvais [1624] 1964. *Speculum Quadruplex sive Speculum Maius*. Vol. 4. *Speculum Historiale*. Reprint. Graz: Akademische Druck- u. Verlaganstalt.

Vladimirov, P. V. [1888] 1989. *Doktor Francisk Skorina, iego perevody, pechatnye izdaniia i iazyk*. Reprint. München.

Wagner, Albrecht. 1882. *Visio Tnugdali. Lateinisch und Altdeutsch*. Erlangen: Andreas Deichert.

Walczak, Bogdan. 1998. "Językowe konsekwencje unii brzeskiej. Postulaty badawcze." *Czterechsetlecie unii brzeskiej. Zagadnienia języka religijnego*. Zenon Leszczyński, ed.

Lublin: TN KUL, 7–19.

Warchoł, Stefan, ed. 1986. *Formacje hybrydalne w językach słowiańskich*. Rozprawy slawistyczne 1. Lublin.

----------. 1989. *Interferencje językowe na różnych obszarach słowiańczyzny*. Rozprawy slawistyczne 4. Lublin.

--------. 1993. *Gwary mieszane i przejściowe na terenach słowiańskich*. Rozprawy slawistyczne 6. Lublin.

Weinreich, Uriel. 1968. *Languages in Contact*. The Hague and Paris: Mouton.

Wexler, Paul. 1971. "Diglossia, language standardization and purism. Parameters for a typology of literary languages." *Lingua* 27(4):330–54.

--------. 1977. *A Historical Phonology of the Belorussian Language*. Heidelberg: Winter.

--------. 2002. *Two-Tiered Relexification in Yiddish: Jews, Sorbs, Khazars, and the Kiev-Polessian Dialect*. Berlin: Mouton de Gruyter.

--------. 2006. *Jewish and Non-Jewish Creators of "Jewish" Languages: with Special Attention to Judaized Arabic, Chinese, German, Greek, Persian, Portuguese, Slavic (Modern Hebrew/Yiddish), Spanish, and Karaite, and Semitic Hebrew/Ladino; a Collection of Reprinted Articles from Across Four Decades with a reassessment*. Wiesbaden: Harrassowitz.

Witkowski, Wiesław. 1969. *Język utworów Joannicjusza Galatowskiego na tle języka piśmiennictwa ukraińskiego XVII wieku*. Kraków.

Wölk, W. and A. De Houwer, eds. 1977. *Recent Studies in Contact Linguistics*. Plurilingua XVIII. Bonn: Dümmler.

Woolhiser, Curt F. 1995. *Polish and Belorussian Dialects in Contact: a Study in Linguistic Convergence*. Thesis (Ph. D.) – Indiana University, 1995.

Worth, Dean. 1975. "Was There a "Literary Language" in Kievan Rus'?" *The Russian Review* 34(1):1–9.

Wyrozumski, Jerzy. 1982. "Benedyktyni słowiańscy w Oleśnicy i Krakowie." *Zeszyty Naukowe Wydziału Humanistycznego Uniwersytetu Gdańskiego. Sławistyka* 3:113–124.

Yeomans, Donald K. 1991. *Comets: A Chronological History of Observation, Science, Myth and Folklore*. New York: Wiley.

Zalizniak, A. A. 1995. *Drevne-novgorodskii dialekt*. Moskva.

Zhuraŭski, A. I. 1967. *Historyia belaruskai litaraturnai movy*. 1. Minsk: Navuka i tekhnika.

--------. 1982. "Dvukhmoŭe i shmatmoŭe ŭ historyi Belarusi." *Pytanni bilingvizmu i ŭzaemadzeiannia moŭ*. Minsk: Navuka i tekhnika.

Zíbrt, Čeněk. 1902. *Bibliografie české historie* II. 758–77.

--------. 1910. *Zlatý jelen na pražském mostě, slepý mladenec, Sibylla a jiná proroctví staročeská*. Praha.

Zoltán, András. 2004. *Oláh Miklós "Athila" című munkájának XVI. századi lengyel és fehérorosz fordítása*. Dimensiones culturales et urbariales Regni Hungariae, 6. Nyíregyháza: Nyíregyházi Főiskola.

**Church Slavonic**

*Edifying Story Told by Faudal the Warrior* (повє[ст] полєзна сиа̀ сказа[н] ѐ фаоудало[м] воино[м]), 52, 59–69, 70, 112, 149, 175–179

*On the Three Lawful States* (ѿ тре[х] в̏законениꙗ[х]), 64–66, 68, 182

*Ostrih Bible*, 7, 50, 88–89

*Reims Gospel*, 32–33

**Croatian**

*Čtenie dobroga viteza Dundula*, 57–58, 70

*Čtenie kako e uséčena glava Ivanu Krstitělju*, 58

*Čti na Pasku evanĵeli*, 58

*Hrvoje Missal*, 47

*Marian Mass*, 37, 44–45, 47–48, 50, 64

*Missal*, 28, 44, 47, 49

*Ot žit'ě svetih trih krali*, 58

*Petris Miscellany (Petrisov zbornik)*, 58, 70

**Czech**

*Apolon, pověst romantičná*, 73

*Bible*,

*Benátská (Venetian)*, 27, 43, 86–87

*Boskovská*, 87

*Cardův Starý Zákon*, 46

*Fojtův Starý Zákon*, 40, 155

*Hlaholská*, 87–88

*Klementinská Neznámého Původu*, 40, 155

*Kutnohorská*, 43, 86

*Litoměřická*, 87–88

*Lobkovická*, 40, 106, 155

*Nymburská*, 40, 106, 155

*Padeřovská*, 39–40, 155–173

*Pražská*, 43, 86

*Severýn*, 46

*Táborská Mlynářčina*, 46

*Talmberská*, 40, 106, 155

*Hospodine, pomiluj ny*, 19, 31–32

*Kronika Česká*, Přibík Pulkava, 30–31

*Kronika Dalimilova*, 73

*Mníšek Bosáček*, 73

*Pasionál*, 58, 83
*Pinvičkův Miscellany*, 72–75
*Piseň o zkáze Českého království pro polepšení života*, 76
*Proroctví Michaldy, královny ze Sáby, třinácté Sibylly*, 76
*Proroctví Sibyllino*, 72–75, 76, 78, 79, 81, 84, 85, 124, 187–189
*Proroctví slepého mládence*, 76
*Skládání o podkoním a žáku*, 73
*Výtah z dvanácterého Sibylliného proroctví*, 76
*Život svaté Kateřiny*, 83

**German**
*Sibyllenweissagung*, 72–73, 77, 85

**Latin**
*Ave Maria, Credo, Pater noster* (Cyrillic Latin Prayers), 48, 50, 148
*Cronica Boemorum*, Giovanni dei Marignolli, 30, 83–84
*De Europa*, Enea Silvio Piccolomini, 3–4
*Defensio verae translationis*, Jan Sandecki-Małecki, 20–21
*Exposicio cantici sancti Adalberti*, Jan of Holešov, 31–32
*Historia Bohemica*, Enea Silvio Piccolomini, 31
*Polonia*, Jan Krasiński, 4
*Sibylla Tiburtina*, 72–73, 83, 85, 149
*Visio Tundali*, 52, 54–55, 57–64, 67, 68, 69, 70, 149, 180–181
  by monk Marcus, 54, 57, 58, 61
  in Helinand de Froidmont's *Chronicon*, 55, 70
  in Vincent de Beauvais' *Speculum Historiale*, 55–56, 58, 61, 67, 70, 180

**Polish**
*Biblia królowej Zofii* (Also as *Szaroszpatak Codex*), 45–46, 88
*Bogurodzica*, 19–20
*Dworzanin Polski*, Łukasz Górnicki, 19–20, 137
*Kronika*, Maciej Stryjkowski, 131, 140
*Kronika wszytkiego świata*, Marcin Bielski, 131
*Lithuanian Statute* (1595), Mamonich edition, 15, 92
*O jedności Kościoła Bożego pod jednym Pasterzem*, Piotr Skarga, 11
*Postylla domowa,* Martin Luther, translated by Hieronim Sandecki, 21
*Przeraźliwe echo trąby ostatecznej*, Klemens Bolesławiusz, 59
*Szaroszpatak Codex*, 45–46, 88

**Ruthenian**
*Apokrysis*, Khrystofor Filalet, 131, 139–140
*Apostol of Krekhiv*, 131

*Bibliia Rus'ka*, Frantsishak Skaryna, 43, 50, 86–87, 100, 103, 105, 107, 108, 132
*Book of Taudal the Knight* (кн̏ига ѿ таоу̑дале рыцари), 38, 52–70, 71, 80, 82, 86, 110–117, 118, 127, 148–150, 174–178
*Book of Tovit* (книга товиѳъ), 38, 53, 86–89, 148, 150
*BOZ* (Biblioteka Ordynacji Zamojskich) *#92 Miscellany*, 59, 175, 182
*Bulla of Pope Eugene IV*, 44
*Historical Notes*, Fiodar Eŭlashoŭski, 13–14
*Khronika*, Maciej Stryjkowski, 131, 140
*Laodicean Epistle*, 108
*Legend of Three Persian Kings* (ѡ житїи и ѡ хоⷤнїи треⷯ королеⷡ҇ персиⷣскыⷯ), 44, 139
*Leksikon slavenorosskii,* Pamva Berynda, 131
*Life of Alexis, the Man of God* (житїє и жиⷥнь чл҇ка бж҇їа ѡ̇леѯїа), 44
*Lithuanian Statute* (1588), 9, 15, 92
*Moscow Synod Collection #558 Miscellany*, 38, 39, 44, 64, 109, 154
*Marian Mass* (каⷦ сѧ м̏ша чтеть римскиⷨ ѡбычаемъ маⷮце бж҇їєи), 37, 44–48, 50, 64, 148, 150
*On the Three States* (реⷱ҇ ѿ треⷯ ставеҳъ), 53, 65–67, 149
*Passion of Christ* (моука гⷭ҇а нашего ї҇сса хⷭ҇а), 1, 64
*Peresopnytsia Gospel*, 16
*Perestroha*, 13
*Song of Songs*, 38, 39–51, 56, 64, 80, 88, 89, 94, 99–109, 116, 127, 148–150, 154–172
*Tale of Sivilla the Prophetess* (сказаниѐ ѿ сивил̏ле п̏рⷪ҇рчици), 38, 54, 55, 71–85, 86, 89, 118–127, 148–150, 183–189
*Wiślica Statute of Kazimierz the Great* (1347), 24–25, 67
*Swidziński Miscellany of Lithuanian Chronicles*, 38, 52–55, 64–70, 75, 86–88, 174

## Subject Index

Antichrist, 55, 72

Astrology, 71, 76–78, 84

Belarusian:
- authors, 44, 53
- dialects, 1, 9–10, 91–95, 100, 110, 118, 129–132, 135–137, 140, 142, 151–152
- documents (*Also as* texts, records), 99, 129–132
- lands (*Also as* Belarus), 1–3, 10, 16, 91, 93, 94, 129, 130, 132
- language, 10, 44, 91, 99–100, 109, 117, 129–131, 147

Bible, 7, 21, 26, 27, 28, 31, 33, 39–51, 86–89, 99, 150

Biblical translations:
- Church Slavonic, 7, 28, 31, 49–50
- Czech, 26–27, 33, 39–46, 49–51, 86–89, 99, 150, 155–173
- Latin, 28
- Polish, 21, 26, 44, 45–46, 88
- Ruthenian, 27, 39–51, 86–89, 99, 150, 154–172

Catholic (Roman):
- Church, 4–5, 7, 8, 9, 34, 35, 46, 62, 150
- Rite, liturgy, 28, 35, 44–45, 48, 49, 51, 148, 150
- Slavs, 28, 58, 132
- source texts, 44–45, 50, 68, 139, 149–150

Catholicism, 4, 7, 8, 9, 13, 16, 17, 29, 34, 35, 150
- conversion to, 8, 9, 29, 34–35, 45
- criticism of, 48–49, 150

Christianity, 8, 30, 72, 77, 121
- Byzantine, 16
- Roman, 29, 48

Christian:
- Church, 22
- texts, 17, 85

Christians, 30, 66, 77, 78, 79, 82

Chronicles:
- Czech, 18, 30–32, 57, 74, 149
- Latin, 57, 149
- Lithuanian, 6, 38, 52–54, 71, 86, 132
- Polish, 33, 131

Church Union, 29, 34–35, 136

Church Slavonic, 5, 10–13, 17, 28, 31, 37, 44, 45, 47, 48, 50, 54, 58, 59–70, 81, 88–89, 91, 96, 98, 100, 105, 109, 118, 120, 121, 124, 127, 132, 134, 136–137, 142, 147, 149–152
- Croatian variant of, 28, 31, 35, 37, 45, 47, 48, 64
- linguistic features, 5, 91, 96, 98, 105, 109, 118, 120, 121, 124, 127, 132, 147
- literacy, 10–13, 118, 136–137, 151–152
- competence in, 11–13, 28, 44, 48, 118, 142
- Ruthenian variant of, 13, 132–133
- translations, 54, 58, 59–70, 88-89, 149–150, 175–179, 182

Clairvaux Monastery, 61–62

Comet Halley, 77

Council of Constance, 22, 34–35

Council of Florence, 32, 44

Cracow University, 8, 19

Croatian:
- origin of Czech, 31–32
- variant of Church Slavonic, 28, 31, 35, 37, 45, 47, 48, 64
- translations into, 54, 57–59, 63–64, 70
- Ruthenian translations from, 46–48
- Glagolite monks, 27–38, 44–46, 48, 50, 52, 58–59, 69, 82–84, 148–149

Crucifixion Tree legend, 72, 78–79

Cyrillic:
- script, 14–15, 28, 32, 37, 44–45, 48, 50, 85, 136–137, 140–141, 148, 150
- literacy, 10, 136–137

Cyrillo-Methodian:
mission, 28, 30–31
translations, 28

Czech:
Bible, 26–27, 33, 39–40, 42, 43–46, 49, 50, 86–87, 150, 156–173
chronicles, 18, 30–32, 57, 74, 149
influence on Polish, 18–21, 128, 137, 144–145
influence on Ruthenian, 21–27, 128, 144–145, 150–151
literary language, 17, 18–27, 30–32
literature, 18, 26–27, 83
translations from, 16, 17, 18, 37–38, 39–89, 127, 136, 140, 148–152

Dialects:
Belarusian, 1, 9–10, 91–95, 100, 110, 118, 129–132, 135–137, 140, 142, 151–152
Central Belarusian, 129
contact of, 9–10, 143–144
East Slavic, 111, 120, 142, 146–147, 151, 152
Great Russian (Muscovite), 135
Greek, 142–143
Kyiv-Palesse, 92
North Russian (Novgorod), 93
North Belarusian, 94
Northeast Belarusian, 92
Northwest Russian (Novgorod, Polatsk, Pskov, Smolensk, Tver'), 94
Novgorod, 93, 94
Polish, 9–10
Polissian, 92, 93
South Russian, 135
South Ukrainian, 91
Southeast Ukrainian, 129
Southwest Belarusian, 92
Southwest Ukrainian (Bukovyna, Pokuttia, Hutsul, Dniester and Sjan), 93
Ukrainian, 1, 9–10, 91–95, 100, 110, 118, 129–132, 135–137, 140, 142, 151–152
West Russian, 135

Emmaus Monastery *Na Slovanech*, 28–37, 45–46, 48, 50, 58, 82–84, 88, 148–149

Eschatological literature, 52–55, 64, 67, 68–69, 71–79, 82–85, 149

Galician-Volhynian documents (*gramoty*), 23, 90.

Glagolite monks (Glagoljaši), 27–38, 44–46, 48, 50, 52, 58–59, 69, 82–84, 148–149

Glagolitic:
script, 28–29, 32–33, 44–45, 47–48
Slavonic liturgy, 27–38, 44–45, 47–48, 148–149
manuscripts, 37, 47, 49, 58, 70, 87

Greek:
dialects, 142–143
language, 12, 13, 142–143
translations from, 16
manuscripts, 32

Hebrew:
literacy in, 14
language, 143
translations from, 16, 31, 49, 50, 90, 100

Hussite movement, 19, 22, 26, 32, 36, 39, 46, 49, 85

Imperfect learning, 137–141, 146, 152

Jesus Christ, 39, 46, 50, 54, 55, 64, 72, 77, 83, 180
passion of, 1, 35, 64
second coming of, 55, 64, 72

Kievan Caves Monastery, 6

Kievan Rus', 5, 6, 15

Kleparz Monastery of Holy Cross, 33–38, 44–46, 59, 70, 84, 148–149

Koine, 100, 110, 142–144, 146, 152

Koineization, 137–147, 152

Krasiński Collection, 38, 52, 65, 70, 71, 86

Language:
accommodation, 9, 135–147, 152
borrowing, 25, 41, 93, 97, 105, 108, 129, 137–138, 142
contact, 10–11, 21, 135–147, 151–152
interference, 10, 15, 23–25, 58, 91, 98, 103, 111, 113, 115, 116, 120, 135, 137–144, 146, 152
literary, 1, 10, 13, 15, 68, 130, 133–134, 136–137, 139, 142, 151–152
mixing, 10, 91, 109, 116–117, 127, 134, 135, 137–147, 152

Last Emperor, 72, 73, 76, 82

Last Judgment, 55, 72, 76, 85, 190

Last Times, 54, 75–77, 82

Latin (Roman):
  Bible, 28, 31, 33, 39, 49, 107
  script, 60, 74, 85, 92, 141, 150
  liturgy, 28, 37, 44, 48, 50–51, 148, 150
  manuscripts, 30, 33, 54–55, 57, 70
  translations from, 28, 39, 54–55, 57, 58, 60, 61-64, 65-69, 72-73, 85, 90, 107, 149

Literacy, 6, 7–8, 10–13, 15, 68–69, 135–137, 146, 151–152
  contact, 10–11, 135–137, 146, 151–152
  in Church Slavonic, 68–69

Lithuania, Grand Duchy of (*Also as* Lithuania-Rus', Lithuanian state), 1–38, 53, 54, 128, 132, 135–137, 142, 143, 146, 148–149, 151
  Christianization of, 3, 4, 5, 34
  chronicles of, 6, 38, 52–54, 71, 86, 132
  Orthodox culture and education in, 6–8
  linguistic situation in, 8–10

Macedonian, 143

Moscow Synod Collection, 38, 39, 44, 48, 49, 64, 109, 154

Oleśnica Corpus Christi Monastery, 33, 37

Orality, 136

Order of St. Augustine (Augustinians), 33, 37

Order of St. Benedict (Benedictines), 5, 27–37, 45–46, 50, 54, 58–59

Order of St. Francis (Franciscans), 28, 30, 36, 73

Order of St. Paul, 28

Orthodox:
  brotherhoods, 7–8
  Church, 4, 6, 22, 34, 48
  culture and education, 4, 5, 6–8
  faith (Orthodoxy), 3, 7, 12, 16, 17, 22, 34, 48, 51, 68, 150
  frescoes in Poland, 4–5, 35
  identity, 137
  language, orthography, 44–45, 47, 49–50, 60, 89, 149
  Rite, liturgy, 27, 44–45, 48, 54, 150
  Ruthenians, 3, 5, 6, 8, 12, 13, 27, 34–36, 37, 45, 52, 148
  texts, 6, 49, 54, 59, 66, 68, 85, 139, 149, 150
  textual corpus, 16, 54, 59, 66, 69, 150.

Pentecost, 30–31

Polish:
  biblical translations, 21, 26, 44, 45–46, 88
  dialects, 9–10, 151
  language, 2, 4, 8–21, 44, 45, 50, 95, 98, 111–116, 119–127, 128–130, 134, 135–147, 151–152
    influence of Czech on, 18–21, 23
    relationship with Ruthenian, 2, 8–16, 21–23, 25, 93, 95, 98, 113, 115, 123, 126–130, 134, 135–147, 151–152
  literary tradition, 18–21, 24, 59, 60, 151
  Ruthenian translations from, 16, 17, 44, 60, 90, 136, 139–140

Polish-Lithuanian Commonwealth (*See also* Lithuania), 1–38, 134, 136, 146, 151

Prague University, 19, 22

Rusyn (*Also as* Carpatho-Ruthenian) 1

Ruthenian:
  as linguistic term, 1–2
  chancery (administrative) language, 5–6, 16, 23–26, 90, 130, 132, 134, 146
  identity, 137
  influence of Czech on, 21–27, 128, 144–145, 150–151
  relationship with Polish, 2, 8–16, 21–23, 25, 93, 95, 98, 113, 115, 123, 126–129, 134, 135–147, 151–152
  literacy, 10–16, 68–69, 135–137, 146–147, 151–152
  polemical literature, 12–13, 90, 132–133, 150
  textual corpus, 10, 16–17, 69, 152
  translations from Croatian, 46–48
  translations from Polish, 16, 17, 44, 60, 90, 136, 139–140
  translations from Hebrew, 16, 17, 50, 90, 100

Sázava Monastery, 32, 33

Speech genres, 132–134, 152

Substratum, 94, 137–142, 146, 147, 152
  interference, 137–142, 146, 152

Superstratum, 147, 152

Supraśl Monastery, 6, 7, 26

Teutonic Order, 5, 34

Treaty of Krewo (*See also* Lithuania, Christianization), 2, 3

Ukrainian:
  language, 10, 13, 44, 91, 93, 99–100, 105, 109, 117, 129–131, 147
  dialects, 1, 9–10, 91–95, 100, 110, 118, 129–132, 135–137, 140, 142, 151–152
  lands (*Also as* Ukraine), 1, 2, 3, 10, 16, 91, 93, 99, 129, 130

Union of Lublin, 3, 7, 94

Vilnius Jesuit Academy, 8, 26

Virgin Mary, 44, 46–47, 49–50, 83–84, 166
  Catholic Mass in honor of (*Marian Mass*), 37, 44–48, 50, 64, 148, 150
  Marian symbols, 46–47
  *Ave Maria*, 48

Visionary literature, 50–70, 174–181

**PERSONAL NAME INDEX**

Algirdas, Grand Duke of Lithuania, 3
Andrzej of Jaszowice, 45
Augustine, Saint, 53, 65–66, 68, 149
Bakhtin, Mikhail, 132–134, 152
Bielski, Marcin, 131
Broniewski, Marcin, 13
Charles IV, King of Bohemia, Holy Roman Emperor, 18, 19, 28–33, 34, 35, 76, 82, 83–84
Claretus de Solencia (Bartoloměj z Chlumce), 18.
Clement VI, Pope, 29, 31, 73
Constantine Kostenecki, 50
Cyril, Saint (Slavic Apostle), 28, 30–31, 32, 33
Dante, Alighieri, 52
Długosz, Jan, 33
Dmitrii Ivanovich (Donskoi), Grand Prince of Muscovy, 34
Elizabeth of Bosnia, Queen of Poland and Hungary, 34
Enea Silvio Piccolomini, 3–4, 31
Eugene III, Pope, 61
Eŭlashoŭski, Fiodar, 13–14
Friedrich the Handsome of Austria, 74, 76, 78–79
Galiatovs'kyi, Ioannikii, 132
Gasztołd, Olbracht, 26
Gasztołd, Marcin, Palatine of Kyiv, 26
Gedyminas, Grand Duke of Lithuania, 3
Gennadii, Archbishop of Novgorod, 49
Górnicki, Łukasz ,19–20, 137
Gregory Tsamblak, Metropolitan of Kyiv and Vilnius, 34–35
Hostovinus, Balthasar (Balthasar Hostounský), 26
Innocent IV, Pope, 28
Isaiah, Prophet, 27, 84
Iuliana Tverskaia, 4
Jadwiga, Queen of Poland, 3, 22, 33, 34, 35, 37, 45, 148
Jagiełło, Władysław II, King of Poland (*See also* Jogaila, Grand Duke of Lithuania), 3–5, 22, 25, 33–37, 45, 148
Jan Čech (Johannes Bohemus), 22
Jan Hus, 22
Jan of Holešov, 31–32
Jan of Prague, 33
Jan of Středa, 83
Jerome, Saint, 28–29, 31–33, 49, 83
Jeroným Pražský (Jerome of Prague), 22
Jeroným Silván Pražský, 22
Jogaila, Grand Duke of Lithuania (*See also* Jagiełło, Władysław II), 3, 4, 34
Kazimierz the Great, King of Poland, 67
Kęstutis, Grand Duke of Lithuania, 3
Konrad II (Piast), Duke of Oleśnica (Oels), 33–34, 35
Konstantyn of Ostrih, Palatine of Kyiv, 7
Kosov, Syl'vestr, Metropolitan of Kyiv, 13
Krasiński, Jan (Joannes Crasinius), 4
Ludwig IV the Bavarian, 76, 78
Malachy, Archbishop of Armagh, 61
Marcin, Palatine of Kyiv, 26
Marignolli, Giovanni dei (Jan Marignola), 30, 83–84
Maxim Grek, 25
Methodius, Saint (Slavic Apostle), 28, 33
Mikuláš Čech, 22
Octavian Augustus, Roman Emperor, 83–84
Peter the Great, Emperor of Russia, 32
Polotskii, Simeon, 8
Prokop (Procopius), Saint, 22, 32, 33
Queen of Sheba, 71–72, 76
Sandecki-Małecki, Jan, 20–21, 137
Seklucjan, Jan, 20
Skarga, Piotr,11–12
Skaryna, Frantsishak, 27, 43, 50, 86–87, 90, 99, 100, 132
Smotryts'kyi, Meletii, 8, 14, 90, 95, 131, 132, 139
Solomon, King, 41, 71–72
Stefan Bathory, King of Poland, 65

Stryjkowski, Maciej, 131, 140
Švitrigaila (Świdrygiełło), Grand Duke of Lithuania, 25–26
Štítný, Thomáš, 83
Václav, Saint, 22
Vanko Kirdeevich of Kvasilov, castellan of Chełm, 24
Vasyl' of Surazh, 13
Vít, Saint, 22
Vojtěch, Saint, 33
Vytautas, Grand Duke of Lithuania, 5
Vyshens'kyi, Ivan, 13, 90, 132
Zamojski, Jan, 65
Zofia Holszańska, Queen of Poland, 45, 51
Zizanii, Lavrentii, 131
Zygmunt III Waza, King of Poland, 15

## Place Name Index

Africa, 142
Athens, 143.
Athos, Mount, 7
Armagh, 61–62
Belarus (*Also as* Belarusian lands), 1–3, 10, 16, 91, 93, 94, 129, 130, 132
Berestja, 94
Bohemia, 18–33, 46, 57, 82–84
Briansk, 3
Bukovyna, 91, 93
Carpathia (*See also* Transcarpathia), 93
Cashel, 61–62
Chełm, 24
Chernihiv, 3
Constantinople, 7, 32
Cracow, 5, 8, 15, 19, 33–36, 45
Croatia, 28
Dalmatia, 28
Dniester, 93
Galicia, 3, 9, 23, 90
Gaul, 61
Greece, 142–143
Hibernia, 62
Hungary, 1
Hutsul, 93
Krewo, 2, 3
Kyiv, 3, 7, 13, 26, 92
Kvarner islands, 28
Lithuania, Grand Duchy of (*Also as* Lithuania-Rus', Lithuanian state), 1–38, 53, 54, 128, 132, 135–137, 142, 143, 146, 148–149, 151
L'viv, 7, 22, 26, 72, 73, 74
Macedonia, 142
Middle East, 142
Moscow, 12
Muscovy, 5, 6, 13, 34, 94, 136
Nevel', 94.
Novgorod, 23, 49, 93
Oleśnica, 33–37
Ostrih, 7
Palesse (Polissia), 92, 93, 130
Pidliashia (Podlasie), 5, 93
Podolia, 3
Pokuttia, 91, 93
Poland (*Also as* Polish Kingdom), 1–38, 45, 50, 65, 148
Polatsk, 3, 6, 23, 65, 94
Prague, 19, 22, 28–37, 40, 44, 45, 48, 50, 52, 57, 58, 69, 75, 84, 87, 88, 148
Pskov, 23, 94
Romania, 1
Ratisbon (Regensburg), 54
Sebež, 94
Senj, 28–29, 31
Silesia, 18, 19, 20, 33, 37
Sjan, 93
Slovakia, 1
Smolensk, 5, 94
Stridon, 28, 31
Transcarpathia (*See also* Carpathia), 91
Tver' 94
Ukraine, 1, 2, 3, 10, 16, 91, 93, 99, 129, 130
Vilnius, 7, 8, 12, 22, 23, 26, 27, 35, 100, 130, 131, 143
Vitebsk, 13, 94
Volhynia, 3, 5, 23, 90
Warsaw, 2, 12, 59
Zabłudów, 6–7
Zadar, 28

**Slavische Sprachgeschichte Bd. 2**

hrsg. v. Michael Moser

**„Ruthenische“ (ukrainische) Sprach- und Vorstellungswelten in den galizischen Volksschullesebüchern der Jahre 1871 und 1872**

Michael Moser

LIT

Michael Moser

**„Ruthenische“ (ukrainische) Sprach- und Vorstellungswelten in den galizischen Volksschullesebüchern der Jahre 1871 und 1872**

Die hier untersuchten galizisch-ukrainischen Lesebücher für die erste bis vierte Volksschulklasse aus den Jahren 1871 und 1872 sind die ersten, die einen mehrjährigen Muttersprachenunterricht in einem auf der Volkssprache gründenden Idiom ermöglichten. Ein Vergleich mit älteren Fassungen zeigt, welche sprachliche Bearbeitung vorgenommen wurde, um das Resultat der Jahre 1871 und 1872 zu erzielen. Bemerkenswert sind die vier Lesebücher auch in inhaltlicher Hinsicht, da sie in unterschiedlichem Ausmaß für die galizisch-ukrainische Nationsbildung instrumentalisiert werden konnten.

Bd. 2, 2007, 272 S., 24,90 €, br., ISBN 978-3-8258-0213-4

LIT Verlag GmbH & Co. KG Wien – Zürich

Auslieferung Österreich: Medienlogistik Pichler-ÖBZ GmbH & Co KG
IZ-NÖ Süd, Straße 1, Objekt 34, A-2355 Wiener Neudorf, Postfach 133
Tel. +43 (0) 2236 / 63 535 - 236, Fax +43 (0) 2236 / 63 535 - 243, e-Mail: bestellen@medien-logistik.at

Auslieferung Deutschland: Fresnostr. 2 48159 Münster
Tel.: 0251 / 620 32 22 – Fax 0251 / 922 60 99
e-Mail: vertrieb@lit-verlag.de – http://www.lit-verlag.de

**Veröffentlichungen des Slavisch-Baltischen Seminars der Universität Münster**
hrsg. von Gerhard Birkfellner, Gerhard Ressel, Alfred Sproede und Friedrich Scholz

Christina Schindler
**Untersuchungen zur Äquivalenz von Idiomen in Sprachsystemen und Kontext**
(Am Beispiel des Russischen und des Deutschen)

Die Wiedergabe von Idiomen stellt ein wesentliches Problem bei der Übersetzung fremdsprachiger Texte dar. Häufig ist zu beobachten, daß innerhalb eines konkreten Textzusammenhangs nicht der im zweisprachigen phraseologischen Wörterbuch angegebene Übersetzungsvorschlag aufgenommen wird. Statt dessen sucht der Übersetzer nach einer anderen Entsprechung. Der Grund hierfür liegt darin, daß sich Idiome in Sprachsystem und Kontext voneinander unterscheiden. Die vorliegende Arbeit macht dies am Beispiel russischer Idiome und ihrer deutschen Entsprechungen deutlich und zeigt, wie eine möglichst genaue Übersetzung gefunden werden kann.

Bd. 9, 2005, 280 S., 27,90 €, br., ISBN 3-8258-8588-7